Alexandra

E. E. P. TISDALL

Alexandra

EDWARD VII'S UNPREDICTABLE QUEEN

Illustrated

THE JOHN DAY COMPANY

NEW YORK

Library of Congress Catalog Card Number: 54-5887

CONTENTS

Part I

NO PROSPECTS

Chapter	I	Poor Relations at Yellow Palace	1
	II	Good from the Ill Wind	6
	III	Birth of a Royal Family	10
	IV	Photograph on the Mantelpiece	13
	V	Missed from the List	16
	VI	An Extraordinary Love Intrigue	20
	VII	Betrothal in Black	30
	VIII	Alix in the Royal Closet	36

Part II

DANISH ENCHANTMENT

IX	The Hazardous Welcome	45
X	Drama at the Wedding	53
XI	Wandering Bridegroom	58
XII	Alix Defies the Queen	67
XIII	Consternation at Frogmore	76
XIV	Is She Dying?	89
XV	The Nile Adventure	99

Part III

MARLBOROUGH HOUSE SET

XVI	Flight from Prince Hal	111
XVII	Nightmare at Sandringham and the Conquest of a Red	130
XVIII	Stars and Clowns at Marlborough House	143

v

Part IV
FULL GLORY

Chapter   xix   Alix and the Elephant Man   163

xx   Archbishop—Pray for Marlborough House   171

xxi   The Worst Snub of Her Life   197

Part V
REIGN IN TWILIGHT

xxii   'Twixt the Boss and the Peacock   209

xxiii   Sorrow Which Nothing Can Lessen   218

xxiv   Murderous Attack   237

Part VI
EDWARDIANS

xxv   An Obstinate Queen   251

xxvi   Sovereigns in a New Pattern   270

xxvii   Her Last Defiance   296

Index   303

LIST OF ILLUSTRATIONS

(*All following page 118*)

The Princess of Wales in 1887.

The Prince of Wales at Homburg in 1896.

The Prince of Wales at the time of his marriage.

Princess Alix of Denmark at the time of her marriage to the Prince of Wales.

The Princess of Wales in the middle 'sixties.

The Princess of Wales with her favorite sister Dagmar (Empress Marie Fedorovna of Russia) in the early 'seventies.

The Princess of Wales in 1889, age 45.

The Empress Marie Fedorovna of Russia.

Prince William of Prussia (nephew "Willy"—the last Kaiser) with his mother, Victoria, Crown Princess of Prussia and Princess Royal of Great Britain (later Empress Frederick) in 1876.

A Press artist's impression of the Princess of Wales receiving guests at the Marlborough House garden party in 1878.

A Press artist's impression of tea in the hall at Sandringham during Queen Victoria's visit in 1889.

A Press artist's impression of the Prince and Princess of Wales with their family in 1871.

Part One

NO PROSPECTS

Chapter 1

POOR RELATIONS AT YELLOW PALACE

THE LITTLE YELLOW PALACE on the Amaliegade in Copenhagen had a rather shabby front in the early forties of the last century. It had only three windows on each side of the porch which opened straight upon the pavement and it looked like a hotel going gently downhill. Inside, the palace was pretty bare, but it shone with polish. To achieve this with so few servants it was necessary for the mistress of the mansion to be active herself.

Every morning a young captain of the Royal Guard hurried out from the porch—his wife made him hurry—and amiably nodding to a groom-batman, who looked easygoing and faintly threadbare like his master, the officer vaulted with surprising agility into the saddle of an inexpensive-looking charger and trotted away to the Guard barracks.

He was Prince Christian of Schleswig-Holstein-Sonderburg-Glucksburg, immensely tall, fair, blue-eyed, whiskered, faintly weak-chinned and in his middle twenties. Prince Christian as he rode glanced about him with the look of a perfectly happy and contented young man. He had no prospects, no ambition other than a dim hope that he might one day manage to qualify for command of his regiment, and his assets were few.

The assets consisted of Louise, his extremely beautiful and capable wife, whom he knew he relied upon very much, and the Yellow Palace which cost him nothing because his elderly cousin the King let him have it gratis. From the monetary angle there were the quite satisfactory presents which arrived from King Christian at birthdays and at Christmas, as well as those which came from his pleasant mother-in-law, Charlotte, the Landgravine of Hesse-Cassel. Still, things were tight at Yellow Palace, good manager as dear Louise was proving to be.

Prince and Princess Christian were often private visitors at the Royal Palace, where Cousin (known as "Uncle") Christian and Queen Caroline Amalie were always kind to them. Princess Christian (Louise) was in fact the King's niece, for her mother, the Landgravine of Hesse-Cassel, was his only sister. In high society the Christians were seen no more than was absolutely necessary for a Guards officer and his wife. Going out meant entertaining at home in return and that they seldom could afford. Besides, during the next few years, like most young wives of her time, Princess Christian planned to be much occupied in bringing a family into the world.

On the whole, then, this couple at the shabby Yellow Palace were lucky, although perhaps the poorest members of the Guards circle and sometimes treated with polite commiseration for their humble way of life.

But what claim had Prince Christian on King Christian VIII of Denmark? To him he owed all he possessed, a commission (unpurchased) in the Guards, his high-born bride Louise, the Yellow Palace when he had married in 1842, and at least enough financial help to make him sure he would never be arraigned as a common debtor. The young man had no claim on the King. Prince Christian was the fourth of the six sons of Duke Frederick of Schleswig-Holstein, etc., etc., who had been so impoverished by the Napoleonic wars that he died leaving his eldest son the misfortune of a crumbling estate and his other boys to the generosity of kind friends.

Since the Glucksburgs were a branch of the ancient Oldenburg family from which sprang the Kings of Denmark, King Christian VIII had "adopted" young Christian of Schleswig-Holstein and put him in the Royal Guard. A few years later when the King's sister, Charlotte Margravine of Hesse, had arrived on a visit to Copenhagen with her two daughters, he had given Prince Christian his blessing when he desired to marry tall and beautiful Louise, the youngest; and the dusty emptiness of the Yellow Palace was at their disposal.

But if this placid young guardsman, who enjoyed his morning rides to barracks knowing that his duties would be only of the lightest description, could have looked into the future, a permanent wrinkle would probably have spoiled the smoothness of his handsome brow. He would have seen himself wearing the crown of Denmark for forty-three troublous years, while from among his children Great Britain chose a future Queen, Russia an Empress and Greece a King.

The first child appeared at Yellow Palace in 1843. He was Frederick, who many years later when the century was spent would succeed his father on the Danish throne. Alexandra Marie Charlotte Louise Julie, the heroine of this story, followed on December 1, 1844. William, the favorite brother and lifelong friend of Alexandra, was born the next year. He would grow prematurely bald and gray in a fifty-year struggle to rule the Greeks, and die by an assassin's bullet. Princess Dagmar, who one day as a stricken Empress would flee from a Russia in revolution, came in 1847. Thyra did not join the family till their fortunes changed in 1853, and Waldemar first saw the light in an accepted royal household six years later.

The earliest recorded English reference to Princess Alexandra comes in a letter from thirteen-year-old Princess Mary of Cambridge written from the old white country palace of Rumpenheim, which stands on its garden terrace on the banks of the sluggish Main near Frankfurt. Rumpenheim was an important and peculiar landmark to the Christian family from their early childhood, as it was to everybody related to the Landgraves of Hesse-Cassel.

The Duke of Cambridge, the most respectable son of George III, had married Augusta, daughter of Landgrave Frederick of Hesse, whose eldest son had married Louise's mother, the sister of Christian VIII of Denmark. Thus Mary of Cambridge and Alexandra had a common great-grandfather, and owing to a strange clause in the old man's will were destined to meet when Alexandra was aged three and to form a lifelong friendship.

Frederick of Hesse-Cassel had willed Rumpenheim Palace to the use of his six children, recording the wish that they and their families would gather there in the summer of every other year, and it was soon customary at these biennial reunions for twenty or thirty relations to take up their separate family apartments with suites and servants. But they would meet to chatter endlessly together on the terrace at the lip of the river, sifting the domestic news and rumor of royal Europe over intricate needlework. Cigars, fishing rods, politics and intrigues amused the princely males below the terrace, and the children played everywhere. At night they danced and dined together in the great hall to the music of peasant violins.

Three-year-old Alexandra at her first appearance among the relations at Rumpenheim already showed promise of that fairy-like beauty, set off by imperiousness and liveliness of spirit, which would one day enchant whole nations. Mary of Cambridge writes of "the little carriage in which we sometimes lead about little Alexandrine." The name would soon be shortened to *Alix* and remain so for the rest of her life. A few years later Mary would record at Rumpenheim that she had "completely lost her heart" to the four eldest Christian children, all of whom, boy or girl, were strikingly beautiful and attractive. The Christians, shabbier than the rest, must have been looked upon as the poor relations of this international group, and perhaps Alix was petted by Mary Cambridge all the more in consequence.

Indeed, the Rumpenheim summer holiday, which soon became an annual event for the Christian children because it was cheap, was the only time of luxury living in their year. Though their parents' suite was almost nonexistent they were always in the apartments of their rich relations and receiving all the attention they wanted from other people's servants. They played house in the bowers and thickets of the eighteenth-century gardens, chased each other through dusty corridors and derelict ghostly guest chambers, learned to fish under the terrace and were taken in boats by magnificent footmen.

At Yellow Palace their mother became their teacher. She spoke English, German and French with fluency, like most of her kind, and the children began to do the same at an early age. Their musical studies started when they were very young, and in this subject Louise was not disappointed in any of the family. They inherited her talent.

The love of gymnastics in the Danish royal family has its roots in those days. Prince Christian returned from barracks at about noon. He summoned his four children to the dining room—Frederick, Alix, William and Dagmar, who had scarcely passed her tottering stage. The guardsman pulled off his high-collared coat, started them off with simple arm and leg exercises and then launched into the somersaults and cartwheels which were his pride. The children with solemn faces followed him. They soon grew highly proficient and liked to give displays.

It used to be the boast of Alix as a young bride that she could turn cartwheels anywhere with perfect propriety—"only a matter of speed"—and her high spirits are supposed to have led her into displaying her unusual accomplishment in the Marlborough House drawing room.

Yellow Palace was situated near the Langelinie, the fashionable tree-bordered promenade beside the harbor, and there the four children were often seen striding in the shadow of their tall father. The memory most often recalled by Alix of her childhood was of sunny walks on the Langelinie, where with spellbound interest she watched the shipping crowding the sparkling water.

Alix and Dagmar shared a bedroom. Two iron beds, one large table and two rubbed eighteenth-century chairs left them plenty of room. Their toys and books needed one long shelf, and the only relief to austerity as time went on was their growing collection of photographs on the walls.

They were encouraged by their mother to think of Papa as a poor man, and perhaps even as a slightly helpless one, who could not give them things which other girls of their acquaintance received as a matter of course.

In after years, Alix in London and Dagmar in St. Petersburg were both famous for their superior style in dress. They always looked right, and this was attributed to the days when economical homemade party frocks had to be worn to advantage in rooms where luxurious velvets, satins and *mousselines de soie* swelled in rich profusion.

High spirits and the family were the keynotes of Yellow Palace days. It was all distinctly bourgeois.

Chapter 2

GOOD FROM THE ILL WIND

*I*T WAS IN 1846 when clouds appeared in Prince Christian's sky.
King Christian VIII knew that his health was failing. He was
a troubled man and an unhappy one. He had striven grimly to bring
Denmark out of the slough left by the Napoleonic wars. The people
did not love him because he refused to grant them a constitution. He
honestly did not believe they were ready for one and ruled them as
a very mild but aloof dictator.

King Christian saw Denmark in her peculiar geographical position, with her dissatisfied people, with the troublous domains of
Schleswig-Holstein tacked onto her foot, as a powder barrel which
might easily set the continent aflame and herself scorch to a desert
in the process; he knew that many shrewd men abroad thought so
too.

King Christian was troubled because of Frederick. Frederick was
his heir and only child. He had divorced Frederick's mother years
ago. Frederick, most unlike himself in every way, was possibly not
his child at all. Frederick, squat, decidedly plump in his middle age,
with flabby cheeks, Hebraic nose and goat beard, had a glint in his
gimlet eyes, a smirk on his tight mouth, that suggested brimstone.
Frederick, last in the male line of Oldenburgs—the beast in a race
of golden giants.

Frederick was the scandal of Denmark, divorced three times by
the wives his father had found for him, the despair of many a remote garrison commander to whose care he had been banished, a
king among pimps and harlots, the doyen of disreputable young

6

men in Copenhagen. Frederick, bland, mocking, totally unconcerned with his country's fate, sitting in pavement cafés with revolutionaries, carrying parcels for his Parisian mistress in the fashionable Ostergarde!

Prince Frederick would have to rule. Probably he would soon drop dead from his debaucheries. Then what would happen in Denmark? His father was sure that Frederick could never have a child, even if he abandoned his mistress for a wife of blood. King Christian was also convinced that if the throne of Denmark stood vacant for even a brief space, a fierce dynastic struggle starting over Schleswig-Holstein might bring in all the great states of Europe. To King Christian the future of the Danes was ominous.

Night and day the ailing King searched his mind for a solution of this dynastic problem, so cruelly complicated by the ulcer of Schleswig-Holstein. By bitter experience he knew that to please Danes and Schleswig-Holsteiners was practically beyond human achievement.

Since the words *Schleswig-Holstein* always reacted like a hammerblow upon Princess Alix and even upon Queen Alexandra of half a century later, since *Schleswig-Holstein* implanted in her an undying attitude of mind, a recurring flash of malevolence astonishing in so sweet a character, the salient points of the Schleswig-Holstein conundrum must be understood.

Across the foot of Denmark lies the state of Schleswig, and below Schleswig is Holstein, with the northern German states beyond it.

For centuries the leading family in both Schleswig and Holstein had been the Oldenburgs, and in both states the head of this family had been regarded as hereditary ruling Duke. But for centuries the head of the Oldenburgs had also been King of Denmark.

Least troublesome subjects under this unfortunate legacy of the centuries were the Schleswigers, because in the course of time they had come to regard their state as a vassal or fief of Denmark. Thus the Danish Kings contrived to satisfy the Schleswigers and rule them in accord with Danish policy by calling themselves Dukes of Schleswig and paying homage to themselves as Kings of Denmark. Lately, however, this comfortable system of administering and taxing Schleswig as a Danish province had grown more troublesome owing to a strong separationist movement which was active in Holstein.

The Holsteiners had long been a headache to the Danes. They too admitted the overlordship of the Oldenburg Dukes. But they had never been vassals of Denmark and were proud of the fact. Until the Holy Roman Empire collapsed with the Napoleonic wars Holstein had been a fief of the German Emperors since feudal times. In those days the Holstein Duke—the King of Denmark—had managed the Holsteiners tolerably well by paying an elaborate but meaningless homage to the German Emperor as his overlord. Since the break-up of the Empire the Holsteiners had been obstinate obstructionists in the Danish camp. Of strong Germanic descent, the Holsteiners began to look across their frontier to the Germans for encouragement in their independence movement, and got it. Meanwhile, they set themselves to poison the Danish loyalty of the Schleswigers.

The leader of this separationist campaign, the most popular man in the two states and the man who intended to rule them when they were free, was Duke Christian of Augustenburg. To complicate the matter further, the Augustenburgs were an older branch of the Oldenburgs, and Christian of Augustenburg was the nearest *male* claimant to the throne of Denmark if Christian VIII's son Frederick died without issue, as he almost certainly would do. Christian of Augustenburg was also a close friend of the British royal family, and his son and heir would later marry Princess Helena.

Yet Christian of Augustenburg was anathema to Danes, and however good his claims, however powerfully he might be supported from Germany, they would resist him furiously. He was a traitor plotting to rob them of Schleswig-Holstein and especially of their great and much-prized Baltic port of Kiel. They forgot that as their king he might be the one person who could hold Schleswig-Holstein in the Danish orbit, in their suspicion that he would bring all Denmark under German domination.

Here were the seeds of an appalling dynastic tussle. It was imperative therefore to find a nearer claimant to the Danish throne than Duke Christian. There was one. But the claimant was a *woman*. At that time nobody seemed to know whether the Salic law did or did not exist in Denmark, but few favored a woman ruler. This lady was King Christian's sister Charlotte, the Landgravine of Hesse-Cassel, Louise's mother. She certainly would not want the embarrassment of the Danish throne if it were offered her, and in any case her German husband would be most unacceptable. Yet King Christian's mind kept revolving around his sister's claim.

Suddenly the mists in the mind of the King started to clear. Why should not his sister Charlotte accept her claim to the Danish throne and then delegate it to her daughter Louise? Then Louise in her turn could pass on the claim to her husband Prince Christian.

Primed with this brilliant idea, King Christian confronted his ministers in council. They listened to him without enthusiasm. There was no unfavorable comment, no eagerness to pursue the matter. They just politely shelved his idea. The subject was changed. But the King had, of course, sounded the principals. His sister Charlotte was ready to do her part. Prince Christian was dumfounded. To Princess Louise her uncle's suggestion came as a profound excitement. Years later, when she had long been a queen, there was a Danish saying, "The King is the Queen!" Louise foresaw the shadow of things to come. Though the jolt that Prince Christian received was considerable, he soon began to look upon it as a kind of horrific jest, so vague and soon once again so unmentionable a topic that he could relapse cheerfully into the old life.

Chapter 3

BIRTH OF A ROYAL FAMILY

TWO YEARS LATER, in 1848, King Christian VIII lay dead and Frederick—King Frederick VII—summoned hastily from his country house, tugged his goat beard and poked into the rooms of the Royal Palace with bland distaste. Beside him was his mistress, Louise Rasmussen, ex-Parisian midinette, governess and ballet dancer. He had just created her Countess Danner. Their public marriage would be in a few days.

This was 1848, the year of European revolution. Thrones were tottering. Even in Buckingham Palace they had watched a revolutionary mob come marching up the Mall. The masses were stirring.

King Frederick summoned his council. They wanted a constitution. He told them they could have one. Let them draw it up according to their pleasure. They could take his throne and burn it for all he cared. He listened silently to their deliberations, with a cool and amiable smile.

King Frederick was a success. He was the right sovereign for that bloody year. Countess Danner likewise proved herself acceptable except in high society. A generous, capable, sympathetic woman, she intended to be of value to her husband and the people. The spirit of anger and unrest died overnight in Denmark.

King Frederick, having eased the tension and with polite unconcern smiled upon the slights of some old courtiers, drove off in his carriage to his country home, to his Bohemian friends and his hobby, archeology. He had done his part. Let the people look after themselves. They would only see him occasionally at Court functions.

There must have been some anxiety at Yellow Palace at the change on the Throne. The Christians had scarcely spoken a word in their lives to the new Sovereign. Indeed, till the old King lay dead it had scarcely been the thing to do. King Frederick certainly had no obligations toward the family at Yellow Palace. The Palace was his property. He might require it of them. He might charge them for it, or ask them to share it with some favorite. His reputation was black enough for anything. They told themselves that the friendship and financial help was at an end.

King Frederick called at Yellow Palace. He walked in with the utmost friendliness. He seemed without saying as much tacitly to accept Prince Christian as his heir. They would soon be surprised to receive the customary presents which they had expected from his father.

Though the Danes had begun to cheer at the sight of their stubby bourgeois monarch, they were less easily satisfied in Schleswig-Holstein. The moment had come. They proclaimed their independence under Christian of Augustenburg, drove out the Danish garrisons, and with arms and volunteers from Germany awaited the answer to their challenge.

Cool and philosophical, King Frederick buttoned himself into his bulging military frock coat and mildly waited for his subjects to decide upon the appropriate action. Then, confirmed in his post as commander in chief, he marched his forces south to open the First Schleswig War.

He won it. It took him three years. German volunteers kept seeping over the frontier to swell the defeated rebels. Prince Christian, with growing respect, served his cousin on the royal staff.

When King Frederick rode north to his country home, as sardonically indifferent as ever, his popularity was tremendous, and Prince Christian, with whom he had pointedly associated himself during the campaign, was as a result more or less popularly looked upon as his heir.

Schleswig-Holstein had surrendered unconditionally. The states were more a part of Denmark than ever before. Christian of Augustenburg was asked to remove himself to Germany, with a generous monetary compensation.

But nobody outside Denmark thought the affair was settled.

Prussia, the rising power in Germania, was known to have naval ambitions. With Kiel in her hands she might drive a canal across the Danish neck and bring a fleet out into the North Sea.

So concerned were the Powers that they summoned a conference in London in 1852. Its object was to "maintain" the integrity of Denmark and to settle beyond dispute her future King. The only tangible item that emerged from this international meeting was due to the Czar of Russia. He suggested that in accordance with a suggestion of the late King Christian VIII the succession should be settled upon Prince Christian of Glucksburg. King Frederick, who was present, seconded the Czar. The Danes when they heard of this had no objection. The Russian suggestion was adopted. Apart from that the London conference was moonshine.

And so the Landgravine of Hesse, to meet the requirements of the Powers, made over her rights to Princess Louise, and Louise triumphantly did the same to her unenthusiastic husband. King Frederick suggested that Yellow Palace was unworthy of the family of the Crown Prince. He gave the Christians Bernstoff Castle, a fine white palace standing in a beautiful park and gardens amid the romantic landscape of forests and ruined castles which surrounds Copenhagen. The family allowance increased in proportion.

Chapter 4

PHOTOGRAPH ON THE MANTELPIECE

THE CHRISTIANS with their four children packed up and set off for Bernstoff. Alix was eight years old, just old enough to enjoy the wonders of Bernstoff—it was like living at Rumpenheim all the year round—and the very modest regal style which her parents maintained there she found thrilling and impressive.

A number of accomplished and quite costly instructors and instructresses now began to call at Bernstoff, and Alix and Dagmar were much occupied in learning deportment, dancing and all those arts considered useful to a royal young lady of the time. The gymnastic department Prince Christian still reserved to himself. He had grown more serious and grave in his attitude to the children since they came to Bernstoff. He had come out with various ideas concerning the upbringing of royal children, which were possibly the result of tips he might have received from the Cambridges at Rumpenheim concerning the training of the English royal family. Punctuality was the strongest of these ideas: royal persons must be punctual to the second. It was simple. Just a matter of habit. Penalties had to be invented to drive home this new maxim.

Fifty years later the booming of a gong would always leave Alix in a flutter. She, who was said to be late for her own Coronation, whose faithful attendants would seek by every kind of trick to keep her to the clock, often ate her meals at Bernstoff in solitary disgrace with no second helping and no dessert. Something always cropped up to hinder Alix at the last moment.

Alix was not really a promising pupil except in deportment—

which came to her naturally—in riding, in music, gymnastics and dressmaking. At this last she soon had great skill—a very complicated art in those days—and although her knowledge would one day give her a reputation for wilfulness and obstinacy among "by appointment" houses, the result was that she always displayed herself to the best advantage.

By rights Alix should have been more often in disgrace than her brothers and sisters at Bernstoff. Her spirits were rather too high. She was too cheerfully incorrigible. But her disgrace was often only theoretical, for she was undoubtedly the favorite of both parents. Alix was, in fact, growing into a child of almost uncanny enchantment. Outsiders, who saw nothing of her more human side, thought her quite perfect, a gem of the finest quality; and as she grew older some news of this lovely creature spread abroad on the continent.

King Frederick often visited Bernstoff. He was interested in his heirs, and evidently he thought that their conduct must be of a rigidity which had not been marked in himself.

The Christian family were often met riding with their father in the country round Copenhagen. They were probably one of the best-looking families in the country. Alix and Dagmar, tall and graceful inseparables, were watched with admiration as they shopped with their mother in the Langelinie. At Rumpenheim their adolescent liveliness disturbed the dusty somnolence of the old palace. In the summer days the Christian family, crammed into one antique coach, came trundling down to the seaside at Klampenborg for the day. A time came when at winter parties in Copenhagen the five eldest Christians with their parents would sit down to perform a musical piece, a family orchestra of immense gravity. When an opera box was distinguished by the presence of Princess Christian with her two eldest daughters, Copenhagen offered the spectacle to strangers with pardonable pride.

Alix, with her brother Frederick, was confirmed when she was almost sixteen in the Royal Palace of Christianborg. King Frederick attended, playing the part of amiable uncle, and the elaborate reception which he gave afterward was considered to have set Alix upon the threshold of womanhood. She came out, and from that time she became a popular figure in Denmark. But outside the country the budding royal family of the Christians cut little ice, compared with many minor royalties or even grand ducal families.

One result of the coming out of Alix was that on the night following her confirmation she slept for the first time in her life in a room of her own. She had really begun to be an individual, rather than a member of a spirited family group.

But although the Christians were still small fry in the world, an event had taken place in the previous year which must be recorded. Bertie, the sixteen-year-old Prince of Wales, came over from his arduous studies at White Lodge, Richmond, to attend his first dinner party with the Cambridges at Cambridge Cottage, Kew, and there he stood and examined a photograph on the mantelpiece in the drawing room with great interest. He made some rather naïve remarks about the charms of the girl depicted. She was Princess Alix of Denmark. The incident was remembered by the Cambridges several years later.

Chapter 5

MISSED FROM THE LIST

IN THE EARLY SUMMER of the year of Alix's confirmation, 1859,
Vicky, the Princess Royal of England, the bride of Prince
Frederick William of Prussia, came home to pay her first visit to her
parents at Osborne. Her father—to whom she was close friend, con-
fidante and indeed disciple—spent much time with his beloved child
on the Osborne terraces. There as they walked to and fro the Con-
sort told her that he and her mother had resolved to find a wife for
Bertie. The Prince of Wales was seventeen: they were worried about
Bertie. His father's disappointment in him was deep. In his soul
Prince Albert was exasperated and bewildered by his eldest son.
Every one of the other boys showed more promise. Next year Bertie
would be eligible for the Crown. The idea was shocking to the
Consort. He confessed that to his brother Ernst, and probably Vicky
also understood. For lovely Vicky was of superior mould. Trained
by her father himself to be a future queen of Prussia, schooled in his
theory of a new European golden age led by England and Prussia,
this earnest green-eyed princess was rich in those qualities he so
ardently searched for in Bertie.

Bertie was on his first trip abroad with his new governor, Colonel
Bruce—Rome for three months, then Spain and Portugal—and his
father hoped the boy's essays and journals of his travels would show
more feeling and receptivity than previous unpromising efforts. To
Bertie his new governor, Bruce, was a happy improvement on Gibbs,
the somber, relentless tutor who had dogged his youth. Bertie
wanted to be a soldier, and Bruce, most scrupulously selected by the

Consort, though with some doubts, had the broader views of the military man. Bruce would have liked to give his Prince more rope; but as a soldier he obeyed orders, which ran strictly to the contrary.

Bertie, knowing something of the program mapped out for him by his father, shrank from the vista ahead. Already he felt that the ring of portentous elderly monitors which hedged him from the world would never break. On the doorstep of manhood, Bertie, having emerged from the most strenuous years of preparation of any youngster in the kingdom, needed urgently a draught of fresh air. Yet, over his next two years, people in England would talk pityingly of "the colossal educational program" upon which the Consort had now launched the Prince of Wales. First it was to be a spell at Edinburgh University for science, then Oxford and then Cambridge: no normal university curriculum for him, but a scholastic campaign waged with unflagging zeal in a scholastic cell. Too often the boy knew he would have to shudder alone under solemn bombardment from the most towering brains of all three places; and behind the amiable façades of those learned faces he saw the spy, waiting to be summoned to report upon his feeble powers. As for Bertie and his father, von Hohenlohe, a future German chancellor who visited Buckingham Palace at that period, has recorded an impression of the Prince of Wales that he (von Hohenlohe) was "dismayed by the signs of the Prince's nervous awe of his father."

Yet there were men of experience in public life who saw qualities of promise in the Prince of Wales: an immense natural courtesy, a surprising power of easy conversation for his years, wide sympathies, ability to find instant friends and a spirit that bubbled up through every boredom. Qualities his father little valued, since he himself had risen to tremendous power and influence without them.

During that summer stay of Vicky's at Osborne, her father gave her a list of six Protestant princesses, the only ones the Queen and he thought eligible to be matched with the Prince of Wales. Since the princesses were all to be found in parts of Germany, Prince Albert suggested that Vicky on her return to Prussia should be able to find an excuse for meeting the six of them. Then she could send him a *frank* report—this father and daughter were very frank with one another—on each one of the young ladies. Vicky was delighted. It was a solemn task after her own heart, a new confidence shared with

Papa, and, indeed, a task which with her great intelligence she could undertake very efficiently.

Oddly enough, rather less than twelve months before Vicky's visit to Osborne, on July 5, 1858, *The Times* had published some remarkable words:

> "To all present appearances our future monarch's choice of wife is positively limited to exactly seven ladies of royal blood—unless he selects a consort much older than himself. This will doubtless appear startling to some of our readers, but is nevertheless true."

The list of *seven* princesses follows. Six of the names on that list correspond with the six given by the Prince Consort to Vicky. The missing seventh, the name marked "5" on *The Times* list, was Princess Alix of Denmark!

And *The Times* at the end of its list had commented:

> "Without venturing upon prophecy, we are disposed to think that *No. 5* will be considered the most eligible lady, Prince Christian being heir presumptive to the throne of Denmark."

The Prince Consort, who read every newspaper, must surely have read *The Times* list, and why he had omitted Alix of Denmark from his list is a mystery. It is heightened by the fact that Uncle Leopold, King of the Belgians—the man who had given Prince Albert to Queen Victoria for a husband, who had attended the birth of Bertie and who had interfered in English affairs ever since—had originally given to the Queen and the Consort the list of suitable princesses handed to Vicky, but with one addition, Alix of Denmark. It can only be said that there does seem to appear later a certain prejudice, at least on the part of the Queen, against Princess Christian, a very obscure hint of "fastness," and they may have heard something at this juncture to make them see the Danish royal family unfavorably. Nor is it impossible that in ill-informed foreign minds the satanic reputation of King Frederick was considered as a blemish on his innocent heirs.

In the autumn came Vicky's report from Prussia. She had toured

Germany. She had met *all* the eligible princesses. One and all, they were impossible! If Vicky said that, the thing was done with in the eyes of her father. Prince Albert, already a worn and ageing man, full of troubles and responsibilities, only forty, bald and looking ten years older, "uncrowned" King of England and almost a Cabinet in himself, put by the problem of Bertie's bride, an act of prevarication most unlike him and symbolic of his weariness.

Bertie, returned from a scientific course at Edinburgh and established with his custodians in stately solitude in his mansion at Oxford, would have to wait for a bride; at least, his father determined he must wait until he had completed his five months' official tour of Canada and the U.S.A., which the Consort with misgiving, reluctance, and as he saw with great boldness, had recommended for his son in the summer of 1860.

Chapter 6

AN EXTRAORDINARY LOVE INTRIGUE

*I*N THE MEANTIME, at New Palace, Potsdam, the home of Vicky, drama was in the making. The leading figure in that opening scene was the charming young Countess Walburga von Hohenthal, who was Vicky's favorite maid of honor because she was the least Prussian one.

Walburga, very pro-English since she was engaged to an English diplomat, was the confidante. The Princess had scarcely returned from her tour through Germany in search of a bride for her brother when she revealed to Walburga the secret of her quest and her conviction that it had been a failure.

At the moment the maid of honor had no suggestions to make; but her womanly love for matrimonial intrigue did not let her forget what she had heard.

Her fiancé, Augustus Paget, the new Minister to Denmark, arrived in Berlin to visit her. From thence on we have Walburga's own words as to what took place.

> "My future husband being an Englishman and a diplomat," she records, "I knew he would be discreet, and I confided to him the dilemma of 'no Princess' for the Prince of Wales.
>
> " 'But I know the prettiest, the nicest, the most charming,' he exclaimed. 'Princess Alix, the eldest daughter of Prince Christian, the future King of Denmark. She is only sixteen, and as good as she is pretty!'
>
> "Armed with this knowledge, I went at once to the Princess and told her all about it."

The information was received with the liveliest interest. It seemed that Vicky had literally never heard of Alix. Walburga was shortly going to Denmark to marry Augustus Paget. She was instructed to secure for herself an introduction to the Christian family at the earliest possible moment and to send her report to New Palace. Apparently, Vicky decided there and then to leave the whole delicate matter in the hands of Walburga. It appears as if she had been seized with a kind of inspiration that this unknown Dane was the one for Bertie. She turned to Walburga and exclaimed, "You must tell the Queen at once as soon as you go to England." This remark was prompted by the fact that Vicky knew that Walburga would be visiting England before she would herself, although it would not be till the autumn of the following year when Paget had his home leave. Vicky's only part in the affair would be to make it possible for the Pagets to meet her mother and father, because Walburga would have something of the greatest interest to tell them.

Walburga Paget had not been long at Copenhagen before she was at Bernstoff.

"Her Royal Highness," writes Walburga, "had asked me to come quite informally, as she knew my husband so well and had often allowed him to visit her in the same way. She was still a very pretty woman, with fine blue eyes and a good figure. Prince Christian came into the room whilst I was with the Princess. There was a delightful charm and kindness about Prince Christian which won all hearts, and the patriarchal and unostentatious setting of the family life of this royal family was most attractive.

"After I had been with the Princess for a little time I said that my husband had so often spoken to me of the Princess Alexandra that I hoped I might be allowed to see her."

Alix was sent for, and at this stage the proud parents must have displayed their gem without the smallest idea that they had a spy in the household.

To Walburga, the girl who appeared was "like a half-open rosebud, so simple and childlike in everything."

Evidently the Christian family circle very greatly impressed Walburga, for she reverts to it.

> "Later on I made the acquaintance of the other children. It was charming to see the still youthful parents and their half-grown-up and growing children, all so happy and united together."

The family was now complete, Frederick, Alix, William, Dagmar, Thyra and Waldemar, though Thyra was only six and Waldemar not yet one. The Christians would scatter to almost all parts of the compass, yet the family bond would always hold them, and as long as their parents lived they would appear year after year at the family reunion in Denmark. A glowing report reached New Palace. The affair lay fallow until the autumn of 1860.

The Pagets reached England in the first week of November. They were dismayed to find the country in a state of anxiety and excitement. *H.M.S. Hero,* bringing the Prince of Wales back from his tour in Canada and the U.S.A., was days overdue. Battered vessels staggered into port out of the terrific Atlantic gales and the number of total losses was mounting. November 9 was the Prince of Wales's birthday and he was to have celebrated it with the family. The Pagets, doubtless through Vicky's machinations, had been invited to the great birthday dinner party at Windsor on the 9th.

No news of the Prince of Wales had come when the birthday arrived, but his parents decided to put a brave face on it and hold the birthday dinner party in his absence.

Walburga found herself sitting next to the Prince Consort.

> "I saw my opportunity," says she rather naïvely, "and when the Prince spoke of his son I ventured to beg him to forgive me if I alluded to a subject that had been kept secret . . . but I now thought the Princess so much searched for had been found, and I told him all I knew about Princess Alix."

When she had finished her breathless recommendation she "heard him repeating it to the Queen, who was on his other side."

After dinner the Queen sent for Walburga. She asked her many questions about Princess Alix. Then she asked her to get any photographs of the Princess she could procure without arousing the curiosity of the Christian parents and send these to England.

Six days later a telegram from Plymouth announced the arrival of the Prince of Wales. His success in the New World had been tremendous. Britons and Americans had been passive and sometimes active enemies since the Declaration of Independence. The young man in his brief visit had literally established an *entente cordiale* with Americans such as he afterward achieved with England's other traditional enemies, the French. To the Consort the triumph of his son was almost incomprehensible.

Not a word was spoken to Bertie about Alix of Denmark, or indeed about the possibility of marriage. A week after his jaded arrival at Plymouth he had returned without protest to his studies at Oxford. The awe of his father was upon him. In the New World he had learned to know himself. It was not without pardonable pride that he stepped on English soil. The atmosphere of Windsor deflated him like a pricked balloon.

In the following spring the Danish affair moved a step further. Walburga received a letter in answer to one of hers to New Palace:

"I am especially grateful," wrote Bertie's eldest sister, "for your last letter, which is so full of the business I have so much at heart . . . my interest increases the more I hear of the person in question. What a pity if she were to make another marriage! In the first place it would be desirable to find out whether she is not coming some time to Germany. I should be so enchanted to make her acquaintance . . . you have a certain flair in making naïve remarks. I should have no objection to your compromising me slightly, not as an official person, but as *my* friend, and if you were to be a little indiscreet about the young lady."

The upshot of this was that Walburga let it be known to the Christian parents that the Princess Royal (Vicky) would shortly be staying with her cousin "Aunt" Augusta, Grand Duchess of Mecklenburg-Strelitz, and that the Christians would be welcome there at the same time. It was clearly understood that the true reason of this visit must be a profound secret, as the possibility of a non-German marriage for the Prince of Wales—especially any move in the Danish direction—must on no account leak out in Germany.

The Strelitz meeting took place, and a letter reached Walburga in Copenhagen:

"I have returned from Strelitz quite enchanted. Princess Alexandra is the most fascinating creature in the world. You did not say nearly enough," wrote the Princess. "For a long time I have not seen anybody who pleases me so much as this lovely and charming girl . . . simply quite charming. . . ."

In June, Vicky came to Osborne. She was Crown Princess of Prussia now. Her father thought her new dignity became her very well. With her were "Fritz," her tall, bearded husband, and Willy (the future Kaiser) on his first visit. It was the last occasion upon which father and beloved daughter were to meet, and left Willy with his one memory of his grandfather—being swung by him in a table napkin in the breakfast room. Father and daughter concerted a plot in which the Duchess of Mecklenburg was again to be called upon to play a part. The time had come for a meeting between Bertie and Alix. Vicky returned home to prepare the ground.

An invitation reached Bertie from his eldest sister inviting him to stay at Potsdam in September. She would take him for a tour in Germany and they would come to "Aunt" Augusta at Strelitz. At this point the Christian parents came into the plot. The Christian family in September would be at Rumpenheim.

September came and Bertie arrived at New Palace. The idea of a German tour seemed to him delightful—but not *too many* cathedrals! He was told that he must see the wonderful old cathedral at Speier, which was near Strelitz. Speier is also near Rumpenheim, and the scene was set.

On that day when Bertie without enthusiasm drove with his sister toward Speier, Princess Christian arrived there with her daughters. It was time they went over the famous cathedral. As Bertie and the Crown Princess entered one door of Speier Cathedral, Princess Christian led her daughters in at the other end of the building. They met in the central aisle.

Bertie was bored by monuments. But it was clear his interest in antiquities had suddenly increased as he escorted Alix of Denmark from point to point. Alix was composed, and it is not quite certain that she was totally unaware of the purpose of the visit.

Bertie and Alix met again next day at Heidelberg. There they found endless antiquities which they could enjoy together.

After the Heidelberg meeting the Consort received a letter, which prompted him to confide in Uncle Leopold, "the young people seem to have taken a liking to one another." It was one of the masterly understatements of that great man.

The girl cousins at Rumpenheim recorded their eager interrogation of Alix after the Heidelberg meeting. Alix laughed at them. She pulled a photograph out of her pocket. "I have got him here!" she said, and slipped it back with an enigmatic smile.

Alix could hardly have been anything but dazzled by the earnest attention of the far-famed Prince of Wales, the first Prince of Europe. She was more or less in love with him after those two brief meetings. Women fell easily under the spell of Albert Edward, Prince of Wales, as she would discover. As for that embryo young man of the world, who was watching life so keenly from behind his bars, those ardent roaming eyes of his gazed upon the loveliest girl in the world, and he would shortly tell his mother and sisters as much.

Yet, scarcely can it be said that Bertie was dreaming of weddings when he brooded distastefully over his books at Cambridge after his return. For Cambridge was now his place of study, and this time his lonely mansion was several miles out of town. The thoughts of Bertie at Maddingley Hall were rather elementary than romantic. How to evade most smoothly the stodginess of his life, how to gather some chosen friends and interests for himself apart from the ageing and ponderous ring about him, how to reach that princely independence to which his age entitled him, how to treat his father—these were the immediate problems of Bertie.

Then, suddenly, it was as if a great black curtain had crashed down upon the scene. With its impact everything shuddered and reeled in bewilderment. The curtain rose again—slowly—and Bertie saw that the old scenery had a brightness and wonder he had never known before.

At Christmas the Consort, who had done so much for his adopted land, died tragically and unexpectedly at Windsor. The half-century had lost its greatest figure. Bertie had lost a jailer. Though he had loved and respected as deeply as he had hated and feared him, not for a moment can it be doubted that he was happier with him in the tomb.

Bertie, very gentle and kind with his mother—the terrible dementia of whose grief seemed best mollified by John Brown, the strange young Highland gillie summoned from Balmoral to Osborne —soon learned that one subject, at least, penetrated through the Queen's awful sorrow; it was Alix of Denmark. His mother talked much of the Princess she had never seen, and Bertie, who knew that at last the mantle of manhood and responsibility had dropped upon him, began to think with purposeful ardor of Alix of Denmark as the future Princess of Wales.

Marriage, moreover, would give him a household and the freedom to move about for which he yearned, and the remembered liveliness and high spirits of this lovely girl seemed to offer him the perfect partner for his new venture. She would be a breath of fresh air to blow away the mid-century cobwebs.

Yet the affair had not moved since Heidelberg. The cautious Consort had in his wisdom let things rest for a space, and Bertie would speak to his mother not of marriage with Alix but of the lady herself. She did not entirely comprehend the depth of his feelings, but that was of little consequence. She knew what she must do. The death of the Consort, far from delaying the matter, was going to advance it decisively. That was because the Queen, knowing how firmly convinced the Beloved One had been that the Danish Princess, whom he had never seen, was the *right* Princess of Wales, was resolved to pursue the match as the first of those wishes or projects of the Departed to which she intended to devote the rest of her life.

It is more than possible that one of the strong motives moving the Prince Consort toward the Danish match was the dangerous Schleswig-Holstein problem. Prince Albert must have become aware through his eldest daughter that there were powerful men in Prussia who harbored sinister designs for Prussian expansion and whose eyes looked toward the mouth of the Baltic. Denmark menaced by Prussia might hazard European peace. Prussia feared Britain. What better deterrent to Prussian hot-headedness than a Danish instead

of a German match for the Prince of Wales? Any political significance in the Danish marriage was publicly denied again and again.
Certainly the Consort would never have contemplated going to war
on behalf of Denmark, yet a cool, firm gesture might find its mark.
Bismarck, who saw well to overlook the Anglo-Danish match with
a sorrowing widow on the British throne, might have held his armies
in check if the great Consort had survived his forty-third year.

The Queen, while still too ill and smitten by grief to listen patiently to her ministers, to be seen by her people, to give anything
but a reproachful glance to State papers which were diffidently thrust
before her, was embarking on a delicate and tortuous intrigue of
the most secret character.

Round and round the Osborne walks John Brown, gentle, grim
and sardonic, led the tiny crawling pony carriage in which the forty-
two-year-old widow drooped in her weeds of woe. Only Brown, they
say, could break in on her thoughts to bring a smile. And doubtless
those somber thoughts concerned her future life, dedicated to the
fulfilment of the plans of the Beloved One and especially the Danish
match. She had heard that the Czar was seeking Alix for the Czarevitch! What would darling Albert—whose spirit walked always beside her—think if she let Alix slip through her fingers to the horrible
Russians? She must stir out of her nightmare to stop that.

Bertie she despatched on February 5, 1862, on a tour of Palestine
and the Near East. A certain lightness of speech and eye, a lack of
melancholy, an eagerness in Bertie, disturbed her. He was better out
of the way while she worked through the spirit of the Beloved One
on his behalf.

Her letters dealing with the Danish match, at first directed to
Uncle Leopold and to Vicky, who dealt with Walburga in Copenhagen, eventually came to be addressed by herself to Prince and Princess Christian. They welcomed the project, indeed, not only for the
glory it would cast upon unimportant Alix, but because they saw in
it a direct assurance that Great Britain ranged herself with Denmark
against the plots of the Prussian brigands.

In Germany an appalling outcry would break out if news of the
Danish negotiations reached the newspapers. England was the German matrimonial preserve, and the political implications would be

seen in the worst light. Warned in the early stages, the Germans might thrust a spoke in the wheels and break the match.

Two factors greatly aided the Queen in her intrigue by dulling the alertness of the Germans to what was afoot. She had already given two of her children to Germany: Vicky to Prussia, and Alice, affianced to the Prince of Hesse-Darmstadt, would marry him that summer.

Though no definite and final proposals had as yet been received at Bernstoff from England, the affair was settled in the minds of the Christian parents within a month of the Prince of Wales's return from the East in June 1862.

For some months Princess Christian had talked purposefully of the Prince of Wales before Alix. She wanted to observe and test her daughter. Alix was seen to blush each time the Prince's name came up. The children made a joke of it, which was not what was intended. Approached alone, Alix was vague and elusive.

"If he really loves me—yes—but how could I know?—I hate an arranged marriage. I would not do it. That's terrible! I think I'm too unimportant and easygoing to suit the English. I couldn't face it. Everybody says they are so solemn—if only I could be certain that *he* really wanted me!"

These are the recorded murmurings of Alix at Bernstoff.

Louise was a decisive woman, and wishing to send some definite news to the Prussian Crown Princess for transmission to Queen Victoria, she began to lose patience. That made Alix worse. The mother, distracted, appealed to the Crown Princess for some reassuring words concerning her brother's sentiments. Vicky could only reply that if her brother were not anxious for the match "it would not have gone so far as this." It was not warm enough.

But when the Prince of Wales reached Windsor from the East he surprised and delighted his mother by displaying some small presents which he had bought for Alix in Oriental bazaars. Then Bertie, who had been a trifle vague himself, proclaimed that he hoped he would be married next spring.

The glad news of this pronouncement reached the parents at Bernstoff. That ought to be enough for Alix. It was the beginning

42154

of July, and Princess Christian attacked her daughter point-blank—would she, or would she not, marry the Prince of Wales?

The vague mutterings greeted her again. "If only I knew if he loved me—if only I knew!" At last Alix exclaimed, "I wish I could see *him* again!"

"That is enough—you want to marry him!" answered her mother.

Word reached the Queen that Princess Alix would accept the hand of the Prince of Wales, with the further comment, evidently in answer to some provisions set by Her Majesty, that "she did not look for *anything else* but Love." Where Alix was concerned this was doubtless exactly true at the moment of writing; but this was not even then the case with her parents, nor would be with the people of Denmark when they heard of it.

As soon as the Queen had seen her daughter Alice married to Prince Louis of Hesse-Darmstadt in a scene of grim gloom in the Osborne drawing room early in July, she began to draft her official letter of proposal for the hand of Alix of Denmark for her son the Prince of Wales.

The happy parents at Bernstoff felt they could reply with easy consciences that nothing was nearer the desires of their eldest daughter. Uncle Leopold, delighted at the news, wrote from Brussels urging the Queen to seek a meeting with her prospective daughter-in-law. Princess Alix would, he assured her, be like "a ray of sunshine." The Queen may perhaps have thought this a quality more suited to Bertie than herself at that moment, but as she had arranged in September to make a quiet incognito pilgrimage to Coburg, the Beloved One's birthplace, and had heard that Princess Alix would be holidaying with her parents in Ostend, she resolved reluctantly to break into the solemnity of her journey to stay with her uncle at Brussels. Would he persuade Prince Christian to bring Alix as his guest for a day or two at Laeken Palace? This was to be the first of the royal widow's solemn Continental tours as the "Countess of Balmoral," which later made her such a legend abroad.

Chapter 7

BETROTHAL IN BLACK

IN THE TWILIGHT of September 3, 1862, there crept into Laeken Palace a funereal little party, bringing gloom with its passage. The Countess of Balmoral, macabre in the shelter of her pouring veils, with her kilted Highlander glowering over her, and her daughters in shrinking attendance, collapsed in grief in her uncle's arms.

Next morning early, Prince and Princess Christian arrived with Alix from Ostend. There was to be a meeting that morning and an interview—a kind of State interview—before the English and Belgian relations and privileged members of the Court. Walburga Paget had also arrived, for she it was who was to introduce the Christians to the Queen.

Just as people were preparing to make their way to King Leopold's Writing Room for the interesting moment, word came from Her Majesty that she must have more time to prepare herself for this "terribly trying ordeal." It was dampening and unexpected: tension was in the air of Laeken's corridors. Uncle Leopold was enjoying himself: bustling, pompous, whispering, making everyone more nervous. He postponed his elaborate luncheon party—supposed to be a kind of celebration after the meeting—until 2 p.m. to suit the Queen.

John Brown came with a message: Her Majesty was too indisposed to attend the luncheon, but she hoped the interview would take place immediately afterward.

Luncheon was spiritless, with Uncle Leopold and Prince Christian pulling out their watches, while Louise anxiously watched the cheeks of her highly strung daughter paling into a green shade.

At last the company were all assembled in the Writing Room. The eyes of all present watched a closed door leading into a little boudoir, and from before this red-bearded Brown observed them with disdainful firmness. Inside waited Her Majesty, alone.

At a sign from King Leopold, Walburga Paget entered the boudoir to request the presence of the Queen. But Walburga closed the door quickly behind her. At sight of her the Queen of England had covered her face and burst into uncontrollable sobs. A dismaying moment indeed for the young German girl to be closeted with this awesome weeping Queen, whom she scarcely knew.

"Oh, you can understand what I feel!" moaned the Queen. "You have a husband you love. You can realize what I have lost!"

Petrification turned to pity, and Walburga, abandoning deference, was able to bring the Queen to compose herself.

The Queen came out to them. They could not know of the heart-rending scene in the boudoir. They froze in the presence of the high priestess of Grief. Only Alix seemed to retain her self-possession. Something within her had gone out to the Queen. Walburga had seen, but of the others it was as if only Alix understood.

Secretly, the Queen was enchanted by the child who stood before her. Alix was "lovely, a beautiful refined profile—a quiet ladylike manner." Outwardly, though gentle to Alix, Her Majesty's chief concern seemed to be to explain to the parents that their daughter would be going to a home of Mourning—she did not say eternal mourning—where Sorrow left little place for high spirits and enjoyments.

It was a stiff, wretched interview. They might all have been gathered at the foot of Albert's tomb in the Royal Mausoleum at Frogmore. Her Majesty's coolness to Princess Christian horrified her uncle. ". . . Must have been quite good-looking, unfortunately very deaf," runs the royal journal. Princess Christian painted her face: a discovery shocking in itself and an affront to the pale-cheeked widow with her tear-swollen eyes. Victoria never would hide her dislikes. Prince Christian, butlerlike in his nervous amiability, ventured to require an assurance of the true affection of the Prince of Wales for their daughter. That he received, somewhat indignantly, and at that moment believed that he was also securing the potent alliance of England.

Parentally, the matter was settled and approved. It was the children's turn, and there doubtless things would soon take their proper course. That bothersome business the Queen could leave to Uncle Leopold to arrange. She retired to rest, leaving the fluttered group in uneasy silence.

Her Majesty dined alone upstairs. But shortly afterward Uncle Leopold entered benevolently with Prince and Princess Christian and Alix, "who had tactfully put on a dead black dress for the occasion."

The atmosphere was warmer. It was the magical spell of Alix which moved them all. When the Queen was alone again she wrote: ". . . lovely—nothing in her hair and curls on either side which hung down over her shoulders, her hair turned back over her beautiful forehead; her whole appearance one of the greatest charm. . . ."

Early next day the Queen, much refreshed, took train for Coburg. Alix had triumphed indeed. As the Queen was leaving she had put into Alix's hand a sprig of white heather from Balmoral. Bertie had picked it for his mother during his last stay in the Highlands.

The heart of Alix thrilled with excitement and relief as they returned to Ostend. In twenty-four hours the Prince of Wales would be with them. Soon she was meeting Bertie. He spent one day with them at the villa at Ostend. They were very happy. He did not propose. He understood Uncle Leopold would warn him when the moment was ripe. Then they all traveled back to Laeken Palace in merry mood. It would be quite pleasant there without the Presence.

Uncle Leopold received them with a grand *déjeuner*. What a difference from his last dismal luncheon! Afterward they strolled out into the sunlit gardens, guests wandering in all directions. Bertie knew that the moment had come. It was only a formality, but in the seclusion of some shrubby corner it might bring a satisfactory reward. Later they presented themselves hand in hand to the Uncle.

Uncle Leopold was now at his best. Next morning they all set out on a deliriously happy expedition to the field of Waterloo. Bertie had quite forgotten his mourning and Alix the sorrowing family into which she was pledged. On the following day came a brilliant review in their honor, with all punishments remitted for the troops and a holiday decreed. Brussels was celebrating the royal engagement in style.

To Bertie those golden days meant more than the blooming of delirious romance. Beyond the wonder of his love for this exquisite girl, he saw freedom and independence at last in sight—the freedom of the world for which his appetite was so keen. With a thrill of delightful anticipation the prisoner imagined himself as one of those envied young men of blood and fashion to whom life was an open book.

While Brussels rejoiced, life was somber in England. People read in the newspapers of the celebrations in Belgium. They knew what must be the meaning of them, although official enlightenment was lacking. Since nothing came from the Throne, nobody dared report the engagement. Rumors of a forthcoming engagement in the Danish quarter had, indeed, been interesting British newspaper readers for more than a month past, and the rumors, moreover, were Government-inspired. The denials which invariably followed were similarly inspired by the highest sources. The truth was that the Queen had considered the affair far enough advanced to prepare the Germans for the shock. And, to use an expression of the time, the Germanic press had been "going it hot and strong." Germans—especially Prussians—did not like it. It was sinister, it was perfidious, with the Schleswig-Holstein question—no business of England—coming to a climax. Vicky—the Prussian Crown Princess, already often referred to rather bitterly as the *Engländerin*—had been indiscreet in the affair and Bismarck was setting the first of many indelibly black marks against her. The "Countess of Balmoral" had not been overwelcome when she passed through Germany, and even loyal Coburgers were pained by her perfidy.

Bertie traveled with Alix as far as Cologne. There they bade each other a sad farewell. The Queen had decided that they must not see one another again until the royal wedding. Bertie, changing his mood, joined his mother at Coburg. She found his manner much improved. He appeared to be taking his marriage seriously. She thought he would have pleased his father. Bertie wrote to his cousin and crony, Victor Count Gleichen:

"I can assure you that I only know now what it is to be really happy, and if I can only prove to dear Alix that I am not unworthy of her love and make her future life a happy one, I think I shall have every reason to be content."

There would be those, including Bertie's wife, who would question the contentment of this restless adventurer, though he looked for no more than most of the fashionable swells and aristocrats in his generation; yet at heart Bertie always would be the good husband and champion of beautiful Alix to the end.

The British public waited until September 16 for the official announcement of the engagement, and the wording of this notice probably reveals the motive for its delay. It was meant to be casual— a private family affair: of *no* significance to Germans or Danes!

"We understand," ran the notice, "that the marriage of the Prince of Wales to Princess Alexandra of Denmark has been privately settled at Brussels, and that it is based entirely on mutual affection and the personal merit of the young princess, and is in no way connected with political considerations. The late Prince Consort, whose sole object was the welfare and happiness of his children, had long been convinced that this was the most suitable marriage. . . ."

One can almost hear the Queen composing aloud this notice for distribution to the Press. This aspect of casualness was further emphasized by Her Majesty herself, who delayed the publishing of her Royal Assent for nearly eight weeks. On November 5 *The Times* printed this as a trifling little paragraph, which might well be overlooked, and without comment. In Prussia, Bismarck, though rattled by the Danish marriage, knew how to read aright into this prevarication. His mobilization plans could go ahead.

Unhappy, hopeful Denmark was on the threshold of a bitter disillusionment. And as for John Bull, always sympathetic to the lame dog, he would grow more pro-Danish week by week. John Bull, indeed, was pleased to have a change from German royalties. Newspapers talked humorously of "understanding the Schleswig-Holstein mystery," and more seriously of "improving England's influence in favor of peace." No wonder, therefore, that Danes could not credit the nonpolitical presentation of the match. The words of a leading Danish newspaper make plain their optimism:

"It is very desirable that England should have an opportunity of knowing more of Danish affairs than is generally supposed to be the case. It would not be pleasant or becoming, on the present occasion, to say anything of the dispute between the Duchies and Denmark, for which other and more fitting opportunities may offer."

Chapter 8

ALIX IN THE ROYAL CLOSET

No sooner had the Queen reached England early in October than she was lying awake in the night watches in terror at what she had brought about. True, the Beloved One, who foresaw everything, had said, "We shall be taking the Princess—not her Danish relations!" But, be there a hundred denials, she knew that to persons not in her closest councils the match might appear both political and significant. The thought of Britain at war, without darling Albert, set her brain reeling and heart pounding. She told Bertie that she had decided to have Alix to stay with her alone for at least a month at Osborne and Windsor before the wedding. She had got to impress firmly upon the Danish girl that her duty lay entirely with her adopted country, that she must hold no kind of partisanship for her land of birth—above all, that she must not dare to influence Bertie, who was impulsive and indiscreet, to favor causes which would be harmful to his neutral position.

Bertie was not told all that by his mother. He simply understood that unhappy Alix was to spend a month being catechized on marriage by her future mother-in-law. He himself was to go on a tour of Italy and the Mediterranean with General Knollys, his new governor. It tore Bertie's heart to picture his beautiful Alix abandoned for a whole month to the solemnity of the Royal Closet.

Bertie appealed in confidence to Uncle Leopold to dissuade the Queen. King Leopold was as horrified as his great-nephew. He wrote to the Queen pleading that sensitive Alix had last year wept for hours at the thought of leaving home to stay with her German grandmother. But it was of no use. *Alix must come.*

A letter—almost an ultimatum—stunned the family at Bernstoff. Prince Christian was to bring Alix to Osborne on November 7. Perhaps he might care to stay for two days while Alix was fitting in, then he could go home and return again for her in December. Princess Christian was not consulted, nor mentioned in any way whatever.

Alix displayed greater equanimity than anybody else at Bernstoff when this awful letter was read. The ordeal had to be faced. Nobody would know what were the true feelings of Alix, for she behaved from first to last with amazing self-possession, and it might have been Prince Christian and not his daughter who had to stay alone with the Queen, judging by his agitation as they embarked on the *Black Eagle* for England.

On the afternoon of November 7 the *Black Eagle,* plunging and rolling, struggled through drifting fog toward the English coast, while rockets and fog signals blazed up to guide her. Very late and exhausted, the royal visitors staggered ashore at Southampton.

At Osborne, excitement and anxiety at the nonappearance of the guests caused Her Majesty, who had "waited and waited," to refuse to sit down to dinner. She would swallow only "a little soup" between nervous questionings to Alice, Helena and Louise, who kept peering out into the mist and blackness.

At last—outside came the rolling of carriage wheels and the clatter of hooves. They had arrived. The Queen and her daughters ran to the hall. There was "dear Alix looking very lovely." The deep family sorrow of Osborne faded in the tearful joy of belated greeting. The Queen herself led her future daughter-in-law to her room. After that first joyous greeting Alix quickly learned that when Her Majesty was present the royal home was truly a house of sorrow: in the Presence lightheartedness was unthinkable, but only in the Presence. The royal daughters and the intimate suite, she discovered, held less somber views. She was destined to spend more time being girlishly occupied beyond the bounds of the Royal Closet than her father grimly anticipated.

Very little is known of what passed between the Queen and Alix within the sanctity of the Royal Closet, what promises and assurances were asked of Alix and how she answered to these. But certain it is that when, in the following year, the Prussian invaders poured into Schleswig-Holstein, the lovely young bride, the idol of England, was an ardent and outspoken Dane, with a husband equally ready to voice his indignation, while a host of chivalrous Britons, bemused by her spell, would shout to a reluctant Government to put arms in their hands. But by that time the magic of Alix would have so bewitched the Queen that she would have to forgive her even this.

Princess Mary of Cambridge, then renowned for her massive beauty, already regarded her cousin Alix with deep admiration and affection from their many meetings at Rumpenheim, and from this time onward she was resolved, and indeed was, to become one of her closest friends. Princess Mary, considered to be the reigning beauty and one of the most fashionable young women in the land—she would soon lose both titles, but she did not mind—was to be entrusted with the supervision of the making of the bride's trousseau, and in her journal are several interesting entries concerning this visit.

At Brighton, two days after Alix's arrival, the Princess writes:

"the Prince of Wales—God bless him—attains his majority (21) today. It blew a gale all night and poured with rain all the morning. After luncheon we watched anxiously for the expected and longed-for arrival of Christian (Pr Christian), who was on his way back to Copenhagen, having installed Alix at Osborne. At half-past three we had the happiness of welcoming him, and for upward of three hours sat talking over the betrothal of Alix and Bertie. We could enter into his feelings of leaving Alix thus for the first time."

Twelve days later the Cambridges arrived at Windsor, where the Court had moved.

"We reached Windsor Castle about twelve," said Mary Cambridge, "and were shown into our old Lancaster tower rooms, where we were presently joined by darling Alix—too overjoyed at the meeting to speak!—and dear Alice and Louis (of Hesse-Darmstadt, her husband); after a while Alix took me to her rooms in the Devil's tower, where Louis was being *sketched;* here the poor dear Queen joined us and remained with us for some time. We lunched with Her Majesty, and Beatrice (aged 5) came in afterward. . . . Went into Alix's room again and played to her *en souvenir de Rumpenheim,* afterward accompanying her into all the State rooms, Mama, Alice, Louis, and Helena being also of the party. On our return Mama and I were summoned to the Queen's Closet, and had a nice little talk with her, ending with tears. We were hurried off shortly before five, Alix, Alice and others rushing after us to bid us good-by."

The Cambridges returned to Cambridge Cottage, Kew, and Mary Cambridge, a good organizer, eagerly took in hand the fascinating matter of the trousseau. What a delight it was to dress and undress such a superbly exquisite creature! Alix, she felt, was her protégée, and many conferences and fittings took place with her during the next few days. Mary's description of Alix as "too overjoyed at the meeting to speak" is probably no exaggeration. The burden of Alix's stay from then on was lightened by the warm-hearted Cambridge girl. With Queen Victoria's daughters Alix, though always friendly, was never really able to get on intimate terms until the end of her life.

On November 24, Mary of Cambridge, writing at Cambridge Cottage, records:

"welcomed dear Christian, whom George (her brother) had driven down *en surprise.* Soon afterward, Alix, Alice, Louis and Helena arrived. . . . As soon as Alix had taken off her things in my room, I left her with her father in my sitting room to an undisturbed *tête-à-tête.* . . . After luncheon we adjourned to the drawing room and conservatory, the suite occupying the library. George and Christian left soon after three, but the others remained till past four o'clock, when they left for Richmond, where a special train awaited them."

Prince Christian was staying at the Danish Embassy, a peculiar lodging for a royal father come to fetch home the royal bride-to-be, but Windsor, the home of Sorrows, had no hospitality to offer him, and it appears that this fleeting meeting with his daughter at Cambridge Cottage was their first sight of one another.

Next day, Mary of Cambridge was concerned with the royal trousseau.

> "I saw Mrs. James with patterns of Honiton lace and models of gowns for Alix's trousseau. Shortly afterwards Christian arrived ... lunched with us ... and after a tender farewell Christian left *en route* for Windsor; he starts with Alix on their return tomorrow."

Calais offered Alix a wonderful surprise. When she stepped ashore with her father, there was Bertie smiling at her on the quay. This was by special concession of Her Majesty. Two glorious days flew by in Hanover and Cologne, and they left him behind at Hamburg. Bertie must on no account appear in the Danish capital. The Queen was adamant about that. It would be too much for the Germans! A little comedy had taken place over this question of Alix and Bertie meeting one another. While Alix was at Windsor Bertie had arrived at Lyons. Here in an especially kindly letter from his mother he read that she was urging Darling Alix to stay on at Windsor into December so that he would find her there when he arrived. Alix, however had not yet made up her mind.

Bertie, full of excitement, wrote rather pompously to his fiancée and his parents, declaring that he felt it only right that Her Majesty's wishes should be followed in this matter. A letter also reached Bernstoff from the Queen. But the Christians had put up with enough. Already the father had been slighted and the mother downright insulted; now, they wanted to keep Alix over December 1, her birthday, the last she might ever spend with them. In terms of unveiled impatience mixed with deferential but firm apology they required their daughter to be returned to them as arranged. Their vehemence was perfectly unnecessary. The Queen entirely understood their motives. All anniversaries were holy to her. Thus, the meeting abroad—outside Denmark!—had been fixed on as a sop to Bertie, the astonishing improvement in whose manner deserved some reward.

Bertie returned home to the bleak silences of Windsor to support his sisters on that awful and dreaded day, the first anniversary of the death of the Consort. But his thoughts, even in the charnel gloom of the Royal Mausoleum at Frogmore, were probably engrossed with the preparations going forward at Marlborough House, the home-to-be, and perhaps with a wider vision of the lights of London which would soon be his. He frequently slipped away from Windsor to spend enthusiastic hours among the men at work in Marlborough House.

A new problem had arisen in this period of supreme sorrow: the date of the wedding. It was difficult, dangerous or impossible to leave Danish ports too early in the year. On the other hand, the most suitable month, February, was already bespoken—Alice of Hesse was to have her first baby at Windsor. Her Majesty suggested to Prince and Princess Christian that they might take Alix and winter with King Leopold in Brussels. Then they could reach England in January: it would be most convenient. The Danish family politely regretted that this would not be possible. March, then, was clearly the month for the wedding.

Some tiresome person reminded the Queen that "Wedding celebration in Lent will cause public disapproval." It was true. In the state of religious revivalism then prevalent Lent festivities might pain many people.

"In my young days there was no Lent!" snapped the Queen; and from Bernstoff they wrote a meek agreement to the royal proposal that the wedding should be on March 10. They would, as suggested, present themselves in London on the 7th, and they would arrive in Brussels on the 2nd for a five-day stay with King Leopold—a final grooming for Alix from the universal Uncle.

All was now in train. Parliament had amiably voted the Prince of Wales a £40,000 annuity (he had £63,000 private income), and the Princess £10,000. Marlborough House awaited the bridal pair, and Sandringham estate, their destined country home, which had been bought by the Prince Consort for Bertie out of the Duchy of Cornwall accumulations in '61, had been brought into a sufficient state of attractiveness to make it from the first sight the most cherished place in England to Alix.

London, practically starved for royal glamour since the Great Exhibition and with nothing but a few crude magazine sketches of this totally unknown but fabulously lovely Danish princess to whet

its appetite, was quivering on the eve of the most amazing and terrifying display of hysteria ever shown to a royal personage.

Some questionings and disagreements had concerned the place for
the wedding. London was known to be agog, and a London wedding might have been thought to offer the most number of people a
chance of participating in some part of it. The Chapel Royal, St.
James's, that almost traditional royal marriage place, was rejected by
the Queen to everyone's astonishment—it was too small, or was
there in her rejection a kind of tragic jealousy because she and Albert had been married there? They offered the ample spaces of St.
Paul's. Such a suggestion had never been heard of! That was where
they buried people like Nelson and Wellington. Westminster Abbey? It was not suitable. The password was Sorrow. This was a
marriage in a mourning family. St. George's, Windsor, was the
place! . . . where nobody had been married since Edward I. The
Queen had her eye on the Royal Closet or balcony, where enclosed
with her sorrow and generous curtains she might gloom dramatically
over the nuptial glitter of the chancel. Dismay spread amongst the
bidden guests at the thought of monstrous ceremonial crinolines
crushed brutally into railway carriages, and as for the mob, doomed
to see nothing, it would be found that their clamor to the railway
company for cheap excursions to Windsor would bring grave embarrassments to that sleepy town.

Part Two

DANISH ENCHANTMENT

Chapter 9

THE HAZARDOUS WELCOME

*I*T WAS February 26, 1863. Copenhagen—indeed all Denmark—was *en fête*. Denmark, little and menaced and fearful, was sending its Princess to marry not merely the Prince of Wales, but a tremendous new ally, the greatest in the world. Immense relief and tearful jubilation was the emotion of that triumphant day.

The wedding party drove to the station through streets mad with excitement. Costly hothouse blooms showered down from windows and balconies, and forests of decorations danced and fluttered in the icy wind. For once Uncle Frederick was cheerful on a day of ceremony as he waited at the railway station. None more relieved than he that the thing was almost accomplished. He had better means than his subjects for knowing what brewed across the frontier. The sands were running out. Cynic as he was, Frederick could not but believe this brilliant match was the salvation of Denmark.

His wedding present was the most magnificent of all: a necklace of 118 pearls and 2000 brilliants, some of which had shone at the Crystal Palace beside the Koh-i-noor in 1851.

Alix with her parents, Frederick, William, Dagmar and Thyra, entered the overdecorated station for the last farewells. An English journalist watching Alix there depicts her as in the highest spirits, "in brown silk with white stripes, and one of those natty little bonnets which seemed to sit better on her head than anybody else's."

Through a rejoicing countryside they came to the sea at Korsor in the evening. They alighted while fireworks blazed into the darkness, lighting the sparkling waves. Alix was walking dreamily as if

45

in some Hans Andersen fairy tale. She was incredulous, knowing nothing of this kind of royal experience, and could not imagine anything more exciting. She had much to learn in the next few days.

The wind howled across the glittering waters and the *Schleswig* put out for Kiel, while the ecstatic cheering moaned away on the wind. The *Schleswig* roared and shuddered from stem to stern, plunging mournfully on the cold crests and abandoned to their mercy. Ship of ill-omened name, her boiler had burst.

Nothing must delay them, and through the freezing blasts sweeping the deserted quay they and their possessions were thrust aboard another less gaudily dressed vessel, and soon they were at Kiel. There was a great banquet in the Ducal Schloss on the following night with the beauties of Kiel, in white muslin and pink scarves, lining the great staircase and a chorus of 14,000 serenading Alix in the cold night outside. Already Alix was collecting addresses of welcome, which she thought were silly and a great nuisance to pack away.

Considering the outburst of German indignation and jealousy at the Danish match, the welcome on German soil was remarkable. Landing at Altona, they drove down the illuminated highway to Hamburg. More flowers and lovely girls and throaty choruses greeted her. Alix was so tired that she delayed arrangements by an hour in leaving Hamburg, a symbol some would say of her almost unfailing unpunctuality throughout her new life.

Through Hanover, in the twilight of its days of royalty and pro-English sentiment, they came to Brussels and King Leopold. "Uncle" Leopold—the beaming matchmaker—waited to receive them in pompous triumph with his ten superb carriages. He was as ready to dominate and advise his new "niece" as years before he had been to direct Victoria herself. To Leopold the celebrations in Denmark and Germany were as nothing: Brussels was the true beginning of all things. Brussels must outdo London in the glory of its welcome, and as it happened Brussels did so, at least in its costly magnificence.

Uncle Leopold revealed his great secret: a wonderful bridal gown of Brussels lace—silence and ghastly embarrassment. The Danes knew that Queen Victoria had also her wedding gown made—one of Honiton lace! It had to be explained to the crestfallen monarch. But Brussels lace was superior! Possibly it was: but Victoria was a patriot. No time for argumentative letters to cross the sea. A combat of blistering telegrams with Windsor, and Honiton lace won the victory.

Such was the enthusiasm of Brussels that Alix was growing tired and nervous before the wedding, and this did not surprise her parents, since she was always considered highly strung. But Alix was a child of surprises, and mercifully she would find her "second wind," these first experiences grooming her for worse things ahead. It was reluctantly agreed by Uncle Leopold that Alix should leave early on the day of departure to escape the hysterical mob. It seemed as if her beauty so worked on all who saw her that they became like persons possessed. King Leopold was chagrined that the Danes were only staying three days for the "preparation" instead of five as decreed by the Queen, but in that time he believed he had imbued Alix with many invaluable hints. Once more they mounted into the ten superb carriages and this time drove quietly to the station en route for Antwerp, escorted by the Grand Master of the Belgian Court.

At Antwerp the *Victoria and Albert* awaited them. At Flushing *H.M.S. Resistance* and *Warrior,* fluttering with bunting, manned yards as the royal yacht drew into the roads. The rigging of the warships was black with seamen. Yet not a cheer, not a gun, not a whisper, greeted them. Alix stood on the paddle-box, bowing to the assembled crews with wonderful grace. Silently, solemnly, shamefacedly the tars waved their straw hats. It was her Majesty's order, received with blasphemous disloyalty, that the welcome must be noiseless and dignified because of the Mourning.

There were to be celebrations ashore at Flushing. Perhaps Alix was glad to hear of the Admiral's decision to sail immediately because the weather threatened. And now it was as if the North Sea, rushing and bubbling in the vessel's wake, had washed away the past for Alix. Soon she would be left to make a life among strangers far from her home, and this was her lot until the end. She kept no diary. We do not know her true feeling. But her spirits appeared to be reviving with each hour that passed.

On March 7 Alix had reached her adopted country, and the Mayor and Corporation of Margate advanced across the deck upon the fabulous nineteen-year-old bride.

Her enchantment worked its spell, as it would so many times in the years ahead. Her loveliness, her grace, her manner, like that of a friendly child yet astonishingly dignified, confirmed all that had been heard of her. Speechless with emotion, they tendered to the lovely Dane their Address of Welcome and retired. Alix, less impressed, was presently found in the cabin beating brother William over the head with Margate's loyal Address.

Meanwhile, in London affairs were not prospering. Confusion, shabbiness and departmental jealousy held sway. It could never have happened in the Consort's time. The Lord Chamberlain and the Master of the Horse were at loggerheads. The former had ordered six open carriages and four with postilions to be at Gravesend, six to cross London, six at Slough for Windsor. The Master of the Horse asked where he should find all the postilions? The quality of the eighteen carriages would vary and some of the seventy-two horses must come from jobmasters!

All were found in the end, but it was a passing shoddy array. The Metropolitan Police quarreled with the City Police, and astonishingly few men were detailed for duty. The military, barring a Life Guard Escort, were ignored. The street decorations were mean and scanty. Only the colored gas illuminations were good, but these the Princess would never see. No conception of the true situation, of the tremendous undercurrent of excitement, of the frantic multitude which would flood London streets, can have occurred to the authorities.

At noon on March 7 the *Victoria and Albert* drew alongside at Gravesend amid a dangerous melee of small craft. Margate gave a warm, orderly welcome; Gravesend gave a warning of things to come.

Alix, in white with shawl and small bonnet, appeared on deck, and the little boats swayed and collided while the air shuddered with the roar of the masses ashore. At this point the Prince of Wales was to come aboard to escort the Princess and her family ashore. He had not arrived. Alix stood at the starboard taffrail, laughing in bewilderment, bowing, and talking excitedly to her mother. Then she would run across to answer the summons on the port side, leaning over to the milling boat parties below, and then return to starboard. It seemed that the deadlock would never end. Alix went below. First her white bonnet appeared at one porthole, then at another, while the crescendo rose and fell with each discovery of the Princess. Bertie arrived to spoil the game; but not before hundreds had fallen in love with Alix.

They passed down the pier through an avenue of sixty young ladies of Kent strewing red and white roses, the Danish colors. Now Alix was clad in the "mauve-colored silk, richly embroidered violet velvet mantle bordered with sable, and white silk bonnet trimmed with rosebuds" in which she was to greet the Londoners. Her crinoline was noticeably small, which the newspapers hoped would be a moderating example to the ladies of England.

The royal train driven by an earl chugged with infinite slowness along the line through an endless cheering throng to Bricklayers Arms, Old Kent Road, the London terminus.

The skies of London were yellow-gray, and it seemed as if the great city was muffled in a hush of expectation as they took their seats in the six carriages. Even the breastplates of the Escort gleamed dully in that light. The authorities must by now have been seized with anxiety, watching the immense purposeful crowds of men, women and children thrusting and eddying round the route of the procession. The temper of people who had bought expensive seats along the way was beginning to rise, since many had no prospect of reaching these. In the side streets horses, carts and smart carriages were drowned in the crowds and scarcely a policeman was in sight to guide things into the appropriate channels.

In the first five royal carriages were the Christian brothers and sisters and the suite. In the last sat Alix and the Prince of Wales, with Prince and Princess Christian facing them. Alix had been warned to expect a tremendous reception. She was about to enter a battlefield. Snowflakes swept down on the open carriages in Old Kent Road. It was half past one.

The crowds were out of hand when they sighted London Bridge. They stopped at the bridgefoot. The Lord Mayor and Corporation, having stayed too long at luncheon, could not break through the human masses.

People were running between the carriages. Shuddering, with the snow in their faces, the inmates of the royal carriage saw a circle of eager faces tightening around them. A man shouting with agony as the people crushed him leaped on the back of the carriage behind the

Prince of Wales. At this dangerous juncture "the smile of the Princess was more enchanting than ever," says an eyewitness.

At last the Lord Mayor's coach appeared as if carried bodily across the bridge on the heads of the throng. The Corporation was lost. His Worship delivered his apologetic Welcome to the City in tones of breathless anxiety.

To cross the bridge was impossible. To sit stationary would soon be suicidal. The Escort were scattered and surrounded. But someone had summoned a squadron of cavalry, which, rearing and clattering, amid yells of terror, pushed its way over the bridge with drawn sabers.

They were moving. They were across. They had entered a scene of combat. Between King William Street and the Mansion House they crawled through a swaying, heaving lane over a carpet of hats, bonnets, crinolines, petticoats, cloaks, shoes and umbrellas. Scarce a human garment was missing.

"Above the cheering the shrieks of the women were painfully audible, and boys in a pitiable state of fright were seen waging a battle for life." Thus this scene is recorded by a member of the crowd. It was at about this time that the people burst forward and the head of a lad caught in the wheel-spokes of the royal carriage. Alix leaned over and disentangled him just in time. With her shoulder painfully wrenched, she still smiled.

Ahead, a frantic mother in a last effort hurled her baby into one of the carriages, and a bewildered Dane later handed over the child safely to the police at Paddington Station. One observer tells of another baby "held up which had all the appearance of being dead."

Only once did the Princess appear really frightened. She jumped to her feet as a Life Guardsman and his horse crashed to the ground in front of the carriage horses. When horse and man were brought to their feet she sat back smiling. By now the casualties collapsing in all directions, some to their death, were tragically obvious, and it was said that the look of gaiety and the continual nodding and waving which the Princess somehow maintained as she was dragged helplessly through this appalling scene had the effect of soothing tempers which might otherwise have reached fever heat and caused a worse calamity.

At the Mansion House the crowd closed and swallowed the five carriages ahead. The royal carriage was alone. Men surged forward, fighting to unharness the horses and drag the carriage. They were driven back. Never in her imagination could Alix have envisaged this. Foreigners in that surging multitude knew that nowhere else in Europe could the royal couple have kept their lives in such a fray.

They were moving again, with the cavalry slapping right and left with the flat of their sabers. Down the Strand they crawled, seeing hatless policemen tossed like flotsam, till the wider streets of the West End seemed to give them a chance to breathe. Not that the crowds were thinner: St. James's Street alone was said to hold thirty thousand people. But frequent blizzards, the sight of the first five carriages, and rumors growing stronger of disaster in the City, had chilled the spectators into passivity.

At half past five the royal carriage joined the others outside Paddington Station. Sick and numb, encircled in a cloud of policemen and soldiers, they crept frozenly to the royal train. A peaceful haven indeed, even though from the lighted windows they must wave and bow to the dancing lanterns outside which greeted them the entire way.

At Slough they dragged themselves out into six more carriages. Closed carriages—and it was blessedly dark once they had left the town; yet in the blackness and sleet they perceived the country road was alive with people.

Windsor had waited for anxious hours: the Queen in the Castle, the townspeople in their icy streets and the Eton boys marshaled round the Castle gate with an Address. Already the frozen Etonians knew that their Address would not be accepted that night, but it was their roars of cheering that apprized the Queen that all was well, that Bertie and Alix had arrived.

It was just seven o'clock when "dear Alix, looking like a rose" and apparently in the highest spirits, though sadly crumpled, fell into the embrace of the Queen. Her future mother-in-law helped her out of her violet fur-trimmed jacket, telling her to take half an hour's rest before family dinner. This, the Queen, tired out with worry and "feeling desolate and sad," feared she could not attend.

It was not an enlivening welcome after all they had been through —Her Majesty appears to have been almost too worn out to notice

Prince and Princess Christian—but Alix was resolved to play her part. Dinner ended, there came a knock on the door of the Royal Closet. It opened slightly and the Queen saw the head of Alix appear: she was alone. The tall, beautiful girl advanced with that grace which so fascinated the Queen. She dropped on her knees at Her Majesty's feet. The enchantment of that moment worked a lifelong spell on Victoria—"much moved," she "kissed her again and again." So runs the royal diary. From that night on Alix could never do wrong, or if she did it could be quickly forgotten. In days to come there would be some moments when irritation was justified; yet always when all else failed with Queen Victoria it would be Alix whom they would summon to go to her.

The next day was Sunday, and in the afternoon the Queen took Bertie and Alix over to the Royal Mausoleum at Frogmore. Perhaps it was a painful afternoon for both the young people as they listened earnestly to Her Majesty telling them in clear hushed tones of the character of the dead Consort; but to the Queen this was plainly an agonizing happiness, which might help to nerve her for an event which she made them see was a truly appalling ordeal: their marriage two days hence.

The Lord Mayor of London arrived next morning with a necklace and earrings, which had cost the City £10,000. Bertie ordered a carriage in the afternoon, and the townspeople running beside the open vehicle were amply compensated for their disappointment of the Saturday night. Bertie decided to show his bride-of-the-morrow to the Etonians. At this sudden appearance of the beautiful Dane the very College buildings seemed to rock with chivalrous excitement; yet the stampede never departed from gentlemanly bounds as might be expected, and Alix was flattered and delighted. There was a personal note about it which she could understand. In London the frantic scenes had puzzled and bewildered her. When congratulated on her wonderful London reception she had answered: "Yes, it was extraordinary. It must have been for the sake of the Queen and the Prince of Wales. They don't know me yet. They have to learn."

When darkness fell on the wedding eve Windsor Park was ablaze with fireworks for hours, and, a gay family party, they stood at the windows of the State apartments to watch the scintillating display— all but the Queen, who sat alone with her grief.

Chapter 10

DRAMA AT THE WEDDING

MARCH 10, 1863, was clear, with sunlight sparkling on the frost. The wedding guests had traveled down from London in full dress in a special train. Their arrival made a dazzling exhibition, since for the first time by the Queen's command colors might be worn by all but ladies of the Household, who must wear grays, mauves and lilacs. At the gate stood the Eton boys in loyal and orderly array. In the court waited the Guard of Honor, looking grim and funereal without a band: by Her Majesty's command no martial music must be heard in the Castle of Sorrow. It was, indeed, by her conception to be a strange medley of mourning and rejoicing.

Inside St. George's Chapel the empty Royal Closet, draped in purple velvet and gold, was the target for every eye. Here was the royal box for the command performance—more important than the players on the stage. It was the first occasion for most people to see the Queen since the Terrible Event. Some believed her a madwoman, or recovering from madness. It was she—the black, desolate figure framed above them—who would cause tough Lord Palmerston to weep, and many a man of lesser fiber, she who for pity would cause her daughters to break down, she who would invest the ceremony with a strange, uncanny atmosphere and make it the most dramatic royal wedding in British history.

From the moment when a lady in waiting was observed in the Royal Closet a hush—almost a horrified hush—came in the whispering and fluttering below.

A figure, flowing with blackness from head to foot, was suddenly

53

standing at the front of the cage—for so the Closet has been described. The Queen sat, crossing her black-gloved hands. The blue of the Garter Ribbon across her corsage held a weird incongruity. The pale face, still young-looking and more beautiful perhaps in sorrow, peered unhappily down upon the brilliant guests, who bowed deeply, with eyes averted.

One guest, Mary Stanley, sister of the Dean of Windsor, watched the Queen intently. Her Majesty was

"restless, moving her chair, pulling back her long streamers, asking questions of the Duchess of Sutherland. . . . At the first blast of the trumpets she quivered all over and you could see the working of her face."

This sound of trumpets signaled the entry of the English Princesses, a dazzling white procession, led by Mary of Cambridge and terminated by "Baby Beatrice," with her golden gleaming hair, last of the Queen's five daughters. "The most beautiful procession," comments Miss Stanley, and looking upward she notes that "a smile did pass over the Queen's face."

A second silvery blast: a scarlet thickset figure, mantled in Garter Blue, walked purposefully forward and halted upon the blue-carpeted *haut pas* by the choir—the Prince of Wales. Undistinguished, slightly too plump, resorting presently to a beard with good results, there can be no doubt of the already tremendous popularity of this young man, who would soon be nicknamed "Prince Hal." For a bridegroom he earned an ecstatic Press next morning.

At this moment, says Miss Stanley, "the Princess Royal (Vicky) burst out crying and cried almost all the time." It was an example presently followed by the other royal sisters and lastly by "Baby Beatrice" in a somewhat bewildered manner.

The trumpets pealed for the bride. She was late, but perhaps on this occasion she merely followed a feminine tradition. The scene which now met the eyes of the spectators was magical, yet how much more would it have enchanted but for their guilty consciousness of that macabre royal figure glooming above their heads.

The Princess seemed to float rather than walk up the Gothic nave. "There was no one present," reported Charles Dickens, "who did not feel the effect of that slowness of progress, which carried the bride so gradually and with such almost imperceptible movement past them."

Her face, says Dickens, "was very pale and full of a sort of awe and wonder. It was the face of no ordinary bride, not simply a timid, shrinking girl, but one with a distinctive character of her own, prepared to act a part greatly."

And Thackeray, watching that breathless advance with that solemn train of bridesmaids following the Princess, wrote of the princesses of the fairy tale who turned into white swans.

"The sun burst forth and it fell on the Queen's cap," writes Mary Stanley. "As the organ pealed forth the first anthem to Prince Albert's own music, the Queen raised her eyes upward as if transfixed."

Then the sweet piercing tones of Jenny Lind, the "Swedish nightingale," broke into the Chorale. It was too much. The Queen was seen to rise in floods of tears and vanish from the box. She had seen a coffin where the bridal pair were standing.

But when the spirit of the Consort had passed and the tremulous voice of the aged Archbishop broke through the stillness the Queen reappeared, and the wave of horrified emotion died away.

One slip only marred the occasion, which was said to have caused a fleeting smile on the bride's lips. The rambling, indistinct exhortation of the Archbishop was suddenly drowned, indeed terminated, by the premature tuning of the orchestra. One member of that congregation—a nephew of the bride from that hour—must be singled out for bad behavior, especially as he was later destined to be condemned as the most detestable person she ever met. He was a four-year-old Highlander with a tiny shriveled arm, Vicky's first-born, Willy (the future Kaiser), who was much occupied in biting the outraged knees of his small kilted uncles, Princes Arthur and Leopold.

When the ring was put on the bride "the guns fired," says Mary Stanley, "and the Queen was very much agitated as if each one went through her. My companions were all as much riveted as I."

It was ended, and a new life had begun both for Alix and Bertie, in their different ways. Let us linger in the Royal Chapel for one moment to experience the warring emotions of the Queen herself, the dark genius of the day upon whom all eyes were riveted. These she has left in the cool, lucid words of her journal.

"When I stepped up to the window (of the Closet)," she says of that moment which had so awed the guests, "the Chapel full of smartly dressed people, the Knights of the Garter, and the reredos in my beloved one's memory, with the bells ringing outside, quite had the effect of a scene in a play.

"Sat down feeling strange and bewildered. When the procession (the Princesses) came in view I felt terribly overcome. I could not take my eyes off precious little baby, with her golden hair and large nosegay, and smiled at her as she made a beautiful curtsey. Everyone bowed to me."

Of Bertie, whom she speaks of as "our boy," she says, "he bowed to me, and during the long wait for his Bride, kept constantly looking up at me, with an anxious clinging look, which touched me much."

Alix, she notes,

"was trembling and very pale. Dearest Albert's Chorale was sung, which affected me much, and the Service proceeded. . . . When it was over, the young couple looked up at me, and I gave them an affectionate nod and kissed my hand to sweet Alix. They left together, followed by all the others, Beethoven's Hallelujah Chorus being played. . . ."

Alix and Bertie departed to the peace of Osborne. It was left to the guests in their ceremonial garments to get a taste of the horrors which the bridal pair had suffered in London on March 7.

The mob had flocked down to Windsor to witness the "going away," and the neck-and-neck race for Slough Station followed. Smart carriages, episcopal hats, tattered coats and frowsy bonnets, crushed velvets, rubies, diamonds, gold epaulets and rumpled trailing crinolines—for many guests had walked from the Castle—crammed together in hopeless riot. The Archbishop reached the station only by clinging to the back of somebody's carriage. Dukes, duchesses, pickpockets, servant girls, navvies and shopkeepers packed frantically into the waiting ceremonial train. As for Mary Stanley, after being locked for half an hour in the station lobby, since the platform was full, she eventually reached it by climbing through a window, where she joined the combat for the next train.

Chapter 11

WANDERING BRIDEGROOM

ID-VICTORIAN BRIDES seldom knew anything of the true characters of their husbands when they returned from the
honeymoon to set up a home. So it was with Alix of Denmark.
Bertie was a tender husband, considerate, chivalrous, generous, obviously deeply in love with her and often very amusing—which last
was most important to Alix. But Alix was disappointed. Bertie was
restless. Bertie hated being alone. She thought she began to perceive
that he relished her sole company only for brief spells at a time.
Bertie was always looking around him—for people.

Bertie frequently took her to the theatres or the opera. He enjoyed
doing that. He was proud to show her to the people, who were always so kind to them both. She would order supper to be waiting
when they returned to Marlborough House. Hopefully and with
care she would choose the items to please Bertie; but as often as not
Alix ate the supper alone with the lady in waiting. On arriving
home Bertie would call for a brandy, light one of his bigger cigars
and send the duty footman to call a hansom cab. Then he would
kiss her with a shade of guilt on his face—in the earliest days—and
go jingling off into the London night. Sometimes, in the morning,
Bertie would talk of what he had done the night before, but not
always.

Bertie was soon a well-known figure about St. James's Street. He
was in and out of all the best clubs. He sometimes attended gambling parties with his aristocratic friends. Alix knew all about that;
though she probably did not know that these gambling parties were

sometimes at the expensive secret establishments which his friends set up for their elegant mistresses in the suburbs.

Bertie was fond of the music halls. He made no secret of that. The Prince of Wales was recognized at Cremorne Gardens, where the swells poured champagne from the balconies on the heads of those below. He was recognized in Leicester Square and the Haymarket, where the crinolined harlots hovered in droves under the flaring gas lamps, unmolested by a well-bribed constabulary. He was recognized in those celebrated gilt dancing saloons where every male was a man of blood and every woman elegant and disreputable. Perhaps these were cases of mistaken identity. He was certainly hailed on many a night after midnight by the crowds which gathered outside the famous Canterbury, across the water, where the hall celebrities rolled up in their smart equipages for a burlesque song and dance after the show, and too often a "blind," before tottering to bed.

Mr. Thomas Burke, the author, in his comprehensive study of London night life, states that the Prince of Wales "set the pace of London night life" in his young days.

> "Social memoirs," he says, "make guarded references to this. . . . One meets stories of a Haroun-al-Raschid kind about a Highly placed Personage, with hat pulled down, being seen in queer places . . . stories of an Important Figure being conducted in disguise . . . his night wandering seems to have belied the Chinese proverb which says that it is the height of folly to seek the person of the Sacred Emperor in the common tea-houses."

Such was one facet of the young Prince whom Alix had married. He craved for friends, and found them everywhere. Presently he would form his own club, the Marlborough, just across the street from Marlborough House. Every man admitted would be sponsored by himself, and he would be running over there at all hours to play in his bowling alley till the neighbors complained about the rattling of the balls. The old-fashioned might think some among the large membership peculiar persons. Besides the aristocrats, such as his crony the Duke of Sutherland, of erratic if not mad reputation, there were famous Jews like the Rothschilds, financiers, Americans and shocking Continentals. But there were also men of the arts, scholars and noted ecclesiastics. Though Bertie never opened a book himself, he could find pleasure in such intelligent company; for he was of very inquisitive turn of mind and a keen listener.

All these people Alix would find herself entertaining continually at Marlborough House and at the celebrated little house parties at Sandringham. With no previous experience as a hostess, Alix soon found in herself an effortless ability to make people depart dazzled with pleasure after her entertainments. Bertie liked this kind of thing, so he should have it. She enjoyed it herself within limits. But it was endless, and thus it would go on with unflagging enthusiasm right up to that day, forty years later, when she would cease to be Princess of Wales and become a Queen.

But alongside all this, Bertie from the first was most anxious to fulfil all kinds of public engagements as Prince of Wales, and here, of course, he looked to Alix to support him. Her wonderful beauty and grace were a tremendous asset to him in such work, and however boring the work in hand he always felt inspired when she was with him and said the right thing to everybody and was affable to the right people.

A visitor entering the hall of Marlborough, a person acquainted with the life lived in the royal homes, felt instantly the different atmosphere. There was a normality, a simplicity about everything, which made visitors feel at home. In achieving this the Prince and Princess owed much to the broad-minded and congenial men and women whom they were lucky enough to have as their suite. General Sir William Knollys, the Comptroller and Treasurer, was sixty-seven and the father of the Household. He had succeeded Bruce as Bertie's governor, and being more sure of his own convictions than his predecessor had insisted that his Prince was given more rope. He was the right man in the right place: he understood Bertie, he believed in him and his belief was going to be justified. His family would serve Bertie and Alix to the end.

Herbert Fisher, a brilliant young London barrister, was the Prince of Wales's private secretary: an appointment of the first importance in those first days when Bertie had to be set squarely on his feet in his new role as the first gentleman of the kingdom. The Earl of Mount Edgcombe was Lord of the Bedchamber. Considerably older than the Prince, he had been with him ever since his first separate establishment at White Lodge in 1859. The Consort had believed that his artistic and cultured tastes would be beneficial to his son. In this connection it can at least be said that Bertie had become much attracted to him. Both of the Grooms of the Bedchamber, younger men, had previously been associated with the Prince. The Honorable R. H. Meade of the Foreign Office had traveled with him on the Eastern tour, and Charles Lindley Wood, Viscount Halifax, had been one of those scrupulously chosen Eton boys whom the Consort had from time to time allowed to come and play with Bertie.

The Equerries were military men, which was in accordance with the Prince's desires, since he hankered after an active Army career. These were Major Christopher Teesdale, V.C., Major Charles Grey and Lieutenant-Colonel Keppel. Bertie had successfully passed his Army exam and had actually completed three months' military training at the Curragh, Ireland, where the Guards and his uncle the Duke of Cambridge had considered him rather an idle young officer. He was in this year appointed Colonel of the 10th Hussars, and immediately a familiar and popular figure at Marlborough House was the ill-starred Colonel Valentine Baker, the commander of the regiment. The sensational scandal which ended the career of this friend of Marlborough House would presently smear much tar on the fraying reputation of the new fashionable set which formed around the Prince and Princess of Wales.

Another valuable member of the Household was M. Holzmann, a German Liberal exile, who was engaged as the Librarian. Since Bertie never read books and Alix looked for lighter fare than the house library could provide, the task of Holzmann was to prepare the body of those brilliant and well-informed speeches which the Prince of Wales was soon delivering all over the country, apparently straight out of his head and with few, if any, notes. With the aid of Holzmann, who always knew exactly what was wanted, Bertie soon turned his natural loquacity to such shrewd account that he became one of the most admired speakers in the country on public or private occasions.

Of the male members of the suite these were the most notable. They, with the Ladies of the Household, amalgamated not only into an extremely happy family, but also a most efficient team in support of a young couple who had to make themselves not only the leaders of a dead society but the leading public figures in a kingdom which, royally speaking, was leaderless.

To Alix, young, totally inexperienced in the exclusive requirements of fashionable life and a foreigner to boot, they had at first to be like mothers or elder sisters. The Ladies of the Bedchamber were the Countess of Macclesfield, the Countess of Morton, Lady de Grey and the Marchioness of Carmarthen. If General Knollys was father of the Household, Lady Macclesfield, the mother of twelve children, was the mother at Marlborough House. It was to her that Alix carried all her problems. The Women of the Bedchamber, people who were not so grand but performed the actual day-by-day work required to maintain a Princess of Wales, were the Honorable Mrs. Grey, wife of Major Grey, a Swede by birth, who was the especial favorite of the Princess, the Honorable Mrs. Cooke, the Honorable Mrs. Stonor and the Honorable Mrs. Hardinge. Alix, by her own good taste and talents, was perfectly fitted to become the smartest woman in the land and the national model, as she instantly did, but doubtless some credit must be given to her more experienced Bedchamber Women.

The London season was dead when Bertie and Alix set up their establishment at Marlborough House. There had been no season since the Consort died, and with little encouragement from the Queen and her late husband the seasons had languished for many years before that.

The year 1863 was the most brilliant season within living memory, the first of a glittering series which would continue until the Waleses ascended the Throne. But 1863 would always stand apart in the memories of all those who partook in its magical season; and although the Prince of Wales played his part very ably, very affably, very adroitly for so young a Prince, it was Alix, the lovely Dane, with her grace and elegance, with her wonderful clothes, with her unflagging spirits, with her beautiful husky voice speaking amusingly correct and delightfully broken English, who threw an exciting spell over the year.

The young couple had barely returned from their nine days' honeymoon when they held their first evening reception at St. James's Palace. The guests felt the changed atmosphere before they even got near the Prince and Princess. It has been likened to the "awakening of spring after a dreary winter." Alix was soon called upon to hold her first Drawing Room on behalf of the Queen. Eagerness and curiosity turned it almost into a blue-blooded riot. Two thousand ladies attended, and the carriages were solid from Cavendish Square to St. James's. By 9 a.m. every beplumed lady was seated in her carriage. At noon the first arrivals were allowed to descend and enter the Palace, but the end of the glittering column, starved and parched by the sun, insulted and pelted by street boys, tottered through the doors several hours later. There was no refreshment for their exhaustion to be found there—Her Majesty would not have it; nothing to revive them but a hard-fought battle and a perspiring glimpse of the glorious Dane, before they were brusquely thrust from the glowing Presence by ushers or carried out by rude footmen. Lady St. Helier has left her record of that epic day.

"The hustling and pressure," she recalls, "were so great that many gowns were almost entirely destroyed before the wearers reached the presence-chamber. . . . *Punch* was extremely witty over it, and the sketches in which he depicted the scenes at Drawing-room were no exaggeration."

If *Punch* and Lady St. Helier are, indeed, to be credited, then what bewilderment, what inward laughter, what wonderment, must have seized upon Alix, the stranger—hot from her own frightful experience in London streets—when dames and damsels, the highest in this crazy land, scrambled before her with their broken, twisted plumes in indecent disarray! It was the suggestion of *Punch* that practice obstacle races in costume should be arranged for ladies attending these functions.

The first great official function was a magnificent ball at the Guildhall, at which the Prince of Wales was to be presented with the freedom of the City. More money was spent by the Corporation on the embellishments than ever before or since. These may be left to the imagination, but there was a carpeted dais with thrones for the royal couple, specially designed and woven tapestries hid the walls, a Prince of Wales's feathers and coronet in spun glass nine feet high were a notable feature, but foremost in the opinion of Alix was a vast illuminated picture of her old home, Bernstoff, which was suddenly disclosed, and there standing on the lawn she saw *herself*.

This congenial function, entirely lacking in pompousness, is best summed up by a contemporary writer. "No wonder," says he, "that the worthy Aldermen flopped themselves about in an agony of delight, and basked in the Princess's smiles like their own turtles in the sun."

Throughout the evening Alix, in plain white satin, was followed intently by every eye. She danced a great deal with the City magnates, and seemed to be totally unaware or cheerfully indifferent to the stir she was causing. Everybody discussed in loud tones the extraordinary fascination which emanated from this Danish Princess. The Corporation was so overcome by her wonderful graciousness in wearing their £10,000 necklace and earrings that it never occurred to them how ungracious it would have been had she failed to do so. Despite the suffocating crush in every room, corridor and passage, curiosity was held within polite bounds, and the royal couple enjoyed themselves, which was more than could be said of many official and private occasions in that year, when ardent admirers put them to considerable discomfort.

Last of the great society events of that season was the famous Guards Ball. This took place in the picture gallery of the International Exhibition in Cromwell Road. For this grand occasion the Queen agreed to lend the committee of the Guards regiments all the accessories used for State balls at Buckingham Palace. This royal gesture caused the great families all over the country to offer the committee their gold and silver plate and most precious ornaments, until it was reckoned that the supper room of the Brigade alone was worth nearly £2,000,000.

This stupendous display was erected for the benefit of only 1,400 guests, but it must be remembered that in the 'sixties this exclusive little body, which the dead Consort might have referred to as "the foxhunters," still practically owned and ran the country for better or worse in spite of the new emancipation, and that the Brigade in entertaining them so spaciously—and, indeed, in well-nigh ruining some of their youthful ensigns—saw themselves as entertaining England in honor of the Prince and Princess.

Eight couples took part in the royal quadrille which opened the ball at 10 p.m.—the Duke of Cambridge with Alix, Bertie with Mary of Cambridge (who was dressed in the Guards colors and was said almost to emulate the Princess of Wales in beauty, though not in animation), and other couples of high estate.

Much has been said of the loveliness of Alix on such occasions as it appeared to strangers, and it may be interesting at this point to hear the words of Bertie himself. These were spoken to the wife of a foreign ambassador at a "small" Marlborough House dance in the early days—there were "only about three hundred guests." The writer tells us that

> "the Princess wore a dress of many shaded reds, and in her hair were red hollyhocks with one large diamond in the heart of each. Observing that I was looking at her with unfeigned admiration, the Prince of Wales said to me, 'This is quite an exceptional occasion. We have asked all the prettiest and best-looking women we know; there is not a single plain one, but,' he added with a pleased smile, 'the Princess is the most beautiful of all.'"

It was said by those who knew Alix well that there was an elusive quality in her beauty, which the artists could never bring out, because it was really a combination of deeply soft blue eyes, smiling mouth and agile figure synchronized in a perfect rhythm of action. Frith, the famous artist of the day, was the first who tried, and he has left an amusing record.

"I soon discovered," he wrote, "that the illustrious young lady did not know that the keeping of her face in one position, for a few minutes only, was necessary to enable an artist to catch a resemblance of it. I did not dare complain till after two or three attempts."

Frith's friend Gibson, the fashionable sculptor, was able to commiserate with his fellow artist after his turn had come. "I saw at once," he said, "what a pretty subject she was for a bust. I modeled it in fourteen days. The princess sat eight times—an hour each sitting. She is a delightful lady, always good sense, but she can't sit a bit."

Doubtless Alix was invariably late for her restless sittings with

Frith and Gibson, though they did not dare to complain; but Constant, the French artist, at a later time has no qualms in doing so. "She was always late for her sittings," he remarked resignedly, "and the manner in which she excused herself made me feel that it was I who should apologize for taking up her time." But the spell of the Princess was upon the Frenchman—"time passed quickly, too quickly, while the Princess's Japanese dog snorted on his cushion."

One society woman, after the glories of that first season, was heard to confess, "I have heard even the men declare that every woman looks frightful in the room with the Princess of Wales!" Unwittingly, the speaker was stressing another of the remarkable features of the Princess: nobody envied her for her beauty. Her sister-in-law Vicky spoke more plainly to her friends. "I have known many women," said she, "who pleased all men without exception, but none like Alexandra, who won the approval of her own sex without exciting jealousy."

Chapter 12

ALIX DEFIES THE QUEEN

THE YEAR 1863, seen in retrospect, must undoubtedly have recurred to Alix of Denmark as the most extraordinary time in her life; but it is probable that the two events which came most vividly to her mind, apart perhaps from her first frantic experience of London streets and the wedding itself, did not concern the glittering events of the season but somber public occasions, both connected with heavy rain. These were her visit with Bertie to Oxford on Commemoration Day, when he received his honorary degree of D.C.L., a solemn occasion which took the wrong turning, and later a day of bleak solemnity in Scotland, when the Queen, making her first public appearance, traveled to Aberdeen with her family about her in awful gloom and there unveiled the earliest statue to the Prince Consort, surrounded by a sea of umbrellas. The Oxford occasion has been most perfectly preserved for posterity by a contemporary undergraduate.

"Commemoration Day! Quotha! No! Umbrella Day! It has been the day of umbrellas and persistent rain. Various showers throughout the morning showed the unkindly disposition of the weather, but its downpour was reserved until the precise time when the Prince and Princess were proceeding up the High Street. A few minutes after the Vice-Chancellor and the most distinguished members of the University arrived at Magdalen Bridge, where the address of welcome was to be presented, the royal cortege appeared.

"There was a momentary pause in order to open the carriage containing the Prince and Princess, which had necessarily been closed. At this moment a mishap occurred which completely ruined the effect of the royal entry into the city. Instead of the volunteers or police, or both, keeping back the crowd, King Mob was permitted to break through every opposition and to crowd round the Bishops and Dons in the most confusing manner. An utterly unseemly, and, at the same time, ludicrous scene followed, the humorous effect of which was certainly improved by the rain, which came down with a pour and compelled everyone who possessed an umbrella to hoist sail.

"You must imagine to yourself Archbishops and Bishops in their lawn sleeves, scarlet robes, and most dignified attire; Heads of Houses in scarlet and black velvet sleeves; Doctors in Pink; Doctors in White; D.C.L.'s, and M.A.'s *ad lib*. You must picture them hemmed in, jostled, pushed, and pinned against the sides of the royal carriage by an unruly, shouting, bawling, hurrahing, but very good-natured and loyal mob—and all this in the middle of a bridge, outlined by umbrellas, while the rain fairly pelted down, and did its best to spoil the beautiful white bonnet of the Princess."

The Sheldonian was "packed like the Black Hole of Calcutta" when the Princess appeared before her throne, bowing and smiling hopelessly, while a fearful din which made the roof tremble roared on and on. Just when she was going to sit down, looking quite exhausted, they started cheering each member of her family in turn, and so it went on for a further ten minutes while the fair Dane kept her feet.

Another exciting day followed, and it was generally agreed with some rancor that in the races on the river the Baliol crew had seized their chance to outdo all in the interest of the Princess. They drew level with the Princess; they should have passed her—but no!—they upset their boat in the water with a great splash and, emerging from the foam chest deep, they cheered her again and again.

It was on October 13 that Bertie and Alix drove over from Abergeldie, the Highland lodge which they had rented near Balmoral, to join Her Majesty's party at the Castle. In the hall the family was collected in readiness, including Vicky and her husband, Crown Prince Frederick William of Prussia. At the door waited John Brown and a group of selected Highland servants in full costume. The skies were leaden and menacing as they started on their dreary way. Everyone was afraid for the Queen: wondering, like herself, whether she would stand it.

The rain poured down as they came out of North Eastern Station, Aberdeen. With cavalry, mounted police and the city dignitaries the carriages splashed through a dense silent multitude to the Northern Club Buildings, where the veiled statue of the Consort stood before a window. Not a sound seemed to stir in the whole of Aberdeen but the hissing of rain and the patter of feet of the royal party as they passed into the billiards room. Her Majesty accepted the Address of Welcome, while her party watched her anxiously, knowing of her state of speechless and agonized agitation during the train journey. They stepped through the window upon the platform around the statue and the rain beat in their faces. Opposite stood the draggled Highland Guard with band and pipers. Below stood John Brown and the servants in their dripping finery. The crowded scene was still and dead, like a picture. Forgetful of the downpour, the Queen looked skyward, as she often did when the thought of the Consort was strong within her. *The Scotsman* takes up the story.

"Her Majesty's appearance was the signal for the multitudes gathered outside to uncover their heads. Her Majesty, who appeared to be deeply melancholy and much depressed, though calm and collected, advanced to the front of the platform, while the Princes, who were all dressed in Royal Stuart tartan, and the Princesses, who wore silk dresses, white bonnets and dark grey cloaks, took up a position immediately behind her. The proceedings were opened by a prayer by Principal Campbell, who spoke for about ten minutes, the assemblage standing uncovered in the rain. . . . During the time that the learned Principal was engaged in prayer, Her Majesty more than once betrayed manifest and well-justified signs of impatience at the length of the oration. At the conclusion of the prayer a signal was given, the bunting which had concealed the statue was hoisted to the top of the flagstaff, and the ceremony was complete. . . ."

Complete, in the opinion of the Queen but for one important detail: of which she would presently complain bitterly to those around her and register her indignation for posterity in her journal. She who had forbidden the bands to sound at the wedding of her own son was hurt, bewildered that not one bugle blast, not one wail from the pipes, was accorded to her Beloved Dead.

"Her Majesty," says the newspaper, "having scanned the statue narrowly, bowed to the assemblage and retired from the platform, followed by the royal party." For the royal travelers the return journey, fraught with the feeling of anticlimax, and lacking that spurious cheerfulness which follows a funeral, must have been more grim and hopeless than the setting out.

In the same month the inhabitants of the Norfolk countryside round Sandringham were becoming intensely interested, for the new squire and his beautiful Danish wife were coming to make their first stay at the House.

Every autumn would see them at Sandringham till the end of their lives. To Alix, who rarely saw Sandringham except under the dying tints of autumn until the death of Bertie, this was always the real home. How often in the years ahead she would wistfully long for Sandringham, even though she knew that by Bertie's wish their stay would probably resolve itself into an endless procession of house parties.

In the diary of the Rev. B. J. Armstrong there are some extremely interesting glimpses of the early Royal Sandringham. The Prince of Wales, who meant to fulfil seriously his duties as the squire, having made a preliminary visit to Sandringham had decided to build cottages and schools. To this end he sought the expert advice of the Reverend Mr. Moxon, a clerical friend of Armstrong's whom he invited to dine at the house.

Armstrong records:

"He (Moxon) describes the character of the house to be one of perfect ease and familiarity—the only 'state' being that the guests and the household assemble in a separate room from the Royal Family, introductions to whom take place after dinner. The Prince asked Moxon if he objected to cards, in which case there should be none. Moxon played a round game of cards called

Chow-Chow—a favourite game with the Princess. They played
for fish at a penny the dozen, Princess Dagmar being very zeal-
ous at it. They talk English but often break into Danish.
They like Sandringham very much indeed. They come into
church just before the litany, for which there is a break, and the
bell rings." (Moxon's uncle was Vicar of Sandringham.)

Armstrong himself held a Norfolk living and after a visit to the
seaside at Hunstanton, ten miles from Sandringham, he notes:

"the most curious thing about this place is the celebrated cliff, so
full of interest to the geologist. Here it is that the Prince and
Princess of Wales are in the habit of taking luncheon, a servant
laying the cloth on one side of the rocks, while the future King
of England sits on another, smoking his cigar."

Of the Sandringham property, Armstrong, after passing it while
on a drive, was evidently surprised by its then state of wildness and
remoteness. He had expected to see one of the stately mansions of
the countryside, but the unpretentiousness of the house disappointed
him. He says that the famous Norwich Gates, one of the features of
the Great Exhibition, looked odd, standing in such "a wild scene."
It was while they were at Sandringham in 1863—it was November
16 and they were in the hunting field—that Alix was given the news
that Frederick VII of Denmark had died suddenly and her father
was King. Spectators claim to have watched the Princess clapping
her hands in joyous excitement.
But four days later joy gave way to dismay. Fresh news from
Denmark. Frederick of Augustenburg—self-styled "the Crown
Prince"—eldest son of exiled Duke Christian of Augustenburg, had
declared himself the rightful King of Denmark and Schleswig-
Holstein. His claim on family grounds was in truth a staggering
challenge to Alix's father, who had only reached the Throne after a
decidedly tortuous transaction. Frederick of Augustenburg with an
army of German volunteers was occupying Holstein, with the oppor-
tunist intention of holding it as a base for further operations. The
Chancelleries of Europe rocked. Because of the London conference,
every great Power was involved. The real crisis of Schleswig-Hol-

stein was approaching, and Bismarck was rubbing his hands. For the moment nothing happened. The Danish troops, abandoning Holstein, sat on their lines defending Schleswig.

It was the period of rumors, accusations, insinuations, secret mobilizations and hot partisanships. Already the cry was going up in Prussia and her satellites that the German "minority" in Schleswig-Holstein were ill-used by the Danes. The theory that Schleswig-Holstein should rightly be German soil would soon be strong on the wind. And among the fierce partisans whom these things would call forth, not the least fiery and plain-spoken would be Alix of Denmark, the Princess of Wales. Thus in fear, anxiety and bewilderment the crisis would hover over Christmastide, while the Queen of England and her Government cast about frantically for means to stop a war in which they must under no circumstances involve themselves.

The family affairs of Alix had, indeed, been worrying since she had left Denmark. In the spring, the Greeks, having thrown out their Bavarian king, Otto, because he was too feeble in his anti-Turkish sentiments, called upon her darling brother William, a seventeen-year-old naval cadet, to become King of Greece.

Greece, the proud new kingdom, which had hacked its way out of the quagmire of Turkish tyranny, the land of bandits, blood feuds, poverty, frenzied politics and unbounded ambitions, was no gift to a stranger boy King in 1863; but the Christian parents, moved perhaps in their wondering bourgeois natures by the glory of the offer, brought William to accept the Crown.

The Queen had watched with reluctance the acceptance of the Greek crown by Alix's favorite brother. One of her own sons had been offered the post before him and she had refused. She and her governments were traditionally pro-Turk, and she knew that a successful Greek king must be a Turk-hater. The accession of Alix's brother might be most embarrassing and troublesome. It brought the turbulent Greeks into the family.

Alix herself seems to have been against it; she perhaps knew little of the dire Hellenic reputation and was chiefly moved by the feeling that she would see more of William if he stayed nearer home—though in actuality this scarcely turned out to be the case; but her dislike of the project is disclosed in a letter written two years later by the Prince of Wales to Lord Russell, the Foreign Secretary, at a time when Grecian problems were taking a troublesome turn in English eyes, as the Queen had anticipated, and Bertie, the loyal brother-in-law, was displaying a brotherly—nay, a fatherly—interest in the nightmares of the amiable King of Greece.

"You can well imagine how happy the Princess is to hear better news (of Greece)," runs a passage in the Prince's letter to Russell. "All the last accounts have caused her great anxiety about her brother, whom she was so anxious should never have accepted his present position. I am very glad to hear that you will keep two English ships at the Piraeus at present—it will at any rate have a good effect." (March 29/65.)

William, then described as a "slight, graceful and elegant boy," had been crowned in lonely state in Athens amid scenes of clamorous Hellenic exaltation on October 31, 1863—his name changed from William to George, in honor of the national saint—and it had been a sharp grief to Alix that she had been unable to be with her brother. George had been able to start well with his headstrong subjects, for, thanks to efforts of Gladstone, he had unexpectedly brought with him a most delectable "dowry," the Ionian Islands, which had long had a British garrison. It was this interest shown by Gladstone, the great classicist, in the affairs of her brother, which was the beginning of the lifelong friendship between the Princess of Wales and the Gladstones.

The family Christmas was spent at Windsor, as it always had been and always would be. It might have been better than the previous Christmas, with Alix there and also Vicky and Crown Prince Frederick of Prussia. It was not: at every turn Schleswig-Holstein seemed to spoil their pleasure.

The affair had now grown desperate. Alix's father, King Christian IX, under pressure by his subjects, had signed a Bill incorporating Schleswig forever in the state of Denmark and granting Holstein independence under his sovereignty. The Danes had vowed to expel him if he did not sign it. Prussia, with her ally Austria, declaring that Danes were unfit to rule Germans in either state, were as yet only threatening to demand, on pain of armed invasion, that the Danes rescind their illegal Bill. Christian IX was the scapegoat, which suited very well the party who supported Frederick of Augustenburg.

Denmark, confident that Great Britain, at least, would stand behind her, faced the world with defiance and truculence. In many a Danish home the portrait of the Princess Alix was proudly displayed, and people spoke of her, though without any concrete reason for doing so, as if she were a national heroine.

At Windsor the flies in the ointment were Vicky and Fritz. They had no use for the Bismarckian outcry of ill-used German minorities. Prussian Liberals themselves, they loathed the man, understanding only too well the true meaning of that outcry. But, intellectuals by nature, Vicky and Fritz were prone to lost causes, which the practical looked upon lightly. Therefore they strongly sponsored the claim of their "house-friend," Frederick of Augustenburg, to Schleswig-Holstein, though not his wider claims. But it was enough! They thought that the Danes had simply no claim at all to Schleswig-Holstein, and never had had any. They felt very hotly about it, and said so. Alix went off like a rocket. They might as well call her father a thief and be done with it. The Princess of Wales was tremendous. Everybody was stunned. Then Bertie declared indignantly for Alix.

The Queen regarded her daughter-in-law with bewildered reproach. Alix did not care; it was only a family party. She could say what she pleased.

When the tussle broke out a second time, the Queen grew angry. She did not care a fig about Frederick of Augustenburg, but Denmark certainly had broken the London Treaty by her Bill, and she imagined also, from what she had heard, by coercion of Germans in the states. Prussia and Austria, being concerned with the London Treaty, were within their rights in protesting. Moreover, she announced that she had looked up an old memorandum of Dearest Albert's. He plainly said that Denmark never had any right to Schleswig-Holstein.

Alix turned furiously upon her royal mother-in-law. The family waited appalled for the name of the Consort to be insulted. That did not come. Her Majesty had suddenly recollected with horror that Alix was nearly seven months pregnant. The child's cheeks were suffused with scarlet, she was shaking with rage. Such excitement might be very dangerous. The Queen declared that the words "Schleswig-Holstein" were not to be mentioned again at Windsor. The contestants continued to repeat themselves behind the royal back.

Chapter 13

CONSTERNATION AT FROGMORE

THEY WERE AT Frogmore after Christmas, the Duchess of Kent's old home in Windsor Park, and nobody expected the event which suddenly happened, for it was two months ahead of time. Perhaps Schleswig-Holstein was responsible.

On January 8 there was a hockey match on the ice covering Virginia Water. Bertie was playing, and he had arranged for an elaborate luncheon to be served to many guests beside the lake. The ice gleamed in the sunshine, and everybody was in the highest spirits. Alix arrived at eleven o'clock. She chatted with all her friends, ate a large lunch and several times during the morning and afternoon she was watched being drawn swiftly around the ice in a sledge. She left for home at four o'clock without Bertie.

They had scarcely entered the hall at Frogmore when Lady Macclesfield was informed by her mistress that she felt very unwell. Bertie arrived an hour later. The household was in a state of inexplicable turmoil. Lady Macclesfield came down to him. The Princess was advanced in travail. Dr. Brown, a local general practitioner, was expected to arrive shortly. She had telegraphed to London for a Court doctor and nurses.

Lucky, indeed, that Lady Macclesfield, that veteran of twelve childbirths, was with the Princess, for nobody else at Frogmore seemed to have any knowledge of confinements.

Dr. Brown arrived at the gallop. He was barely in time, but with the help of the Lady of the Bedchamber he delivered the child safely, a boy. It had been a difficult birth, as every one would be for Alix.

Lady Macclesfield wrapped the child in one of her petticoats, while a carriage hurried off to Windsor to arouse the local drapers and buy baby clothes, since the elaborate royal layette had scarcely begun manufacture. It was two o'clock next morning before the nurses arrived. The Princess was exhausted, but doing well, and Dr. Brown had ensured himself a knighthood.

One little item, however, was causing doubts downstairs. This child was the heir to the Throne after his father. Suppose some officious person should challenge his right to succeed: the Home Secretary had not been present at his birth! Naturally one could not foresee calamities of this kind. It was very awkward. However, by luck Lord Granville was one of the guests in the house party at Frogmore. It was decided that it was best to put on a bold face about this unfortunate irregularity and assume that without question Lord Granville would do just as well. Then everybody would probably forget about it. Everybody did forget.

National rejoicing followed, and the boy was christened in St. George's Chapel with much pomp. He was known to the public as Prince Albert Victor until the Queen created him Duke of Clarence on his twenty-first birthday.

Madame Jerichau, a well-known Danish portrait painter who shortly afterward came over to paint the Princess of Wales, tells an interesting story about the first days of this boy.

"The little Prince Albert Victor," she says, "had as wet nurse a handsome Irish woman of robust health. Some time after entering on her duties, however, she suddenly began to decline without any visible reason. The doctors who examined her were quite unable to detect the cause, nor could she herself offer any suggestion. The Princess's maternal instinct, however, solved the riddle. She inquired the whereabouts of the nurse's own infant, sent for it, and suddenly placed it in its mother's arms. The effect was instantaneous. The mother's joy at seeing her child again was so great that she recovered at once. The child remained about a week at Marlborough House and shared the life of the little Prince."

Thirteen days after the birth of Albert Victor the Prussians and Austrians invaded the Duchies, and *Punch* saw fit to involve even this little boy in the Schleswig-Holstein question. The "Nursery Song for the New Baby" caused no little amusement, and was anti-Prussian propaganda of a kind. Decidedly it must have embarrassed Her Majesty if she read it.

> O slumber, my darling, thy sire is a Prince
> Whom Mamma beheld skating not five hours since.
> And Grandpapa Christian is off to the fray
> With Germans, who'd steal his nice duchy away.
>
> But slumber, my darling, the English are true,
> And they'll help him for love of Mamma and of you,
> And the Channel Fleet's coming with powder and shot
> And the Germans must run, or they'll catch it all hot.

Bismarck, of course, knew enough of the secrets of Westminster to laugh at this rhyme. But the Prussian public believed the last verse of this doggerel would come true. So did the British public. They set to cursing one another. Alix had probably been receiving letters from home for some time urging her to push the cause of Denmark with the English, but while she was in bed after her confinement these took on a more urgent note. No sooner was she on her feet than she forgot about confining her feelings to the family circle, forgot about her promises to the Queen before the wedding, and became an ardent partisan of Denmark among her large circle of friends. Her friends—especially her male friends—in their turn broadcast her views. With her beauty, her grace and the legend of her wonderful enchantment, she could scarcely have done more for her country had she traveled round speaking in the town halls.

Even in Ireland "100 Irish volunteers of good family, led by a gentleman of Cork noted for his success in the hunting field" prepared themselves at their own expense for the fray. "The Alexandra Cent Gardes"—for thus they named themselves—set a chivalric example, which many ardent admirers of the Princess were clamorous to follow in England. Alix, like Joan of Arc, might have brought armies into the field. She wanted to do so for her father. It was her mission. But the Queen with her eldest daughter sitting in the Prussian camp and dear Fritz leading his division against the Danes observed the upheaval with rocklike calm from the battlements of Windsor; while the Government, fearful of a second Crimean catastrophe and knowing the weakness of the armed forces, declared their earnest desire to mediate between the combatants. Denmark, who had challenged adversaries totally beyond her own strength, hung on in dismay while her troops died bravely.

"It is my strong conviction," wrote Professor Max Muller of Oxford—an authority who was then publishing some notable articles on the subject in *The Times,* "that the war was mainly brought about by the encouragement given to Denmark and the taunts levelled at Germany by a portion of the English Press."

Bertie had openly declared himself for Denmark, as was to be expected. He abused the Prussians in all the clubs. "The Danes," he declared, "are a brave people who prefer death to any kind of humiliation." He expressed bitter contempt of his own government to the French Ambassador. He had the new Austrian Ambassador informed that the Princess of Wales did not wish to meet him.

The Queen herself was speechless with indignation when she heard that the terrible Palmerston had told the Austrian Ambassador that "if the Austrian fleet went to the Baltic it would have to reckon with the British Navy." That was not her intention; and when they brought her a draft of the Royal Speech to be read—in her absence —at the Opening of Parliament, she declared that it committed England to war, and refused to sign it. The Queen, already becoming much criticized for a number of reasons, was held to blame by the country for England's perfidy. But, for all the clamor and heroic gestures, there was only one ending: Denmark lost the Duchies, and Bismarck got Kiel.

Alix was left in bitterness: bitterness with the Queen, bitterness with the people who had given this mad empty acclaim and abandoned her in need. Her sudden popularity had gone to her head. She was too young to weigh it at its value, too young to understand the very sane point of view of the Queen. But as that year wore on, the tone of Alix's bitterness changed. She forgave the British, forgave her mother-in-law. Her bitterness turned against herself. She had failed, and had betrayed her father and her country. She was nothing but a beautiful doll with nothing but sawdust inside her. They had raved about her as children might do about a lovely doll in a shop window. But she herself, Alix, her soul, her personality, that had meant nothing to them. It was too feeble. They had not been moved at all. She was no good to her own countrymen—nor to the English.

Bertie, the kindest of men, was full of sympathy. He understood, if nobody else in the royal family really did so. When a member of the household too callously announced another Danish defeat before the Princess, he swiftly drew the offender into another room and revealed what his anger could be like. It was he who suggested that they should travel together to Copenhagen in the autumn to visit her parents. At first the prospect much comforted Alix. She wanted to go home to explain things to her father, at least.

Bertie set to work to persuade his mother and Palmerston that this visit would be a good thing. His mother was most reluctant. He had said so many terrible and unwarranted things about the Germans that she trembled to imagine the indiscretions he would perpetrate in Copenhagen. Even Lord "Pam," the old Lion of England, was not overenthusiastic. However, having formed a high opinion of the real acumen of the Prince of Wales, he agreed to approach the Queen.

The Queen decided to agree with her Prime Minister. But only on two conditions: they must visit Germany as well, and the visit must be incognito. The Prince's letter of September 1 from Abergeldie to Palmerston touches not unamusingly on one aspect of the coming visit.

"I have to thank you for your letter of the 23rd, and feel much obliged to you for having told the Queen that you thought the expression of my feelings and opinions on the late sad events in Denmark would be tempered with due discretion.

"I sincerely trust that nothing I may say during our visit to Copenhagen would give annoyance to the Queen or H.M. Government."

Meanwhile, rumors of the coming visit had reached Denmark. The Danish Press announced bluntly that if the Prince of Wales cared to come he must recognize that whatever his personal sentiments were known to have been during the war, he would be treated as the official representative of the country which by un-ashamed perfidy had allowed an ally to be "robbed" of its most precious territories. For Bertie the prospect was scarcely inviting.

As the day of departure grew closer, desolation and dread over-whelmed Alix. She was ashamed. She never wanted to go home. The Danes would break her heart. They might insult, even stone, poor Bertie, who had been so good to her. Perhaps Papa did not much want her, either. Bertie, with good cause to dread the coming visit, had firmly to exhort his wife to visit her own country. He had still to find in himself his brilliant flair for successfully visiting sore foreigners, which would later serve his country so well, but he set off in stout heart with his nervous Princess in the royal yacht *Osborne,* well loaded with bouquets of rockets and colored fire flares to illuminate the rails and paddle-boxes in joyful greeting of the sullen Danes.

Alix, pale and drawn as she stepped upon Danish soil, need not have worried herself. Soon the color swiftly came and went in her cheeks as she bowed again and again to the crowds which roared a welcome. They had brought with them their infant son, and al-though the Danes looked somewhat coldly on the young man in plain clothes and a rather immature beard who stood beside their Princess, they one and all felt that his son Albert Victor was their son too, and were half ready to thaw toward him.

An Englishman who was present when they reached Denmark has recorded his impressions.

"I have never seen her (the Princess) look better or more handsome. Surrounded as she was by the greatest in the land, she stood out peerless and beautiful. Her equal was not there. As an Englishman I could not help feeling proud as I looked upon her charming, sweet face and thought she was *our* Princess.

"She seems to have been almost idolized in Denmark. The love for her here is intense. People tell stories of her young life, little incidents of her goodness and courtesy, probably quite forgotten by her. 'She is ours still,' they say; 'she is Danish!' "

They joined the Danish family at Fredensborg Castle. The in-cognito was thin from the start. The Prince and Princess of Wales had to meet every important personality in Denmark and they were proudly displayed to the foreign diplomats. The Prince even had to dine—in plain clothes—with the officers of the Danish Fleet. For Alix everything was easy, but Bertie had to make his way. He so impressed the naval men that they confused him with his naval brother Alfred. His final triumph came with a visit to the opera, where the ovation directed at the royal box was obviously mainly for him. Next morning the Press declared that "he had conquered the Danes, as his wife had conquered the English." And he had not uttered one indiscreet word, though everybody felt that the Prince of Wales had silently conveyed his sympathy to them.

An interesting guest was with them at Fredensborg. He was Grand Duke Nicholas, Czarevitch of Russia, a distant cousin of the family, and his object in being there was to seek the hand of Alix's sister and one-time inseparable companion, the beautiful Dagmar. It was a match highly approved by all, doomed not to take place because of the sudden death of Nicholas; though for Dagmar, the most ambitious, forceful and intelligent member of the family, affairs would turn out equally brilliantly. Czarevitch Nicholas's next brother, just as towering and handsome, would conveniently step out of the wings to solace that broken romance, with practically no time lost and, indeed, at his dying brother's request.

The time for their German visit arrived. Needless to say, they did not call at Berlin. The Prince of Wales, certainly, would not have been welcome. Those words of his, that "the horrible war they had brought on will be a stain forever on Prussian history," that Prussian ministers only "lit their cigars" with notes of mediation, had been very ill received. They visited Hanover and Hesse, but at Cologne at the railway station they did have a brief meeting with Vicky and Crown Prince Fritz. For a meeting between relations it was a frigid occasion. Bertie examined coldly the new medal glinting on Fritz's chest, and wrote to his friend Lord Spencer.

"I can assure you," he ironically reported, "that it was not pleasant to see him and his A.D.C. in Prussian uniform flaunting before our eyes a most objectionable ribbon which he received for his *deeds of valour???* against the unhappy Danes."

They reached home in the first week of November, but on the way an incident had occurred which surprised even Bertie, and revealed his wife to him as a girl of more adamantine character than he had believed.

The *Osborne* approached Kiel, and according to the time-honored usages of the sea the captain ordered the Prussian flag to be run up. The answering flags went up in the Prussian shore stations and the batteries fired. Perhaps it was one of the first ceremonial sea visitations for the Prussian authorities. It had been all perfectly correct. Now they were doomed to insult.

Livid with rage, the Princess of Wales regarded the Prussian flag fluttering at the masthead.

"What is the meaning of *that?*" she hissed.

She was told by a member of the suite that it was in order. To fail to acknowledge would be a great discourtesy.

"That doesn't matter in the least," said she. "Go and tell the captain from me to take it down. I won't have it on any ship which carries me." She went and placed herself in a position in which she could be observed from the bridge, and stared stonily upward at the commander. "Tell him," she snapped, "that I refuse to move one inch from the spot where I now stand until he does haul it down!"

Ashore, the astonished Prussians watched their flag sliding ignominiously down the mast of England's royal yacht.

George Frederick Ernest Albert was born at Marlborough House on June 3, 1865. He would one day become George V. Albert was added to his names as an afterthought at the request of the Queen. Much of these years of the 'sixties for Alix was occupied in childbearing, or the prenatal or antenatal effects of it, and after that first brilliant year she was seen less frequently outside the family and Marlborough House circle than many people would have wished until the turn of the new decade.

It was the year 1866, in which the Queen was to open Parliament for the first time, and to hold some of the Drawing Rooms herself.

On this account the Opening of Parliament in February might almost be called a social occasion, with a packed gallery. It was a peculiar ceremony, especially arranged to soothe the hysterical fears of Her Majesty. She had to have the obnoxious Brown with her, to the disgust of officialdom. She could not bear to wear the State Robes or the Crown. The Mantle had to be draped over the back of the Throne and wrapped gently round her shoulders by the Mistress of the Robes when she was seated. The Crown had to be carried on a cushion. The Lord Chancellor, after tending the Speech to the Queen, had to receive it back and to inform the House that "by Command of her Majesty I shall now proceed to read it." The only ordeal remaining for the Queen, therefore, was to make a regal entrance before the company; and this by her own confession was so awful a moment that she thought she was going to tumble in a faint to the floor. Yet, in spite of her blind terror before the gimlet eyes of that tense multitude—almost as keyed to the drama as they had been for the wedding—there was one face among the royalties ranged behind the Throne which caught the attention of the Queen. We know from the Press reports that

> "as her Majesty passed in front of the Princess of Wales to the foot of the throne, she paused for a moment while the Princess kissed her hand; she then ascended the steps and took her seat, the Duchess of Wellington drawing the State robes slightly around her."

After her first Drawing Room the Queen handed over to the Princess of Wales a considerable time before the end and she took a drive in an open carriage through the park. Taken by surprise, the people in the streets were delighted to see the Queen once again. They ran to give her a clamorous greeting. She was moved. Pathetically she wrote to Uncle Leopold:

> "Everyone said that the difference shown, when I appeared and (when) Bertie and Alix drive, was not to be described. Naturally for *them* no one stops, or *runs,* as they always did, and *do* doubly now, for *me.*"

The picture of the neglected Prince and Princess of Wales seems to be a trifle inaccurate, although there were certainly occasions when Bertie would have been exceedingly outraged if chased by inquisitive crowds. Bertie had a private life, which he liked to live according to his own plan, and it was about to be brought home to the people of the country that Her Majesty also had a peculiar kind of private life, which, although she seemed careless of keeping it as a secret, she yet meant to follow without hindrance.

It may be that the embarrassment caused by Bertie to his mother went beyond his indiscreet words in affairs of high policy, beyond his constant request to peruse State papers, which she would seldom allow, beyond his frequently expressed desire for useful State employment, which she did not want to give him, and that something of the Bohemian nature of his personal life was becoming known to her; but during the next few years the Queen herself was to be the subject of much graver embarrassment to her eldest son and her daughter-in-law than ever the heir to the Throne can have been to her.

For the Queen, 1866 and the years following were the Brown years *in excelsis*. John Brown, the tough gillie, who seemed to combine the offices of groom, custodian, lady's maid and Closet companion to the Queen, had now reached the point in his life when he was to be hailed as "The Great Court Favorite." Long hated by the Court for his rudeness and disdain, he was now to become the guy of the nation. The Prince of Wales disliked him heartily. He is said to have been refused access to the Royal Closet from time to time by Brown and to have been treated like a schoolboy. What was more, Brown, who practically regarded himself as one of the family circle during the seasonal meetings at Osborne, Balmoral or Windsor, and was constantly slipping in familiar asides to the Queen, naturally did not see any reason why he should accord to the young Princess of Wales a deference which he never gave to Her Majesty.

It was in 1866 that people in society began to refer jokingly to the Queen as "Mrs. Brown." The habit grew widespread, and astonished visiting foreigners. Some people really believed Her Majesty had married him. Others remembered that George III had been mad, and declared that Brown was secretly the keeper of a lunatic. Others, still, thought he was a spiritualistic medium who kept the Queen in touch with the dead Consort, or pretended to do so, and this was perhaps a part of the secret. But not all of it; it was obvious to everybody about the Court that the Queen was perfectly infatuated with the large red-bearded Highlander.

Punch was openly tilting at Mr. Brown in the summer of 1866, the Scottish papers stressed the bibulous qualities of this remarkable Caledonian—these were well known at Court, and the odor of alcohol sometimes lingered in the Closet—and although Brown was doing a service for the Queen which nobody else could do, he was a shame and humiliation to the whole family. When in August of the following year *The Tomahawk* published the cartoon entitled "A Brown Study," depicting Brown propped meditatively against the empty Throne, with pipe in hand and the Crown in a glass case behind him, while the British Lion roared up at his feet, Bertie is said to have been so enraged that he ordered a special train and arrived at Osborne to tell his mother that the time had at last arrived when Brown must go.

The Brown crisis reached its head with the projected Hyde Park Royal Review of '67, when the Queen was warned that riots were planned to break out if John Brown was seen to be traveling on the rumble of the royal carriage, and even her cousin, the Duke of Cambridge, and Lord Derby were popularly supposed to have made a strong protest. The Review was, luckily perhaps, postponed. But the plaintive royal letter of remonstrance, addressed to Lord Charles Fitzroy, declaring that "She (the Queen) is much astonished and shocked at the attempt to prevent her faithful servant going with her to the Review, thereby making the poor Queen, who is so accustomed to his watchful care and intelligence, terribly nervous and uncomfortable," gives some hint of the odd state of affairs prevailing about the British Throne at that time. It also illuminates the difficulties which faced Bertie as eldest son and heir, and Alix as the daughter-in-law.

"Good Mr. Brown" was to linger on through the whole of the 'seventies and beyond, the royal bogey, his sharp ways tending to mellow somewhat, or at least grow blunt with usage, to all but the Prince of Wales, who reciprocated the murderous hatred of the servant without concealment. But in their time prince and princess of the blood, peer, minister of the realm, great lady and sergeant footman alike, seem one and all to have quivered at the royal portals before the eagle glare of the grim-kilted custodian, like recruits before some awful sergeant-major.

It was in 1866 that early one summer morning police were called to move a TO LET notice mysteriously fixed to the gates of Buckingham Palace. Republicanism was a live and growing force in the Victorian 'sixties, and unconsciously one of its most potent propagandists was the Queen herself. Against this force there stood out before the eyes of the nation one young couple, cheerful, friendly and energetic, the Prince and Princess of Wales.

It has been said of Alix that after the Schleswig-Holstein calamity she never meddled in politics, and in a direct sense that is true. But during the 'sixties, as also to a lesser extent during the decades which followed, her sisterly loyalty to the helpless and hopeless and very earnest King of Greece caused her to encourage her husband to support the cause of Greece, which was highly disconcerting to his mother and on several occasions to Ministers of the Crown. For a young man of his age Bertie had worked up for himself a great many high political contacts. The continual snubs of his mother were actually of advantage to him here, as ministers out of sympathy were ready to listen to his views and reveal to him matters which they felt in his position should have come to him through the Queen.

Thus, when his distracted brother-in-law wrote to him from Athens in October 1866 "how would not your name be blessed could they (the Cretans) know that you take some interest in their destiny," he was not entirely overrating the power of the Prince of Wales to help Greece in her struggle against Turkey. In this instance the Cretans were attempting to drive out the Turkish garrisons from their island with the aid of Grecian troops from the mainland, and the Prince, who made no secret of his views, called upon Lord Stanley, the Foreign Secretary, to discuss the situation. Lord Stanley agreed that something might be done for the Greeks. It was, however, one of those intricate problems involving the Powers, and the Queen, hearing of her son's action, grew exceedingly nervous. She sent for him. The interview at Windsor was private. The result: Bertie, doubtless to the chagrin of Alix, wrote to his brother-in-law saying he could only advise him for the present to moderate his anti-Turkish activities, as a consensus of the Powers was against him. This, for a space, the unhappy George seemed able to achieve at the expense of abuse from his ardent subjects, and the Cretan insurrection temporarily died away.

Another foreign event of that October of much importance to the

Marlborough House couple, and of no little significance to Great Britain, was the marriage of Princess Dagmar in St. Petersburg to Czarevitch Alexander of Russia. When his elder brother had died the Czarevitch had promptly arrived at Copenhagen to claim the beautiful Dane: a young lady well fitted by character to become the wife of an autocrat Czar, and especially one who himself was not notably a strong-natured man.

For Britain this match was of importance, for by the family tie it established the basis upon which this country and Russia could draw together after the Crimean War. Alix, to her regret, was again unable to attend a family wedding through pregnancy. But both she and her family were most anxious that Bertie should attend. The Russians, hearing of this project, seemed to be pleased. The pressure put upon Bertie sent him to the Queen. She was reluctant. What might Bertie say in St. Petersburg? He could truthfully assure the Russians that he was a Turkophobe, which would please them very well. It did not please her. Her Government seemed to think the visit would do good.

The Queen waived her own views. Bertie, with promises of the utmost discretion and bearing messages from Alix to her favorite sister, departed for St. Petersburg. It was the first of those unofficial semipolitical missions which he always performed so admirably, and although this Russian *rapprochement* was only a very tentative beginning, he himself, the grand cosmopolitan in embryo, was a tremendous success in the Russian capital.

Chapter 14

IS SHE DYING?

ON FEBRUARY 18, 1867, newspaper readers were informed that the Princess of Wales was confined to her room at Marlborough House with acute rheumatism. There was "no cause for anxiety." Some of those hardy Victorian matrons probably doubted this, for it was known that a new baby was expected at Marlborough House in a month or so.

Three days later Louise, afterward Princess Royal and Duchess of Fife, was born. Once again the Home Secretary could not be called in time, and confusion reigned. This time it was serious. Alix lay in a high fever before she started in travail.

Several days elapsed. Sir James Paget saw that her condition was so critical that, without consulting either her husband, who was fulfilling an official duty, or the Queen at Windsor, he telegraphed to Copenhagen for her parents.

Queen Louise arrived at Marlborough House, and two days later King Christian. The Queen, in London for a Drawing Room, was anxiously watched as she drove to Marlborough House. When Her Majesty arrived she discovered Queen Louise in charge of the sickroom. This was no time for dignified tepidity. The two women were probably more cordial than ever before or afterward as they discussed the patient in an adjoining room. Alix seemed to have recovered well from the birth, but spasms of agonizing rheumatic pain left her stiff and moaning. The Queen, perhaps, was skeptical when Queen Louise declared that since she had taken over the sickroom the spirits of Alix had revived in a wonderful way and she believed

89

this had helped her to turn the corner. But it was probably true. If her mother was decisive and brusque, she was also amusing and understanding, and Alix was deeply attached to her. It was the opinion of Sir James Paget that the appearance of her mother had saved her life.

The guarded nature of the bulletins pinned outside Marlborough House, as also of the reports in the papers, was a mistaken policy. The arrival of the Danish parents and the news leaking out of Marlborough House gave them the lie. Press statements issued by the royal physicians that "rumors are afloat as unfounded as they are extraordinary" were ignored. A wave of frenzied anxiety swept the country. It was in the nature of Alix that she always affected people's emotions violently. Huge crowds lingered all day outside Marlborough House, pressing forward hungrily toward anybody who struggled out of the house and drove away.

Alix was now to learn the true measure of the love of the people for her. This was no demented outcry from hysterical and battening mobs. This was human. The real thing. Probably Alix found it as difficult to understand as the maddened crowds at her first arrival. But it was much more delightful, in spite of the delirious pain which tore through her body.

Every few hours bulging postbags with letters of sympathy—some very ill-spelled—were dragged into Marlborough House. Parcels began to arrive. In one month more than one thousand bottles of medicine, embrocation and patent cures were received. Had she tried one quarter of the "cures" recommended to her she would certainly have died. Rolls of oilskin, felt pads and an amazing variety of splints, many secondhand, had also to be accepted. One working man, who had read that the Princess suffered sleepless nights, called at Marlborough House and left a hop pillow which had been of great comfort to his wife.

On one day—it was the anniversary of their wedding—the crowds outside Marlborough House were observed to be in a frenzy of anxiety. They refused to believe the bulletin that was posted up and grew clamorous and abusive. The story that the Princess was then dying passed from mouth to mouth. It actually looked as if they might try to storm the house to learn the truth. At last the Prince sent out that indefatigable warrior, Major Teesdale, V.C., to explain personally to the people that there was no special cause for anxiety.

The royal physicians had watched with indignation the arrival of the unsolicited medical stores at Marlborough House, and at last they caused an official request to be published that these should cease. It was only a matter of time now before the Princess regained her health, though she would, of course, long be an invalid. Scarcely had they announced this than, in the middle of April, Alix slipped into a dangerous relapse. This time they declared frankly that the Princess was in high fever, and in such pain, especially in one knee joint, that they were giving her doses of chloroform. Once more the bottles of medicine and the letters began to arrive; but this time Alix quickly turned the corner. It was as well, for the physicians had in *The Times* of April 15 announced with astonishing honesty that they were practically helpless to aid the Princess and that the obstinacy of the "inflammation was baffling to the last degree."

Alix was so much better on May 10 that, hobbling on two sticks, she was able to attend the christening of Louise in the drawing room. There now seemed no reason why Bertie should not take his departure for Paris, where the Emperor Napoleon III's Great International Exhibition was about to open. Alix urged him to do so, for she knew how much this chance of intimate contact with the fabulous Second Empire court would mean to him. Napoleon III—the "Parakeet"—was Bertie's hero. When Bertie was thirteen he had gone with his father and mother on that celebrated official visit to the Emperor and Empress during the Crimean War, and it had been on the Tuileries terrace that Bertie had remarked quite seriously to the Emperor, "I should like to be your son!" If Bertie did not exactly model himself upon the Imperial parvenu, whom the old royalties inclined to regard with suspicion, there can be no doubt that the personality of this remarkable Frenchman offered a pattern which Bertie found highly attractive. The Marlborough House "set" when in full flower, and the whole broadening outlook in Britain which began to follow upon the example set by the Prince and Princess of Wales, were indirect results of a young man's admiration for Louis Napoleon.

Bertie had slipped over to Paris with a male friend or two on several occasions since his marriage. He had yet to make the statement "I am a true Parisian—a Frenchman at heart!" but he already regarded himself as a true *boulevardier*. Yet this was different: this plunge into the glorious flamboyance of the Second Empire court. And there he would mingle with all the crowned heads of Europe—only his own mother would be missing, thank heavens!—and he would learn how a royal court really should be conducted. For this occasion was Napoleon's great triumph: at last he was recognized, at least patronized, even by the great Autocrat of Russia.

In Paris, Bertie received hints that the Czar of Russia, the Sultan of Turkey and the Khedive of Egypt would all like to visit England. Anything of that kind would clearly have to be official. He wrote to his mother about it. The Queen could not bear the thought of the Czar. She would send him the Garter in an official parcel, and he would have to go home from Paris. Bertie, whose anti-Turk sentiments had somewhat modified, urged the desires of the Sultan. Distasteful as this idea was to the Queen, it was from the Governmental point of view sound policy. The persuasions of the Prime Minister and her son convinced the Queen. After all, Bertie would be good enough for the Sultan and his vassal the Khedive. They could lodge at Buckingham Palace and Bertie could look after them: she might see them once or twice. The Czar might have been a more embarrassing proposition. The invitations were sent out and enthusiastically accepted.

Alix, meanwhile, was recuperating. She could walk only the shortest distances, and then only with a metal support round her knee. The lameness and weakness in the knee joint would gradually right itself, and rather astonishingly in the following year she would be dancing again with Oliver Montagu, Lord Carrington, Harry Chaplin, Montague Guest and Louis of Battenburg, those tall partners whom she so greatly favored, and who as her devoted slaves soon learned to cover up her limp on the dance floor. The "Alexandra Limp" was before long to be a fashionable affectation, which for several years was displayed with more or less grace by society women. Another effect of the rheumatic attack was that Alix, who for many years was to be a well-known figure in the hunting field, could no longer use the normal sidesaddle. From 1868 her beloved mares *Victoria* and *Viva* had to learn to carry her in "reverse."

Alix was unable to help her husband when the Sultan arrived on July 11. She was much disappointed, for the visit promised to have its humorous moments, and Bertie was anticipating it with the glee of a schoolboy. A small stand was built for her in the gardens of Marlborough House from which she could watch the potentate pass with Bertie on his State drive from Charing Cross to the Palace. It was from this same stand that Alix, as long as she lived at Marlborough House, would appear almost daily to watch the Changing of the Guard at St. James's Palace, a ceremony which never tired her.

On the great day as the Sultan's carriage drew abreast of Marlborough House, Bertie called his attention to the waving Princess. The Sultan sprang up in the carriage, saluting and bowing till he almost overbalanced. As soon as the State procession was ended the Sultan declared that he must go and call upon the Princess of Wales. He arrived unexpectedly with Bertie, who had to maintain a more than usual solemnity when he caught his wife's eye. Oriental potentates in those days looked and acted the part. Alix did not kiss the Sultan and his heir, as Queen Victoria had to do—she being a sister sovereign—but she became great friends with the Turks with the help of a good interpreter. The Sultan departed, declaring that the Princess of Wales would be welcome in his palaces in Constantinople at any time she liked to come. By such a declaration the scintillating potentate literally slashed through every tradition of his race, and he would shortly prove that he meant his words.

This ended Alix's connection with the visit of the Sultan, and her disablement caused her to miss one of the great comedies of the reign, doubtless recounted to her in delightful detail by that born raconteur Bertie: that unforgettable afternoon on the royal yacht at the Spithead Review when the Sultan, gray with seasickness, staggering on the reeling deck, received the Garter Ribbon from the Queen—a secondhand Ribbon confiscated brusquely in full view by John Brown from the bewildered Prince of Hesse, since the new Ribbon had been forgotten.

Bertie took Alix to Wiesbaden in August for the waters. She was carried in a sedan chair specially made for her. Perhaps the waters did her good, for her sister-in-law, Alice of Hesse, presently reported to the Queen that "Alix can walk upstairs with the help of two sticks, although her knee is still stiff." At Darmstadt that impressive military figure King William I of Prussia arrived to call on the Princess of Wales. Anger welled within her at the name of the King of Prussia. Personally, she had no wish to meet him; but she realized that the harsh-looking bewhiskered monarch was doing the right thing and she must receive him civilly. He tried to be friendly to this beautiful girl. He was proud of his coarse soldierly manner, but much more the pawn of Bismarck than a "blood and iron man" himself, and momentarily she was not unmoved by his approach. She informed her mother-in-law that "the meeting had been satisfactory to both parties; bearing ill will is always a mistake besides being not right." But this did not last. When King William died she would refuse to go to his memorial service in London.

Early in 1868 Bertie's friend Napoleon III wrote to offer Alix the use of his spacious villa at Algiers, where she might recuperate in the African spring under ideal conditions. But Alix felt so well that she was insisting that she would go with Bertie on his visit to Dublin in April. Perhaps Bertie's lone visit to Dublin in the previous year for the Exhibition of Arts and Industry had worried her so much that she had decided that if Bertie was going to be murdered she would prefer to die with him. His visit had been a huge success. But you could never tell in Ireland, as she herself in her time would have good cause to know.

Several ministers, including Mr. Disraeli, had an idea that the Prince and Princess of Wales ought to have a residence in Ireland, and that nothing would be more likely to tame the Irish and curb the ferocious Fenians. The Queen would not hear of this. But Disraeli, who was Prime Minister now, persuaded the Viceroy, the Marquis of Abercorn, directly to approach the Prince about an official visit to Dublin. Bertie went to his mother. This was clearly the wrong line of approach. She was shaken with indignation at this backstairs intrigue to get him to risk his life in Ireland, and her anger was not diminished when he told her shortly that *in two centuries British sovereigns had spent twenty-one days in Ireland!* In the end she gave way, as she usually did when her Government was against her. She saw this granting of permission to Bertie as a purely domestic affair.

This first Irish visit of the Prince and Princess of Wales, which started when they landed at Kingstown on April 15, is in detail of little interest, just because it was so successful and so much like any royal visit anywhere. It was certainly most unlike that adventurous and dangerous tour which Bertie and Alix endured in Ireland several years later.

Doubtless the first appearance of the wonderful Princess of Wales played its part in sweetening the Dubliners, who in any case were always more broad-minded than the rest of Ireland. If any Prince was suited to the Irish it was Bertie—or "Prince Hal" as they liked to call him affectionately behind his back. Bertie could make wonderful speeches without any notes. He wore a green tie wherever he went in Dublin, and Alix, not to be outdone, was seen in a green gown of the celebrated Irish poplin. Whatever the Dubliners may have thought of this gown, it seems to have been viewed less favorably in England. Alix appeared in it for Cup Day at Ascot. She knew that the Irish would read in the papers that she had worn the same dress at Ascot as she had done at their own rather happy-go-lucky Punchestown Races. A remark from a member of the royal family was that "dear Alix was looking a little less than her very best in a green gown trimmed with yellowish Irish point lace and a white bonnet with shamrock."

That visit to Punchestown Races, incidentally, was frowned upon by the Queen. It was risky, undignified, not in good taste. Bertie could never resist a race-meeting. His letter explained to her that their attendance enabled a vast crowd of Irish people "to display their loyalty to you and your Family." She expressed entire satisfaction.

A curious story is told of Alix while at Viceregal Lodge. Ernest Hamilton, the eight-year-old youngest son of the Viceroy, had his hands covered with warts, which he tried to hide from the Princess. His mother explained to her the boy's shame and distress.

"Come here, Ernest," said the Princess of Wales. "I can cure those hands for you. Go and fetch a little hazel twig from the grounds."

Presented with the hazel twig, she performed a kind of magical incantation. She was perfectly solemn.

"The warts will all vanish," she assured him, in her slightly husky foreign accent.

There is no denying that starting from the day of her departure the warts did vanish with astonishing rapidity. She did not herself know of this till she met Ernest twelve years later as a young cavalry officer.

"Where are the warts?" were the first words she addressed to him.

"Your Royal Highness dispersed them with a magic touch!" came the answer.

On July 6 another daughter was born at Marlborough House. Once again the birth was a premature one. Only the day before, Alix, in the highest spirits, had been applauding Patti at a gala concert at the Crystal Palace. This time there were no serious after-effects, and when September came Alix was ready to join Bertie in a scheme they had secretly been discussing for some time. They were at Abergeldie, and the Queen was at Balmoral. Balmoral was always the best place to approach the Queen upon any subject which you thought she might not like.

Feeling rather nervous, they reached Balmoral, and presently were vying with each other to secure a favorable opening to reveal their hopes. Alix won. It seems to have all come out in a rush. Alix was really rather tired after her long illness. She would very much like to spend a family Christmas in Denmark, and Bertie felt it would do her so much good if they could combine it with quite a long foreign tour, including a visit to George in Athens and a visit to the Near East. Bertie declared his great interest in De Lessep's Suez Canal, which was almost completed. He was convinced that it would be of enormous importance to Britain. He thought he should inspect it. He also thought it only right that Her Majesty's friend the Sultan, likewise the Khedive of Egypt, who had been so enthusiastic about their reception in England, should be given an opportunity of returning the hospitality. He believed that King George of Greece might be glad to have some conversations with him. Finally, and he was very frank about this, he had heard that tall stories were abroad about excessively high play at Marlborough House and about the fast style of life of some of the friends they regularly entertained there. This was, of course, sadly exaggerated, he assured his mother: nevertheless, it would perhaps be a good thing for them to be away from the country for a time to give people a chance of forgetting all the nonsense.

The Queen listened more sympathetically than they had expected. She knew what Alix had suffered. She said they could go. But there and then she could lay down the conditions upon which she gave her consent. They must promise to observe them to the letter. They agreed.

They were to travel and visit strictly incognito, even in such places as Constantinople and Cairo. Bertie knew that was going to be difficult. "Lord and Lady Renfrew," the Queen thought, would be as good a name for them as any. She must know all the places to which they intended to go, and they must visit no others without telegraphic communication with her. Finally, whatever the custom of the people they were with, they were always to regard Sunday as a day of rest and take no light amusement. They joyously departed to make their elaborate plans.

Alix never ceased to live in a state of delirious excitement till November 15, when she and Bertie, with the three eldest children and a lovely collection of new dresses, calculated for all climates, set out for Denmark.

First they went to Compiègne to be the guests of Napoleon III and Empress Eugénie. By temperament they were perfectly suited to be a glowing success in a French court, just as they would shortly find themselves uncomfortable in the stiff absurdities of the Austro-Hungarian court. The redoubtable Princess Mathilde, the Emperor's cousin, a much-dreaded figure in Continental society, well summed things up when she said of the Prince of Wales, "He is open—he says what he has in his heart and is not like other princes who have always the air of having something to conceal." It was plain from her cordiality to Alix that *"la terrible* Mathilde" included her in the same category.

They left Paris on the 25th for Cologne, from there to Düsseldorf to be the guests of the Hohenzollern-Sigmarin family, to Lubeck, to Copenhagen. At Fredensborg, where the traditional family party was gathering, Bertie left Alix and the children and departed for Stockholm to spend six days with King Charles XV of Sweden. It was here by King Charles' sponsorship that he became a Freemason, of which craft he was afterward such a very distinguished leader.

He rejoined the great family party now assembled at Fredensborg for Christmas. As the years went by those remarkable Fredensborg parties would increase in size and glory. This year there was a Czarevitch of Russia and his wife. The King of Greece and his Russian bride, Olga, could not attend. But in future years, besides the Prince and Princess of Wales, there was often a Czar of Russia, a Czarina, a King and Queen of Greece, an exiled King and Queen of Hanover—for Thyra, Alix's second sister, was to marry the son of the exiled Hanoverian monarch—and many a less exalted person from across the frontiers. Alix delighted in those cosmopolitan gatherings. She would look forward to them all through the year. How they would all laugh and chatter, while the men swapped vital international politics in the most inconsequential manner. Bertie also came to enjoy those parties, and in his letters home during many years there occurs an almost identical formula—"we are an immense family gathering; quite a Babel, seven different languages spoken, never sitting down to dinner less than fifty or sixty."

Sending the children home from Denmark, Bertie and Alix came to Berlin on January 18, 1869, as the guests of Vicky and Fritz. Relations between the Waleses and the Crown Prince and Princess warmed a good deal, but neither found the three-day Prussian stay very enjoyable. For the first time they met the fabulous Bismarck. Bismarck, always well-informed, was aware that the Prince of Wales regarded him with suspicion, but that the Princess heard his name with disgust and hatred. He did not underrate the power of England, nor the influence such a beautiful woman as the Princess might wield behind the scenes. He resolved to do his best with her. The giant Prussian draped his Danish Order of Dannebrog around him, and at the State banquet his bulging steely eyes fawned amiably upon the lovely Dane. He might have saved his time. At Berlin their incognito wore pretty thin. They could not help it. At Vienna it vanished altogether.

The Emperor Francis Joseph did not recognize incognitos. Besides, having just been ignominiously crushed by the Prussian armies, he was most anxious to flatter England. The brilliancy of the Imperial Viennese reception was surpassed only by its freezing decorum. This was so alien to the Waleses' way of life that they were discomfited. To Alix the only highlight seems to have been her visit to the Imperial stable of five hundred superb horses, followed by an inspection of the amazing collection of six hundred Imperial coaches of all periods. They had been sustained through the trying days of this visit by the exciting thought that the real adventure was almost upon them.

Chapter 15

THE NILE ADVENTURE

ON JANUARY 27 the Prince and Princess were at Trieste and in lighthearted mood. *H.M.S. Ariadne,* embellished as a royal yacht, waited to take them to Alexandria. Egypt was agog. They said that no European princess had visited Egyptian shores since the Crusades, and the wondrous beauty of the Princess of Wales was celebrated even in that land of female repression. French-educated Khedive Ismail, the most profligate and generous man in the Near East—his bankruptcy would soon give to England the Suez Canal shares and cause her to occupy Egypt—had lavished fantastic sums of money on the coming entertainment, which was to be a bewildering, almost nightmarish, display of French Second Empire at its worst and the Arabian Nights at their best.

Heavy seas brought them two days late into Alexandria, while Egypt had waited in hourly expectancy in ceremonial array. Soon their weirdly painted engine had drawn them into the Khedive's private station before Kasr-el-Nil Palace in Cairo, and they were alighting from their Orientally festive saloon coach into the golden sunlight. Russell, the famous *Times* correspondent who accompanied the visit, and Mrs. Grey, the favorite lady in waiting, have between them left some picturesque and amusing glimpses of the Egyptian visit. It was a page in the lives of Bertie and Alix which could never be repeated. It brought them closer together as human beings. In the shades of the after years, which sometimes glowed and sometimes darkened, it was never forgotten.

They were to be lodged at the immense Esbekiah Palace, and as they took their seats with Khedive Ismail in "a handsome carriage drawn by a pair of fine English greys, ridden by English postilions in faultless tops and leathers and jackets," they gazed about them at

"the broad sheet of the Nile crisped by a fresh breeze, which drove a regatta-like fleet of vast-sailed lateen-rigged boats upwards against the current; the opposite shore lined with palm trees, shaking their tufted crests in the wind; the forests of yards and masts lining the course of the stream; and, rising above them again, the tops of the Pyramids of Gizeh; the irregular outlines of the houses over which peered the domes and minarets of many mosques—formed the background to a brilliant picture, framed in a sky of heavenly blue, of which the foreground was composed of the colonnades of the barracks crowded by soldiery, the strict line of troops under arms, and officials in uniform."

At the Esbekiah the sleeping chambers of the guests were "so large that, even when the candles were lit, there might be somebody sitting at the other end without you knowing it." One member of the suite had a fountain continually hissing in the middle of the bedroom. Much supplication was needed before the officials would turn it off at night. Solid silver bedsteads were the order of the house, sheets of beaten gold covered furniture or entire walls, hangings of the richest silk drooped everywhere and hundreds of huge ornamental mirrors reflected the dim glittering interiors. The royal bedchamber was "more like a State drawing room at Windsor than a bedroom."

While Bertie was occupied with the Khedive, Alix was taken to dine at the Khedival harem at the Palace of the Nile. Here, La Grande Princesse, Ismail's immensely fat mother, presided with a company of gigantic eunuchs over her son's wives and daughters and more than five hundred female slaves. When she entered those gorgeous, crowded halls she faced a scene such as the most fantastic pantomime has never staged. The princesses shone with precious gems, which dazed and dazzled the senses, the slave girls were scarcely less glittering, and heavy perfumes stifled the atmosphere. Bangles jingled and rattled and the waters of fountains tinkled everywhere and sprayed the heated visitor as she passed, pursued by a huge excited cluster of smiling women. With La Grande Princesse leading her by the hand, Alix arrived in a room where "in the middle was a kind of round silver table, one foot high, with large square cushions placed all around it."

A tortoiseshell spoon with a coral-branch handle was placed in the hand of the guest—a mere ceremonial, for the better part of the strange and endless repast which followed was more safely and correctly eaten with the fingers. Alix did not mind the rice and chicken dishes, she found sausage omelette messy to the fingers, she could taste without wincing the vermicelli and sugar confections, she swallowed rosewater and tapioca good-naturedly, but gracefully repudiated a sauced onion offered in the fingers from her neighbor's plate. She refused a gemmed cup of spiced vinegar, and also rejected the long Turkish pipe set with diamonds. She toyed with a cigarette in a holder "one mass of precious stones."

Alix was overjoyed with the harem band of twenty female slaves "wearing trousers, frockcoats and gold buttons, quite European." She applauded the dancing girls and everybody was delighted, and, asking for a *yashmak,* she tried it on while a slave girl held a mirror. They clapped their hands and everybody crowded into the room. In a few minutes Alix and Mrs. Grey were clad from head to foot as Oriental slaves of the first class. The reception was turning into a hysterical riot. A Khedival wife suggested that she should return home to the Prince of Wales thus garbed to give him a surprise. To the astonishment of the officials and grooms waiting outside the sacred portals, the two veiled ladies mounted the royal carriage and drove away for the Esbekiah. Here such mystification reigned that it was doubtful if they could be admitted, for naturally no man dared raise their veils. Eventually they were forced to disclose themselves.

On the morning of February 6 a remarkable flotilla started down the Nile, proudly watched by Khedive Ismail. First went an escort steamer, bright with flags and bristling with troops and officials. The *Ornament of the Two Seas* followed, the chartered steamer of the Duke of Sutherland's party, with Russell of *The Times* aboard, forever watchfully looking back. Behind them steamed the *God Protected* in solemn pomp, for on her tow-rope glided the royal dahabeah *Alexandra.* They said that even Cleopatra had never seen anything like the *Alexandra*. Blue and gold inside and out and paneled in mother-of-pearl, it suggested some giant caravan in a super-circus. Each mealtime the Prince and Princess left their floating palace to join the suite aboard the *God Protected*. But what is that shabbier craft with greasy-gowned natives at the rail which forges officiously at the stern of the dahabeah? It is the "kitchen steamer" with its string of dirty barges towing placidly behind her: the food barge, the drink barge, the fuel barge, the luggage barge, the riding animals' barge and the French washerwoman's barge. Behind the menacing rear escort the Nile is cluttered with a fleet of inquisitive native craft. Never had the simple fellahin dwelling by the Nile watched the passing of so glorious a pageant.

> "I would be ashamed," wrote Russell to *The Times*, "to say how much more we were interested in watching the progress of the royal yacht, and in observing those on board of her, than in scrutinizing the sites of the famous places on both sides of the river above Cairo. 'There is the Princess! You can just see her in the saloon on deck!' "

Frequently the flotilla had to heave to, for the Princess wished to go ashore, and the string of barges banged together amid Oriental curses. She liked to stroll in the moonlight when "the country looked as if covered with thick gray gauze and only the tops of the palm trees were visible." They sometimes lost the dahabeah in the darkness.

Other newspaper correspondents—less lucky than Russell—were watching from hired native craft. Mr. Cook had chartered a steamer for forty English tourists. Through a mistake their pursuit was tardy, but the thought of them filled the *Morning Post* with indignation.

> "A cat may look at a king, and doubtless Mr. Cook thinks he and his forty British Toms and Tabbies are quite entitled to gaze on Royalty at the First Cataract. Imagine Thebes, the hundred-gated city, with a tourist at each portal to intercept the royal visitors! Picture the most enterprising of Cook's party perched among the ruins of Luxor and Karnak, armed with the

newest binoculars! Conceive the feelings of the occupants of the royal *dahabeah* on finding themselves convoyed to the Catacombs by a motley flotilla, manned and womaned by a Cook's company!"

At last the writer in his wrath envisages "one of the party getting near enough to secure as a memento an empty beer bottle whose amber contents may have been quaffed by the Princess herself"!

Russell's fellow passengers were also disturbed by the impudence of Cook's people. Every morning they hurried on deck to look out for them. There was always smoke on the skyline. Each time it turned out to be a merchant craft. But the shout of "The tourists are coming!" would wake the late sleepers again the next morning.

The readiness of the Princess to buy rubbish preceded her. Bold dragomans would jostle after her, shouting: "De mos' lovely dings in Egypt! Cleopadre's neglace! Look, Highness. I find her myself!" Bertie was resolved to shoot a crocodile. He asked for one whenever he stepped ashore. They seemed to be scarce, but it was a point of honor that the men of the Nile must find him one. He found his crocodile.

The picnic expedition to Karnak was a notable occasion. Russell followed

"the Princess on a milk-white ass, caparisoned in red velvet and gold, the Prince on another of darker hue, attended by some two hundred people all in full cry and as merry as the morn; all the suite; Egyptian *valetaille;* French cooks; *Ariadne* sailors careering gloriously on donkeys; Peter Robinson, the Prince's Highland piper, in his kilt ingeniously adapted to the latitude in which he is travelling . . . the gay noisy throng cantering in a long stream over the irrigated lands of sandy desert strips, now spreading out like a fan of many colours, again condensed in an undulating cord-like strand over the plains in clouds of dust, all bright with fantastic dresses, turbaned and loose-robed."

Alix's health was perfectly restored. She was tireless in her explorations under the burning sun. Bertie, more plump, was quicker to tire. Alix at Philae trotted to and fro on an old donkey bareback, because her girth was broken. She must go back to Karnak by moonlight. Her project was known. She approached the ruins. They burst out into hundreds of blue lights. In the immense ruined halls, gleaming under their weird illumination, she sat meditatively on a carpet for close on an hour. Suddenly she jumped up, "riding away on her white donkey full canter amid a crowd of syces running with lanterns."

At Assouan, Bertie and Alix called upon the celebrated Lady Duff-Gordon, who was dying of consumption.

> "The Prince," she recorded, "was most pleasant and kind, and the Princess too. She is the most perfectly simple-mannered girl I ever saw. She does not even try to be civil, like other great people, but asks blunt questions, and looks at one so heartily with her clear, honest eyes, that she must win all hearts. They were more considerate than any people I have ever seen."

At Assouan the Nile narrowed. They had to abandon their flotilla and ship on a smaller craft. Alix seems not to have fully understood this necessity. She was desolated when she discovered she was meant to leave behind her motley company. Everybody adored her, and every European had got alongside her by this time and spoken with her, or boasted that he had. "Nonsense!" she cried out, if Russell is to be believed. "It is decided that you must all come on with us!" But this was impossible, and she left each one of that extraordinary company behind with a feeling of aching personal loss.

It was as their vessel started on its course for the Second Cataract that Mr. Cook's tourists arrived, and the baffled occupants of the craft fanned themselves out along the banks.

They were back in Cairo in the middle of March. With the Khedive they inspected the Suez Canal, which was to open that autumn, and Bertie chatted earnestly with the great De Lesseps. After the romance of the Nile, the great ditch stretching across the sands bored Alix. She could solace herself, however, with anticipation of the longed-for visit to dear George at Athens. Also, she wanted to see Olga, his grand ducal Russian bride, whom she was sure must be much too young—barely eighteen—to help poor George in his troubles. To her dismay, the Greek visit had all but been forbidden by orders of the Queen. Once again the Turkish trouble had rushed to boiling point. Then, suddenly, the kettle had stopped boiling. On the way back to Cairo a royal telegram had told them they might proceed.

The *Ariadne* had not cleared Alexandra harbor, the plaudits of the Egyptians had scarcely died away, when two merchant ships crashed into the royal vessel. The collision was not too serious. But the blow unluckily had struck near the royal quarters. Alix seems to have been rather thrilled, even by the sight of their splintered saloons, and in spite of the inspection of many ruined dresses.

The *Ariadne* with naval escort and the Sultan's yacht entered the Dardanelles, and soon they were experiencing the unsurpassed glories of the Golden Horn. Constantinople—more Orientally hidebound than cosmopolitan Cairo—offered a less warm welcome. But the Sultan, true to his promise and risking severe censure from his subjects, had cast aside all tradition in their honor. The Sultan never ate with any subject but his Grand Vizier, and that seldom. He dared to give a banquet in the French style for the visitors. Twenty-five guests attended this unprecedented occasion in the Dolmabakshi Palace, among them only twelve vaguely disapproving Turks. The Sultan himself silently regarded his guests with amiable nervousness, as if apprehensive of what he had done. His broadmindedness went further. He astonished the foreign colony by appearing with an impressive following at a grand ball given at the British Embassy, and he even apologized to the Princess that religion forbade him to dance with her. He was, however, seen to take her arm, which was sensational enough. A ferocious tyrant, this Sultan Abdul Aziz—he died by assassination—yet Bertie and Alix had nothing but good to say of him, which, burdened with his Russian fears and his anti-Greek indignation, was exactly what he intended of them.

On April 12 the *Ariadne* had carried the visitors to the Crimea. Russell of *The Times* and the Russian general commanding the district showed them over the still-scarred battlefields in two days: it was interesting, and indeed, occasionally embarrassing, to hear both points of view exposed, not always without rising heat. By the

Czar's invitation they spent the night of the 14th in the Imperial villa at Livadia.

Five days later they were entering Phalerum, and for Alix the thrilling moment had arrived. There stood George with a carriage, waiting to rattle and bump them away over the plains to Athens.

George lived in a monstrous white palace overlooking the dusty, stony, tree-bordered square at the end of Kifissia Road. Neglect was outside, and space and drafts within, but he cheerfully assured them it was cool in summer. The kilted Evzone bugler disconcerted them, lurking in the Doric portals and darting out to blow a blast at every royal entry or egress, or, indeed, at anyone who might chance to be royal. Poor George was very democratic. He had to be. He would receive anybody in his blue room powdered with gold stars. He wished he did not yawn so easily. It was catching for visitors, and embarrassing. When he and Olga wanted to go to the seaside they hired the first old cab in the square. The Greeks liked that. George was wan, but bubbling with boyish cheerfulness, his troubles set aside for the moment. Only the bandits were troublesome just then, but that was several miles outside Athens.

Olga was at Corfu with his two tiny sons, Constantine and George, and they were going to join them. That would be much pleasanter. Olga rather impressed them. She was an earnest, strong-minded girl. She might one day be very useful to George, who needed some stiffening. For Alix that rural week in Corfu fled all too quickly. It was the end. The week they yet had to spend in Paris at the Tuileries sampling the splendors of the Second Empire with Napoleon and Empress Eugénie hardly counted, even though she had much exciting shopping to do after the Alexandria collision.

At Paris a letter of welcome awaited them from the Queen. Dismally black-edged, it brusquely jolted them back into the everyday. "You will, I fear," wrote Her Majesty, "have incurred enormous expenses, and I don't think you will find a disposition to give you any more money." She had been looking after the children for them, and did not seem much interested in the girls; but she thought the two boys "little dears" and the elder (later Duke of Clarence) "very sensible when you have him with you alone." The Queen knew that Alix—and Bertie—had the children more about them than she really thought right, and took the opportunity for suggesting that "they ought not to be downstairs too long at a time and one at a time is much the best."

The Waleses' children, some people thought, were too much in evidence at Marlborough House and elsewhere. The Prince of Wales often had children fiddling around him when he was writing letters in his study, and their head nurse, Mrs. Blackburn, has said of their mother: "She was in her glory when she could run up to the nursery, put on a flannel apron, wash the children herself, and see them asleep in their beds."

In London it was a regular afternoon sight to see the Princess of Wales driving in an open carriage without a lady in waiting and with her children grouped around her. At Sandringham she drove them about herself in a pony-cart, and if she passed other children on the road who looked tired she would tell them to hang on behind. A guest of Sandringham House a year or two later writes in a letter of the Waleses' children:

"All were in high spirits and seemed very fond of their nurses, who sat down to tea with them and treated them without ceremony. They were easily amused, and I never saw such a battered set of toys, and such rickety old dolls. The two boys were very happy over some boats the footman had made for them."

With the birth of Princess Maud that November the family had reached its limits, for Prince Alexander, born two years later, died within a few hours.

Maud was christened on Christmas Day of 1869. It was the last event of their first wedded decade. In Mary of Teck's journal we hear of that Christmas at Marlborough House.

"*December 24.* We started about one o'clock for Marlborough House, where the grand christening took place in the inner hall. I represented Adelaide Nassau, and held the baby, who was named Maud Charlotte Mary Victoria. The Bishop of London officiated. There was a stand-up luncheon in the dining-room. . . . I between Wales and Alix. We were home soon after three. . . ."

And on Christmas Day Mary of Teck was there again.

"We dined at Marlborough House, and sat down seven to dinner. Afterwards we went to the servants' hall to see them have
their tree with prizes for all on it. We returned to the drawing-
room; tree relighted by magic. Received charming presents, and
saw all the present tables. *Beautiful things!* The Knollys family
(seven in number), the Fishers, Holzmann (librarian), and Grey
(equerry) were present. After plundering the tree we left at
11.30."

Part Three

MARLBOROUGH HOUSE SET

Chapter 16

FLIGHT FROM PRINCE HAL

THE 'SEVENTIES STARTED BADLY for the Waleses with the Mordaunt Case. On February 16, 1870, before Lord Penzance and a special jury, Lord Mordaunt petitioned for divorce from his twenty-three-year-old wife. Lady Mordaunt had been one of the beauties of the Marlborough House set—had been, for she was considered insane at the time the case came up—but apparently she had not been so looked upon when she confessed her relations with certain men to her husband. The case rested solely upon the confession, in which she ramblingly seemed to reveal herself in a promiscuous light. The two men selected by Lord Mordaunt as co-respondents, Viscount Cole and Sir Frederick Johnstone, were both close friends of the Prince of Wales. But Mordaunt, who showed strong dislike for the Prince, upon the advice of his counsel, Serjeant Ballantine, subpoenaed him to answer in court an accusation of undue familiarity. Material evidence against the Prince was nothing but one dozen letters, indiscreet yet scarcely more than society gossip chronicles, but the "confession" seemed to involve him more closely, in the petitioner's opinion. Here was a *cause célèbre*, indeed, and the whole country woke up to it. It confirmed many people in their prophecies that sooner or later something of this kind was bound to crop up at Marlborough House.

Momentarily Bertie was panic-stricken. It was a cruel shock to Alix and the Queen. The Cambridge ladies dared not speak of it. Bertie was reminded of the immunity of his position. Should he refuse to appear in the witness box? He could ignore the summons.

III

Alix firmly and quietly urged him to obey the summons. He went to his mother. In a real crisis the Queen was a strong woman. She had sought advice of the Lord Chancellor. She told him he should certainly present himself before the court. It would be best, however much they tried to hurt his reputation.

On February 23—after a postponement—the Prince of Wales stood in the witness box. He was cool and restrained. He spoke throughout in even, unruffled tones. He answered the cross-examination with resolute denials of improper conduct. He retired unshaken. In the opinion of intelligent men the Prince had done well to take the witness box, and had cleared himself as much as was possible in such an insidious affair. The nation at large, with many scandal-lovers anxious to see the Prince sensationally exposed, drew their own conclusions as to all that lay behind the Mordaunt disclosure.

Marlborough House was not in good odor. It had been hoped that the tall gambling stories would die down during the long absence abroad, but this inevitably was not the case, since the gambling recommenced at Marlborough House. Some of the participants, though of blue blood, were notoriously mere professional gamblers; nor were such meetings confined to domestic premises, but caused Bertie to be seen at less respectable rendezvous. Exaggerations of facts—and stakes—necessarily followed. Bertie and Alix could scarcely be expected to give up their frequent theater visits, or Bertie his race-meetings, his betting on horses or his jockeys and generally quite reputable sporting friends, but there was a powerful nonconformist body who watched all this activity with grim disfavor. Disraeli had labeled him Prince Hal, but he was more widely referred to behind his back as "Teddy," and one of the friends of Teddy at this time coined an apt description of his occupations. His life, he said, "was a perpetual search in daytime of hours he had lost at night." Though his daylight hours might be filled with public works, there were too many people perpetually gazing into the darkness.

Among the misfortunes of Bertie, one to which his most eminent and authoritative biographer, the late Sir Sidney Lee, bears witness, is that he could not resist an attractive woman. He collected them at Marlborough House, and his boyish enthusiasm did not stop at home: a hobby unfortunate in a prince, chased by the ruthless floodlight of publicity, and a discomforting trait in any husband, which could not but leave Alix secretly ruffled or with deeper hurt.

It was not the least of his indiscretions at this period that when the notorious "Skittles"—Catherine Walters from a Cheshire public house—"the last of the great English courtesans," abandoned decaying Paris after the Franco-Prussian War to set up her three smart establishments in Mayfair, in ultra-respectable Brown's Hotel and in South Street, the Prince of Wales and his friends were some of the first to attend her tea parties and evening baccarat sessions. Bertie appears to have been previously acquainted with "Skittles," though he could scarcely have been so in her youthful English days when she was mistress of his friend "Harty-Tarty," Lord Hartington, and the celebrated equestrienne heroine of the Town, Rotten Row and the Quorn. "Skittles," now thirty-three and in the full glory of her womanhood—"her language should one tread on her dress is a caution!"—once more became a byword for her carriages and horses, surpassed only, it was said, when Lily Langtry appeared some years later.

The friendship of the Prince of Wales was the making of "Skittles." She was the grand dame of the demimonde, with a unique manner of regal disreputability so respectable that in her brilliant and intellectual salons even the great W. E. Gladstone could happily discourse over a teacup on the classics. Thirty years later, "Skittles," thanks to an unflagging royal respect, would daily make her queenly passage through the Park in a Bath chair, while such stirring figures as Lord Kitchener walked proudly beside her.

Alix had been hurt, angered and humiliated by the Mordaunt affair, and she had gone off for a long stay with her close friend the Duchess of Manchester at Kimbolton. While there she visited Reading, and the quite ecstatic reception she received, coupled with a fan mounted in mother-of-pearl and gold, bearing a dozen loyal words, in place of an Address of Welcome, was almost certainly a manifestation of sympathy with her at her husband's shortcomings. She had, moreover, decided to make a long—an indefinite—stay with her mother in Denmark.

They had not exactly quarreled. Alix might be a volcano where Prussia was concerned; her own sorrows she always chose to keep inside her. Nevertheless, Bertie was punished. Innocent of the Mor-

daunt business he might be, but that affair only skimmed the surface. Bertie, respectful and attentive, accompanied her as far as
Calais. With the memory of the wonderful tour still upon them it
must have been a sad, even a painful, journey.

The parting was not destined to last long. Affairs of State inter-
vened. Only one week after Alix's arrival at Copenhagen the outbreak of the Franco-Prussian War caused the Queen to demand her
instant return to London.

It was strongly believed that Denmark intended to go in with
the invincible armies of Napoleon and get her own back on the
devilish Prussians, and the Queen did not doubt that all too soon
the Princess of Wales would be openly voicing her enthusiasm for
such a heroic course of action. The Queen had always liked Napoleon. She had once thought that astute adventurer must be positively in love with her, but she would hate to join him against her
beloved Germans. In any case, her commander in chief, the Duke of
Cambridge, had shouted out before witnesses, "What the hell can
we do without an army!" She knew he was right, and was praying
that the Germans would not invade through Belgium, when her
forces would have to take the field.

Bertie traveled to Copenhagen to fetch Alix at the end of July,
fervently exhorted by Mr. Gladstone, the Prime Minister, to preserve "an extreme reserve . . . on this miserable war," and with the
warning that his stay "at this moment might be the subject of
comment and suspicion."

In Denmark he kept his views to himself. He himself would have
been proud to fight as a volunteer for the man who held so much
of his admiration. But back at home he was supposed by the Prussians to have declared at a London dinner party that he hoped they
would get a thorough beating. Possibly he never said any such
thing so publicly—he sharply denied it—but nevertheless he *was*
expressing such sentiments to his friends, an immense circle which
could hardly be called watertight. Thus the Prussian surmises were
by no means inaccurate.

Though Vicky was Bertie's favorite sister, and Alix liked her very
well, knowing she could scarcely help her Prussianism, such commu-
nications from the Crown Princess as the following, written when

the Germans were carrying all before them, left them in cold silence. Paris was encircled. German unification was in the wind.

"The feeling of belonging to one great nation for the first time is very delicious to experience," Vicky assured them. "What will Bertie and Alix say to all these marvellous happenings! Gay and charming Paris! (Under bombardment.) What mischief that very Court and still more that very attractive Paris has done to English Society! What harm to the young and brilliant aristocracy of London!"

It was September the 11th: ten days after the surrender of Emperor Napoleon at Sedan. To Bertie the savage bombardment of Paris and crushing defeat of France was a personal affront. That day news reached Abergeldie that Empress Eugénie had escaped across the Channel. She was in England but she had disappeared. Bertie's chivalrous soul was stirred. She was in dire distress and he wanted to help her. He discovered that the news was also known at Balmoral. His cautious mother, though she, too, knew Eugénie well, was less ready to seek out and publicly succor the exile. It was better to wait and see.

Then they heard that the young Prince Imperial with his tutor had joined the Empress. Their whereabouts were a secret. Several days passed, and at Abergeldie they were much disturbed, feeling that they ought to be offering help, or at least a welcome to the country.

Empress Eugénie with her son appeared at Chislehurst. She herself had reached the French coast in disguise and crossed to the Isle of Wight in the yacht of an Englishman. Bertie, not knowing that Eugénie had decided to settle at Camden House, Chislehurst, which was the gift of an admirer, and believing her to be a wanderer, without any consultation with the Queen was moved to write to her from Dunrobin Castle, where the Waleses were then guests.

"The Princess and I feel that a residence near London would be nice for you. I venture to offer Your Majesty our country house at Chiswick, which is entirely at Your Majesty's disposal, and shall be most happy if Your Majesty will accept it."

No secret was made of this offer and a copy was shortly forwarded to Lord Granville, the Foreign Secretary, from Sandringham. Granville was distinctly worried. If he approved the generosity of the Prince and Princess, he thought he knew what the Queen and some others would think. Whatever the new French government might turn out to be, it would have to be dealt with, and for the royal family to succor and sympathize openly with the old disinherited regime would scarcely make for smooth relations. Unhappily, also, an escaped French general, Bouraki, had been observed at Chislehurst, in disguise. The matter took on a sinister aspect, which, in fact, was perfectly illusory.

The Queen was the only one in a position to talk of the conduct of her son and daughter-in-law as "presumptuous," but many thought that the Waleses were once again involving the family in their foreign intrigues. How could the Prince and Princess be made to withdraw their offer to the Empress? This was seriously debated in official circles. Since Eugénie had permanently established herself, no answer was required.

Meanwhile Bertie and Alix, unrepentant, had arrived at Chislehurst to assure the Imperial mother and son of their friendship and eagerness to help in any way that they could. Aware of this move, the Queen fell to pondering the matter. At last she felt shamed. In November she herself arrived at Chislehurst to commiserate with her one-time Imperial hostess.

It was from this time onward that Bertie and Alix began to take a strong interest in the lively young Prince Imperial. Before long he would appear in London as one of their protégés, a most vivacious and enterprising member of the Marlborough House set in the colorful heyday it would presently achieve, until his tragic death in Zululand. It was largely by the persuasions of the Waleses that the French Prince entered the Royal Military Academy and subsequently the Royal Artillery: such an active career as Bertie might have hankered after himself. By this sponsorship of the Prince Imperial, Bertie had set himself a delicate task, which in the opinion of ministers he by no means tackled unsuccessfully. With his numerous French contacts and his ardent Gallic enthusiasm he would be expected "unofficially" to forward British interests with the Republicans, while at the same time he cultivated the friendship of the Royalists; for who knew that they might not seize power again in France? Bertie, especially where Continental matters were involved, was on the threshold of becoming a man of affairs—a man of affairs who never, or scarcely ever, read a State paper, but who often was fully aware of the trend of events sooner than his mother.

From the family angle the interest which chiefly occupied the minds of Bertie and Alix in 1870 were the improvements and enlargements at Sandringham. Despite their great expenditure in the previous year, some of which was spent on at least semiofficial occasions and for which, as the Queen had dismally prophesied, they had got no reimbursement, they were able to lavish large sums not only on the house but on the grounds and the home farm. As a result, the house parties in which Bertie so delighted were much less cramped and confined, and gave the very varied collection of guests invited—some with the scantiest previous acquaintance with their host and hostess, such as club friends or the attractive wives of club friends—a much better opportunity of enjoying themselves in the unfamiliar atmosphere of a royal home. Sandringham guests were often not Marlborough House people: they might be clergymen, scholars, and people concerned with affairs, science or the arts. The aspect of things at Sandringham was not only quite unlike the hectic feel in the air of Marlborough House, but also unlike those rather wild and intense house parties in many great houses inspired by the Marlborough House example. That this was so was due in a large measure to the charming hostess of Sandringham, who regarded this as her real home.

But male guests at Sandringham had to reconcile themselves to one strong probability, that, even if they were clergymen and exempt from card playing, they would be expected to sit into the early hours chatting and smoking with the Prince. Card stakes at Sandringham were usually low, since the host was unwilling to deprive people of money they might ill afford, and he was quite happy to smoke his endless cigars while he won or lost penny points.

We have a view of life at Sandringham from one clerical guest of this period. He enjoyed his stay, calling it "pleasant and domesticated, with little state and very simple ways." He was an Irishman,

Bishop Magee of Peterborough, and he gives an intimate glimpse of the afternoon of his arrival.

"I arrived," says he, "just as they were sitting down to tea in the entrance hall, and had to walk in all seedy and dishevelled from my day's journey and sit down by the Princess of Wales. . . . I find the company friendly and civil, but we are a curious mixture. Two Jews, Sir Anthony de Rothschild and his daughter; an ex-Jew, Disraeli; a Roman Catholic, Colonel Higgins; an Italian duchess who is an Englishwoman, and her daughter, brought up a Roman Catholic and now turning Protestant; a set of young lords and a bishop. . . . We are all to lunch together in a few minutes, the children dining with us."

The Prince's friend, Lord Sandwich, records another house party of this time.

"On November 5th I went to Sandringham. The guests were Prince Eddy, the Duke and Duchess of Edinburgh, the Landgrave of Hesse, Vicomte and Vicomtesse Grafuhle, Comte de St. Priest, Baron von Holshausen, Captain von Strahl, C. Vivian, C. E. Sykes, Oscar Dickson, Lady Emily Kingscote, Francis and Miss Knollys, and A. Ellis in waiting. Tuesday and Thursday there was partridge driving; Wednesday, Commodore and Dersingham Woods; Friday, Woodcock Woods. Friday, the 9th, was the Prince's birthday, and he received innumerable presents from all sorts and kinds of people, and there was a ball, which lasted till 4 a.m. In connection with this party I must give an extraordinary instance of the Prince's memory. Many years afterwards he was referring to the death of Creppy Vivian, when he remarked on the number of members of this party who had died, and he really ran through the names of the people I had met at Sandringham on this occasion. I remember telling him with wonder of his marvellous memory."

Mary of Teck at this time gives a picture of Sandringham in the spring in a letter to the Dowager Countess of Aylesford. This was a distinctly family party, with only two privileged commoners.

The Prince of Wales at Homburg in 1896.
(After photo Voight of Homburg)

The Princess of Wales in 1887.

Princess Alix of Denmark at the time of her marriage to the
Prince of Wales.
(Portrait Lauchert)

The Prince of Wales at the time of his marriage.
(After the portrait by Winterhalter)

The Princess of Wales with her favorite sister Dagmar (Empress Marie Fedorovna of Russia) in the early 'seventies.

The Princess of Wales in the middle 'sixties.

The Princess of Wales in 1889, age 45.

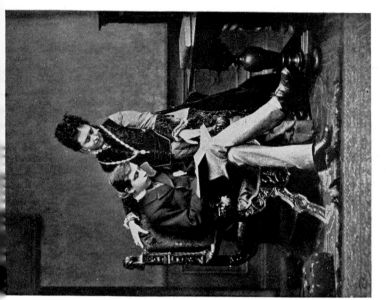

Prince William of Prussia (nephew "Willy"—the last Kaiser) with his mother, Victoria, Crown Princess of Prussia and Princess Royal of Great Britain (later Empress Frederick) in 1876.

The Empress Marie Fedorovna of Russia. Her son was the last Czar.

A Press artist's impression of the Princess of Wales receiving guests at the Marlborough House garden party in 1878. Sir Dighton Probyn, V.C., her faithful attendant who always referred to her as "the Beloved Lady," stands stroking his beard by the tree.

A Press artist's impression of tea in the hall at Sandringham during Queen Victoria's visit in 1889. The Queen sits in the center foreground and the Princess of Wales at the tea-table right. Careful inspection will show a parrot on top of its cage in the right background. This small green parrot had been taught to give three cheers for the Queen in the pauses of human conversation.

A Press artist's impression of the Prince and Princess of Wales with their family in 1871. The children (*left to right*): Prince George (George V), Princess Victoria (*top*), Princess Maud (Queen of Norway), Prince Albert Victor (Duke of Clarence, died 1892), Princess Louise (Duchess of Fife).

"We came down here yesterday," she writes, "and are, I believe, going to stay till Monday. We are a family party of seven, consisting of, in addition to the Prince and Princess, Princess Louise, my brother and sister, and our two selves (she had married the Duke of Teck); and with *la suite,* your son who was my neighbour at dinner last night. Mr. Charles Hall and Christopher Sykes number fifteen. Today, alas! for us, and especially for my poor sister, who has never been here before, it has rained without ceasing; but in spite of the elements we have been out for two hours this afternoon, lionizing Augusta, over the garden, cottage, kennel and stables. This place is looking its prettiest in its bright spring dress. Weather permitting, we are to make expeditions to Houghton, Lord Cholmondeley's place, now, I hear, for sale, and Castle Rising, where stands the ruined castle in which Edward III kept his wicked mother, Isabella of France, a prisoner for thirty years. . . ."

The Rev. B. J. Armstrong, of the neighboring parish of Dereham, whose diary has already been quoted, saw the Princess of Wales twice in the early 'seventies. On the first occasion she passed through Dereham in Lord Suffield's drag. The news had gone round and the townspeople were in the streets. "There was much disappointment. Everybody struggled to peer into the interior. No Princess of Wales. They never noticed the lady sitting on the box beside Lord Suffield till it was too late."

On the second occasion when the diarist saw the Prince and Princess, he noticed that the Princess "was terribly pale and thin— the Prince just as much too fat." Armstrong further observes that he had been told, "the Princess of Wales saves her husband from much unpopularity."

One of the peculiarities of the regime at Sandringham House was that by order of the Prince all clocks were kept half an hour fast, a matter of much bewilderment to guests. The reason was the unflagging unpunctuality of Alix upon every occasion. Bertie, meticulous and bustling by nature, had found this habit disconcerting from the first. Half in fun, half in angry desperation, he had first ordered the alteration of the clocks. It brought little improvement, since Alix, remembering that the clocks were fast, made allowances for this, exceeded the time she had allowed herself and still appeared late. But the clocks remained fast till the end. The Queen when she visited Sandringham was disgusted and ordered the clocks to be returned to the right time while she was in the house. "A ridiculous custom and a lie," was her comment. In later days, when Bertie's views had become more settled, when he had developed into something of an arbiter or dictator to those around him, the unpunctuality of his wife began to irritate him intensely. But she was unmoved, and continued to be late. Though the putting forward of the clocks was not enforced in Marlborough House, it was a ruse which from time to time was adopted by the suite in the Princess's apartments in the hopes of having her ready for some official occasion.

Three notable changes took place in the suite in the early 'seventies, and it may almost be said that at this point Providence stepped into the lives of Bertie and Alix to supply them with the three persons most perfectly suited to serve them, and, indeed, to display them to the world to their best advantage.

In 1870 Francis Knollys, the second son of General Sir William Knollys, replaced Fisher as private secretary to the Prince of Wales. He was a personal choice of the Prince when Fisher retired, and the Queen was reluctant, thinking him too young. He was, however, appointed. Francis Knollys perfectly understood the complexities in the character of his master and served and managed him with remarkable wisdom and faithfulness till the day of his death. Bertie by virtue of his own abilities was destined to achieve greatness and to serve his country well both as Prince and King, and it is certain that the measure of his success was heightened by Francis Knollys, who himself from 1901 to 1910 was one of the first men of the land.

Charlotte Knollys, the sister of Francis, came two years later and with her Colonel Dighton Probyn, V.C., of the Indian Cavalry. Charlotte Knollys, who was thirty-eight, became Woman of the Bedchamber, and would still be loyally accompanying her mistress everywhere when her reign as Queen was ended. She was perhaps the closest woman friend and intimate of Queen Alexandra throughout a strenuous and not untroubled life. Like her brother, in a rather different sphere, Charlotte Knollys would become a byword, a figure whom nobody would think to trifle with, and as token of her industry it used to be one of her proud boasts that she could, and had, written as many as sixty letters a day in the royal service.

There must be many alive today who remember seeing Queen Alexandra followed by a tall, ageing military figure, distinguished by moustache and chin-tuft, which some officers affected in the 'seventies. You rarely saw Queen Alexandra or, indeed, the Princess of Wales, in earlier times without Sir Dighton towering behind her. He adored her. He worshiped her. In reverent tones he spoke of her as "The Beloved Lady," and the name spread. He was thirty-nine when he joined the Household as Comptroller and Treasurer, an arduous task which Bertie would always maintain that nobody else could have fulfilled successfully; but as far as the public was concerned, Dighton Probyn was the faithful guardian and courtier who unfailingly followed behind the Beloved Lady, and, like Charlotte Knollys, followed her into the Shades.

The year for the Waleses was now beginning to form into a perceptible pattern, which was followed with slight variations year upon year till the end of the century. From Sandringham they traveled in early March to Cannes, Biarritz, or the fashionable French resort of the moment. On the outward and the homeward journey they stopped at the Hotel Bristol, Paris, and Bertie might pay a further visit to the beloved city from their resort. They were back at Marlborough House in time for the season, in which they had to play the leading rôles. Goodwood and Cowes followed. Both loved the sea and yachts, and the headquarters of the Royal Yacht Squadron became a brilliant and fashionable mecca, where the lawns of the celebrated enclosure were much more greedily sought than the decks of yachts. From Cowes they went to Baden, Homburg or Marienbad to take the waters, and partake, with archdukes, barons and the numerous scions of royalty then existing, in the cosmopolitan life of these smart Teutonic spas.

The swaggering highly-colored hothouse life of fashionable German spas with their atmosphere of intrigue and archducal gallantry appealed less to Alix. She might stay on the royal yacht *Osborne* with the children and cruise till it was time for Scotland. She might take the family for a quiet visit to her parents in Denmark, or she might accompany Bertie to Germany and in company probably of Charlotte Knollys—as an ordinary person whom few people recognized—visit the Bayreuth Music Festival and seize any other musical opportunities which were available. Once, but only once, in their lives did she to her delight get Bertie to go with her to Bayreuth. He was good-natured about it, but he preferred baccarat.

In September they were with the children again at Abergeldie, and Bertie, like his father, became the great huntsman. Guests at Abergeldie were few, but the men were expected to be distinguished shots, though not quite so skillful in marksmanship and fieldcraft as their slightly rotund host. At Abergeldie they and the family saw much of the Queen at Balmoral, and this they found a much more enjoyable experience than elsewhere. Even dear Mr. Brown, constant as a rugged Highland crag, always referred to by Her Majesty, always listened to—the Rasputin of Scotland, as some of his countrymen have liked to call him—whose fiery gaze seemed to shift only from his mistress to menace some other person with a shrewdly crushing remark, fitted better into the Balmoral picture.

From Scotland they came with the family to Sandringham and their house parties. From Sandringham they would travel from time to time to attend the house parties of other people of their set. During the country house visits, somebody started the idea of asking the beautiful Princess of Wales to scratch her signature with a diamond on one of the windows of the mansion. The custom soon spread. Everybody was asking her to do this, till her name decorated windows throughout the length and breadth of the land. Some of her first efforts were crude, like the writing of a child, but many of the later examples are finely done; and one of the reasons for this was that one of those male admirers whom she favored begged for the honor of presenting her with a gold stylus with a diamond point, which from then on she always carried with her.

These visits, however, were really anticipated with greater pleasure by Bertie than his wife. Once she was settled at beloved Sandringham she wanted to stay there with her children. At first this tendency to immovability in Alix exasperated Bertie, but as the years went on he would find, apparently, that his lone visits to country house parties were by no means uncongenial. A kind of legendary literature would in fact come into circulation, embellished no doubt by the celebrated Stock Exchange story mill, about happenings in country houses patronized by the Prince of Wales.

At Christmastide they often left Sandringham for Fredensborg, again with the children, and, as everybody else also brought their young families to the festive celebrations, the babel at the castle was caused not only by the adult mixture of foreign tongues. They returned to Sandringham for the remainder of the winter, where they stayed until they left for France in the early spring.

It will be observed how the children were almost always with the Waleses. At Marlborough House during the season they generally gave an elaborate children's ball for their family, as well as the two expensive adult balls which were the highlights of the London season. There is a hastily scribbled note written by the Prince of Wales in the House of Lords on the afternoon of February 21, 1873, to Lord Granville. It had been necessary to rise and depart in the middle of his lordship's carefully prepared speech, and he hoped it would not cause offense. The reason for this action displays Bertie in an attractive light as a father. It was the birthday of his "eldest little girl" and "the Princess and I are going to take four of the children to the circus at 7.15, and it is now 6.30. I have not a moment left."

With Alix the favorite child was the eldest, the Duke of Clarence. He was the one who had suffered most from the premature births, and was much more delicate than his brother George, who from an early age was inclined to dominate him. There may perhaps have been a jealousy here, for George adored his beautiful mother, who, loving as she was, did not feel for him the deep emotional sympathy which welled up in her whenever she was with her eldest boy. From the time her first-born's legs were strong enough to carry him any distance she liked to go for long walks alone with him at Sandringham, and as soon as he was big enough he would take her arm or put his arm round her waist. In many of the photographic portraits that exist of the Princess of Wales with her two sons, it is noticeable that the handsome, dreamy-eyed Clarence stands close to his mother's shoulder with a possessive look, while the less distinguished George is somewhat apart, gazing rather sadly at the world on his own. The eldest himself perhaps best summed up the relationship with his mother in his own words, to one of those who looked after him when young. "Mamma is so nice," said he. "She is fond of everything I like. There is nobody like Mamma."

Augustus Hare, that celebrated and most copious diarist of the last century, who went everywhere in society, records glimpses of the Princess of Wales on several occasions in the 'seventies, which are interesting because they are typical pictures of her activities at that period.

In July 1874 Hare traveled down in the specially chartered train packed with guests to the great party at Hatfield House, the magnificent country mansion of the Marquis of Salisbury. A column of smart carriages bore the army of blue-blooded guests from the station to the house, and they passed through triumphal arches of flowers, with excited country people lining the road. Royalty was coming to honor the Marquis and the Marchioness of Salisbury: the Prince and Princess of Wales, the Prince and Princess of Prussia (Vicky and Fritz), the Duke and Duchess of Teck (Mary of Cambridge), and Prince Arthur of Connaught, the youngest brother of the Prince of Wales.

The skies grew black as the guests gathered before the great mansion—the party was to be on the terraces—and then a fearful storm broke. Thunder pealed, lightning flashed and the rain splashed down in torrents. They fled into the Golden Gallery, and at that moment the royal procession trotted into view and drew up before Hatfield House. In bustle and confusion the royal ladies were rescued out of the downpour. Hare thought the prettiness of this sight quite entrancing. The spice of drama increased the enjoyment of the guests. The rain ceased, and the royalties were escorted to the celebrated labyrinth. There was to have been a sumptuous dinner for eight hundred in the gardens. Everything was now rushed into the Armory by footmen. There was no delay. The royalties with their hosts went to dine in state in the Marble Hall.

But when the long dinner was over and darkness had fallen, the guests emerged to see the great gardens gleaming under colored illuminations. At the same time the royalties emerged and, splitting up, wandered unescorted among the guests in the wonderful gardens. It seemed to Hare that there must be many more royalties than there actually were, for he kept running up against one or another in some glistening glade or arbor, and although he scarcely had their acquaintance they were always very affable and never at a loss for something to say to fit the occasion.

Such were the monster parties given by the great families, at which the younger royalties were constantly a feature, in that heyday of aristocratic opulence.

In the following summer Augustus Hare was the guest of Lady Waldegrave at Strawberry Hill. An elaborate breakfast was prepared in a vast tent on the lawns. But a heavy rainstorm had ruined everything. Gallons of water poured through the tent roof. Half the food on the tables was ruined, and appalling confusion reigned inside, where the guests had fled for shelter. This time there was no Marble Hall for the comfort of royalty. Those who could seized on dry chairs, and royalty were not the first to reach the tent. In a free-for-all spirit the guests were devouring what food they could find. Perhaps the crockery had been smashed. For Hare observed the lovely Princess of Wales, in a pink gown under black lace and small matching hat, standing cheerfully in a dry corner, drinking tea out of a common tumbler.

Three years later Hare was at a great party at Holland House, that famous London landmark of Victorian high life, off the Kensington High Street, which has recently been destroyed. There were clusters of royalty on the lawns: the Prince and Princess of Wales, the Duke and Duchess of Teck with their small daughter Princess May (later to become Queen Mary), and others. The Princess of Wales was much concerned that day with the activities of her two little girls, both dressed alike in pink frocks with red trimmings. There were wonderful performing dogs on the lawn, and Hare watched entranced the ecstatic joy of the pretty royal children, watched over by their attentive mothers.

It may be of interest, since the movements of the Prince and Princess of Wales throughout their year have been set down, to include a contemporary computation made by an observant journalist of the actual activities of the Prince of Wales, in so far as these applied to England and in so far as these were publicized, during the first nine months of the year, before the annual "rest" at Sandringham. The Princess, of course, would have shared many of these occasions with him, and the time would have been broken up by the spring visit to France and Cowes and perhaps terminated at a German spa. The actual year these figures denote is of little significance, for the volume of activities varied little between the 'seventies and the late 'nineties.

The Prince attended 28 race meetings, 30 theatrical performances, 45 official ceremonies, 43 dinner parties, banquets, balls or garden parties, and 11 sittings in the House of Lords. Some of the ceremonies in days when a special train was the quickest form of travel would probably have occupied several days, and some of the dinners, banquets and the like could be regarded as official or semiofficial occasions, though not as ceremonies. There would also have been a great mass of correspondence to be dealt with almost daily—he was by nature an ardent letter scribbler himself and required the most meticulous care from Francis Knollys—newspapers to be scrutinized, since he had to read these if nothing else, discussions with ministers and other important persons, and on the social side many private activities not listed. In many years he would also have some foreign mission of a more or less delicate character to perform.

He possessed one of the most remarkable qualities of the father he was so unlike: an ability amounting almost to genius to fit many things smoothly into an inadequate space of time. Privacy cannot have been a feature of this life. He did not hanker for it, though no man loved more the crowded fireside of his homes. We know that this restlessness and craving for human society was to his wife his most painful characteristic—as discomforting to her as her vagueness and unpunctuality were to him. His mother, also, was much disturbed and bewildered by these traits in her son, and dear Mr. Brown summed up the matter shrewdly as he did most things when the chance offered. "The Prince," said he, "preeferrs the preevacy of the public road."

In the August of 1871 after Cowes week, Bertie promised to accompany Alix to the Oberammergau Passion Play on the way to Baden. Rumpenheim was often a stopping place on the German visit, and it was convenient for Oberammergau. Mary Cambridge—now Duchess of Teck—was there with four-year-old May, and Queen Louise of Denmark, "wonderfully young-looking, reminded us of Alix" and "Thyra, the grown-up young lady, extremely charming, the eyes very fine."

The time came for the arrival of the Waleses with their family, and Mary has left an intimate record of this Rumpenheim occasion in her diary.

> "*August 15* . . . Alix was expected at four o'clock. I wrote till she was in sight, then ran down to receive her. It was quite half-past five before we had dinner, and Alix came in even later. . . . The five children arrived and I helped to take them over to their rooms. *August 16* . . . Wandered about the garden, and worked all together on the terrace, the children playing in the bowling alley. Alix came up to my room afterwards and visited the nursery. Luncheon over, we sat in front (water side) of the house at work. . . . Grand dinner of twenty-eight at five, and coffee in the gala-rooms . . . we wandered on the terrace. *Aug. 17* . . . Louise and I watched all the children at play in the courtyard from the Waleses' nursery windows. . . . To Casino to tea, and we sat up till nearly twelve o'clock waiting for Wales, who never arrived till one. *Aug. 18* . . . Down late, for me, at 9.30 breakfast; Wales was there before me. . . . Then worked with the rest on the terrace, while Wales entertained us. Dinner of thirty-three, to which George (Duke of Cambridge, her brother), Lord Clonmel, Knollys, *père et fils,* and Holzmann came over. Early tea in honour of Alix and Wales, who departed with Mrs. Hardinge at 9.30 for Frankfurt *en route* for Oberammergau. . . . After dinner the children romped together in the courtyard (11 in all) and we elders had a game of croquet in the sand! *Aug. 22* . . . Alix and Mrs. Hardinge much impressed by the Passion Play and delighted with their expedition. . . ."

At Oberammergau, where the Waleses had stayed as Lord and Lady Renfrew, nobody in the modest hotel which they chose had any idea of their identity. Lord Renfrew distributed his big cigars among the men and was doubtless considered most attentive and attractive by the ladies. Lady Renfrew in a green Tyrolean hat drew a good many eyes as she bought wooden carvings at the bazaar held in the hotel lounge. Her spirits soared so high at this glorious escape that she was perhaps rather inadvisedly lively if she wished to call no attention to herself.

Then a man walked into the hotel who knew the Princess of

Wales quite well. He stood still at the entrance, snatched off his hat and drew himself up, preparatory to bowing low. She glared at him. "You don't know me!" she hissed in English. He stopped himself just in time.

They had not booked seats in the open-air theater because they had feared that the negotiations might cause someone to become suspicious and spread the news which they hoped to avoid. They waited with the crowd before the ticket booth at the gate, and the long delay so tedious to the others was a novel delight to them.

After that long, amazing performance from which the tired spectators always seem to depart stunned and exalted, Alix was silent for some time. Then she addressed her husband. "I want to meet the man who was the Christus," she said. "He was wonderful. I'm sure he must really be rather like that."

"If we do," came the reply "we shall have to disclose who we are, and Heaven knows what may happen then. He doesn't receive visitors after the performance. He's not an ordinary actor."

"I don't care. I want to talk to him. He's different from other people. Do you really think he is the kind of man who would give us away?"

"No," answered the Prince, after reflection.

The man was Joseph Meyer, a notable figure in Oberammergau, and one who was Christlike not only in his appearance but in his way of life. They sought him out, and when he understood who they were, he agreed to receive them privately.

Alix had a very valuable ring on her finger, and after she had talked for a while with Meyer, who sat before them still in his biblical robes, she removed it with a struggle. Meyer was a man not given to anger, but that anyone should think to tip him like a street performer disturbed him. When the Princess held out the glittering ring to him he started to refuse it. Then he perceived the earnest light in her eyes. He heard her saying that she wanted him to keep it as a token of her gratitude, because she would never forget his performance and believed she would be the better for it all her life. Meyer gently took the ring and painfully forced it upon a little finger, the only place it would fit on his rough woodcarver's hand. After that he abandoned the somewhat platitudinous conversation that had previously taken place, and held the Princess of Wales spellbound for an hour as he discussed the Passion Play scene by scene, revealing the hidden truths which lay behind it.

Perhaps after Oberammergau Bertie had some important engagement at Baden, for there is no mention of Wales in Mary's diary after the return from the Passion Play. Alix presently departed again from Rumpenheim with her sister Thyra, Mrs. Hardinge and the "General" (perhaps Knollys senior); but on September 7 the diarist has more to say of her.

"Lunched in garden and garden-house, after which we sat quietly, for the heat was intense, till three; just as we were going in, we espied a carriage coming over the water, and in it sat Alix, Thyra, Mrs. Hardinge and the General, all hiding their faces in order not to be recognized! A charming surprise for Louise. (It was her birthday.) I went with them to Alix's rooms, but after a few moments we all discreetly departed, leaving the two sisters with their mother. Gala dinner of twenty-six at five. Coffee in the fine rooms; established ourselves in front of the Casino. *Sept. 8* . . . Early walk, breakfast, then to my room to change my dress. Before I was ready Prince and Princess Charles of Hesse Darmstadt arrived, and, on going down, I found the whole party sitting out in front of the house. . . . At two Alix and Thyra took leave of us, and Adelheid, I and Tilla had a long quiet talk in the Japanese room downstairs. . . . It had been a glorious day for the haymakers, and it was a pretty scene on both sides of the river, as cart upon cart laden with hay drove off."

Chapter 17

NIGHTMARE AT SANDRINGHAM AND
THE CONQUEST OF A RED

IT WAS THE ICY NIGHT of December 8, 1871, and around Sandringham the moon shone on a countryside still and dead under snow. A little silent party emerged from Wolferton station: the Queen with John Brown striding behind her. Gently the grim servant handed her into the waiting carriage. Perhaps she gazed at him imploringly and then upward at the starlit heavens, that peculiar habit of hers, when her mind was heavy, which puzzled others. That day of horror in the year was almost upon them when dearest Albert had died. It was ten years ago. Without a word spoken the carriage padded away over the snow to Sandringham.

Scarcely a light shone in the windows of Sandringham House as they drew up at the front door. There had been something almost hearselike in the moonlit carriage as it crept to a standstill. No door flew open to show the welcoming lights inside. The bell tinkled away into a kind of emptiness. Then the door did open. No Alix—it was Lady Macclesfield who stood shivering in the lonely hall.

"How is the Prince?"

"He is very bad, Ma'am."

"There can be no doubt it is typhoid?"

"The doctors say so, Ma'am."

That was what his father had died of ten years ago. She went straight up to the sickroom. Alix and Louise sat beside the bed in the light of a single lamp and Bertie lay on his back in the gloom. There was a terrible sound in the room: his muttering and frenzied breathing. It was horribly like that dreadful scene ten years ago.

Two days passed and there was no change in the patient. The newspapers had given the nation their ominous reports. Foreigners, knowing all the wild stories told of the famous Prince of Wales, were staggered by what they saw or heard. The whole British nation seemed to be trembling. The people who had been so shocked by this amiable Prince of Wales were praying in their churches and sending telegrams to the royal home as if he were a relation.

At half past five on the morning of the 11th they called the Queen to Bertie's bedside. She came in her dressing gown and there was Alix. She had not been to bed. They gazed down helplessly at the dim form, shaken from head to foot by fearful spasms. They knew by the manner that he might not last. Ten years ago in the early morning on that last agonizing day the Queen had been summoned like this. In her terror she almost collapsed. Alix led her from the bed. A screen was brought, and there behind it she sat wild-eyed and speechless for several hours, while Alix, as panic-stricken as she, strove to help Bertie. The face now was almost that of a corpse.

She knew there was little hope. The heart could not stand much more. Then Bertie fell quiet and still. Was this the end? He was still living, said the doctors. They thought he had passed a crisis. They were watching the Queen, too. They advised her to leave the sickroom.

But the newspapers could say nothing to reassure the nation. And now perhaps the most astonished people in Europe were the French republicans. They read that their comrades in England, the members of the London republican clubs, had joined in sending a message of sympathy to the Queen.

"While not concealing our decided preference for a republican over a monarchical form of government," said they, "we, yet, desire as Englishmen, to record our sorrow for the serious illness and protracted suffering of the Prince of Wales, and our heartfelt sympathy with the Queen and the members of the Royal Family under their present deep affliction; and we also desire to express our sincere hope that the life of the Prince of Wales may yet be spared."

The Queen, perhaps, was moved. She was not surprised, for she had never taken republicans seriously. And yet, such was their influence in the country at that time, such was the case against the Throne, and such were the numbers hovering indeterminedly on their fringes, that but for this dire sickness of the Prince of Wales, which has been called a decisive historical moment in the tale of British royalty, they might well have achieved their declared object. But here unknowingly they had signed their swan song. An almost miraculous royal conviction had suddenly overwhelmed the British people.

Bertie was fighting hard, and it almost appeared that the nation was in the sickroom fighting with him.

"Death," declared one paper, "appeared to play with its royal captive as a young panther with its victim. Again and again he struggled to free himself from its grasp, only to be drawn back, stifling and helpless, as if for the final sacrifice."

When Alix had been desperately ill a human note had been struck: as if people were desperately frightened for someone whom they loved. This, the illness of the heir to the Throne, was different: it was an emotion of the British race, very deep and indescribable.

The 13th of the month dawned. Bertie was worse. They could make no secret of it. All day the Queen and Alix looked at one another and moaned, "There is no hope." Alix, at last, had broken. For many days and nights she had scarcely slept, scarcely left the bedside. The day wore on. The entries in the Queen's journal reveal a strange sense of fatalism as the day of Prince Albert's death—the 14th—drew upon them. The doctors admitted that they did not think the Prince would last so long. It was useless to keep the truth from the nation. But at one minute after midnight Bertie still lived. He had reached the fatal day. A stricken nation had already got out their mourning.

Just before dawn Bertie slipped into a peaceful sleep. The mother and the wife thought he had gone. The doctors were incredulous. The Prince of Wales had survived. It was the end of the delirium and the fever. They knew that the last climax had left him.

Throughout that day the doctors did not publicly commit themselves. "No change," announced the bulletins outside Marlborough House. But at midnight when a silent crowd still waited outside in the freezing wind, the bulletin bore a different message. "The Prince is passing the night quietly." Somehow, everybody grasped the full meaning of that message. The night rang with cheers, which traveled away up St. James's Street and down Pall Mall, and the cries of "Saved! The Prince sleeps!" could be plainly heard above the tumult.

The brass lectern in Sandringham church was presented by Alexandra, the Princess of Wales, and inscribed upon it are the words:

TO THE GLORY OF GOD
A THANKSGIVING FOR HIS MERCY
14th DECEMBER, 1871, ALEXANDRA

"When I was in trouble I called upon the Lord, and He heard me."

The manner in which this event was seen in France has already been noticed, and it shows up the British of the period, as seen in contemporary foreign eyes, in such a revealing light that it is worth closer examination.

Here are the words of one Parisian journal when our national agitation was at its peak:

"This England, which we were told was ready to become a Republic, which was accused of despising its Princes, and, having got rid of all its old-fashioned ideas of loyalty—come and see it today, note its grief, and be instructed!

What a spectacle! What a lesson!

The Prince of Wales is dying, and yet upon the other side of the Channel no one laughs. The Princess quits the bedside of the dying man, not to seek necessary repose, but to hasten to the church to pray and to listen to prayer—and no one laughs. The Queen, whom calumny sought to wound but the other day, kneels with her veil of widowhood beside the probable deathbed of her first-born—and no one laughs. The Council—Gladstone, the Lord President, the Lord Chancellor, all whom England holds in the highest esteem for talent, or position, or age—address themselves to the Archbishop of Canterbury and call upon him to prepare new forms of prayer. . . . And the people, instead of mocking, rush to obtain copies of these prayers. Lutherans, Calvinists, Methodists, Anglicans, Catholics, Jews, all implore the Deity to prolong the days of the future Sovereign of England. The people have the courage, the good sense not to disown either their history, their Government, or their God, and yet they are a free people among all—who will dispute that?

Such a spectacle affects us Frenchmen greatly, and we look around us with bitterness. In vain, alas! do we look for one of those powerful bonds of union upon which we might rely in a moment of trial. When shall *we* learn to pray altogether for anyone?"

It is said that the French Ambassador, the Duc de Broglie, was so impressed by what he witnessed that he not only made public declarations in praise of British government at the expense of his own national institutions, but in reports to Paris he almost insulted his countrymen, who, if they themselves had not been so thunderstruck by what had occurred across the Channel, would probably have deprived him of his post.

"May sweet darling Alix be preserved and blessed . . ." These are the words to be found in the Queen's diary, written when the height of the fever had passed. The writer knew how magnificently her daughter-in-law had acquitted herself both for her son and for herself. Delicate and highly strung, Alix had stood the strain: nor did she seem to suffer from after-effects. The Queen and Alix had drawn much nearer one another during December 1871. There is a story told of Alix—it had great currency at the time—that before her husband's illness had grown really desperate she appeared at the door of Sandringham church before the morning service, looking less groomed than usual. She asked for the Rector. "I can't stay till the end of the service," she explained, "but please put in some special prayers near the beginning so that I can join in with the others."

Alix certainly showed her good sense over the matter of the suggested Thanksgiving Service at St. Paul's. Disraeli was the Prime Minister at the time, and this was his idea. He put it to the Queen. She did not like it. She thought it sounded too much like a "show." She agreed, however, to consult the Princess of Wales upon her views, since it was she who in the eyes of the nation had emerged as the heroine of the December month. Alix did not like the idea much better than the Queen. To her it had been a very terrible and a very personal thing, and she knew that to be put "on show" in this way could scarcely appeal to Bertie. But Bertie was convalescing, and not to be bothered at present. She replied to the Queen:

> "I quite understand your feelings about the public thanksgiving, for it seems to me also to be making too much of an outward show of the most sacred and solemn feelings of one's own heart, and I quite agree that a simpler and more private service would be in accordance with our own wishes. But, then, on the other hand, the whole nation has taken such a public share in our anxiety, it has been so entirely one with us in our grief, that it may well feel it has a claim to join with us now in a public and universal thanksgiving."

This letter decided the matter. Bertie was informed that a great national Thanksgiving Service at St. Paul's in which all the royal family would take part had been arranged for February 27. Weak and drawn as he was, the prospect of being dragged in an open carriage through a vast concourse of commiserating people seemed to him positively humiliating, but recognizing the rightness of the idea he agreed cheerfully, as he always did when any duty had to be fulfilled. Some have thought that Alix was moved by other than the motives stated in her letter to the Queen to press for a public Thanksgiving: that although she herself was the lively hostess and leader of a gay and reputedly fast set and the wife of a Prince whom at least she did not actively discourage from an indiscreet way of life, yet secretly she was ashamed and troubled by the scandalous talk and by the wild stories which it was well known the Continental Press were always publishing. She may have believed that by identifying her husband so intimately in a great Thanksgiving with the nation a new relationship might be established with the people. If this was so it was perhaps inevitable that in a measure she must be disappointed.

Thanksgiving Day was more moving than even they expected, for there had been nothing before like it: a deep and fervent acclamation, achieved again only at the Queen's Jubilee, at the Diamond Jubilee and at King George V's and Queen Mary's Silver Jubilee. It not only established royalty, at last, as an institution desirable to the British race, but it dedicated royalty in their turn to the service and guidance of the nation in a more solemn manner than before.

Bertie and Alix spent the spring traveling in France and Italy. In Rome there were meetings with the Danish family and other foreign relations. Bertie enjoyed it all with the zest of a small boy, and long before they returned his activity and eagerness for something new was as great as ever.

On January 9, 1873, the exiled Napoleon III died suddenly at Chislehurst. To Bertie, who had found so much to admire and secretly to copy in the great Frenchman, the blow was personal. It was astonishing—at least, to the French—that all England, which had raised her somber volunteer battalions and her amateur batteries to combat his imagined menaces, was now acclaiming the dead Emperor and friend with real emotion. The phrase was coined that Napoleon was more mourned by his foes than his countrymen.

The presence of the French Imperial family at Chislehurst had always been an embarrassment to the shrewd men of government, and secretly to their friend the Queen as well. Nobody knew better, for instance, than the Prince of Wales that underground royalist activity was extremely active. Though not himself concerned with it, though its activities were across the Channel, yet Chislehurst was the target. In governmental circles there was no relief that the Emperor was dead; since the young Imperial Pretender was still with them and a protégé of Marlborough House. They were only anxious, as far as possible, to stay aloof from a too official display of sympathy with the Imperial son and widow.

Where their friends were concerned the Waleses would always put humanity before the subtleties of policy. Bertie declared he would take a leading part in the funeral of his old friend, and Alix affirmed her resolve to give any comfort she could to the Empress and her son.

The Queen, nervous of the international aspect, declared that a participation at the funeral of one of her younger sons would be quite sufficient. By that time Bertie and Alix were at Chislehurst, asking to see Empress Eugénie. She was too stricken to see them, but she sent messages of gratitude. The nation and France soon knew of the action of the Prince and Princess of Wales, and among the English public there was general approval. They returned to Sandringham; but shortly afterward the French Republic learned to its indignation that the Prince of Wales had been at Chislehurst, mingling with the leading Bonapartists, who had crossed over to attend their Emperor's lying-in-state.

On the day of the funeral the Prince and Princess of Wales were notable figures at Chislehurst. While the Ambassador of Republican France glowered in London, the Prince and Princess were observed to be warmly commiserating with the great Bonapartists. That they did so purely as friends of the family was scarcely believed. This cordiality led to an incident at Chislehurst which was admittedly extremely embarrassing. A party of Bonapartist artisans, moved by the royal sympathy for their dead Emperor, prepared an enthusiastic Address for the Prince of Wales in which they hailed him as "the true Friend of Bonapartism." This they sought publicly to present to him at Chislehurst.

This time even Bertie was shaken. It had to be stayed at all costs. Perhaps it was the resourceful Francis Knollys who persuaded the Gallic artisans to leave the Prince in his grief and post the Address to Marlborough House. Unfortunately, the post office delivered it safely. At first both Prince and secretary shrank away from the dreadful object as it displayed itself on the study table. In the end an acknowledgment of the briefest and most guarded description went on its furtive way to Paris.

With 1873 the annual program of the Prince and Princess of Wales returned to its normal form. It had been hoped by statesmen that the great Thanksgiving occasion would not only have cleared the air for the Waleses, but also have cleared the Queen's mind to the extent that she would now agree to give her eldest son some useful and important full-time employment which would absorb his immense activity and tap the high abilities which they believed were his birthright. But it was not the case: his mother had nothing for him. The ever-restless Bertie had to look for employment for himself, and it is scarcely surprising that a being so rich in the im-

pulses of common humanity, so blessed with wealth and so stimu-
lated by the adulations of a heterogeneous multitude of friends,
should have sought much diversion among a welter of unimportant
ceremonies. Thus the temptation to present him to the world as a
super-playboy Prince, for whom Europe had no rival, was too good
for many people to resist.

There are two events of 1874 which stand out as interesting in the
lives of the Prince and Princess of Wales: their attendance at the
confirmation in Potsdam of nephew Willy of Germany (the future
Kaiser), soon destined to play the part of sinister bogeyman to his
English uncle and aunt; and, secondly, their sensational visit to
Birmingham—the Radical city—and the conquest and conversion of
Mayor Joseph Chamberlain, the forceful Radical-Republican, by the
charms and enchantments of the Princess of Wales.

It was 11 a.m. on September 1, 1874, when nephew William with
the Crown Prince and Princess entered the cloisters of the Friedenskirche, to undergo the most dreadful and embarrassing three hours
of a Hohenzollern's life. There the shrinking victim with his parents, equally nervous—parents always feared that their children
might disgrace themselves—waited for the tardy coming of the Emperor and Empress.

The body of the *Kirche* was bare of chairs but packed with glittering notabilities. Below the altar rails stood a low platform draped in
the ancient coffin pall of Emperor Sigismund of the Holy Roman
Empire, and on the grim platform was a prayer desk and a chair for
the Imperial candidate. Close beneath the platform on a row of
chairs sat Uncle Bertie, Aunt Alix and other royal guests and relations.

The high moment of the ceremony was the awful *Glaubensbekenntnis,* the Confession of Faith, which the candidate must compose for himself and read aloud to the critical assembly. The *Glaubensbekenntnis* must be long—it must not be outrivaled by that of any
previous candidate—it must be suggestive of original thought, it
must be orthodox, for no Hohenzollern had ever delivered a mildly
heretical Confession of Faith. The *Glaubensbekenntnis* was the signal for the ladies to weep with emotion, and a candidate revealing
his soul from the plaform might gauge the measure of his success
by the number of handkerchiefs fluttering before him.

Willy, according to the testimony of his tutor Hinzpeter, had "found considerable difficulty in formulating his Confession of Faith. With this aim in view the Prince would go for solitary walks along the Scheveningen to meditate." The strange mind of the unhappy cripple was a maelstrom which would one day engulf the world. He had faith in nobody but himself.

But when William stood on the platform with the pitiful shriveled hand supported nonchalantly on his hip—that gesture of concealment already habitual within him—he declared himself in brusque, faintly braggart tones of spurious self-confidence, which in a lad was not unimpressive to the listeners.

Then came the Forty Questions of the examining pastor. He did not hesitate. He firmly threw back answers which filled his exacting mother with pride and caused heads to nod with wise satisfaction. Three long addresses by the clergy followed, which, according to Vicky in a letter to her mother at Balmoral, "might have been better and shorter, still they did not spoil the ceremony!" followed by the added titbit, "as you like to hear little details I was in black with a plain white crepe lisse bonnet. Sometimes I feel too young for the mother of a son already confirmed, and then at times too old!"

Uncle Bertie also wrote to his mother after the ceremony:

"Willy went through his examination admirably. I was only too glad to take the Sacrament with Vicky and Fritz and Willy, after the ceremony, and the service is almost the same as ours. Willy was much pleased with your presents which were laid out in my sitting-room. Your letter to him and the inscription you wrote in the Bible I thought beautiful and I read them to him."

When Willy came to the apartments of Uncle and Aunt Wales after the service the present from his grandmother which pleased him most, or which he declared delighted him the most, was a portrait of his grandfather Prince Albert.

The Prince and Princess of Wales came to Birmingham in the first week in November. Many people thought they would have been wiser to find an excuse for avoiding Birmingham. It was the provincial stronghold of militant Radicalism, and Mr. Joseph Chamberlain, the celebrated or notorious Mayor, was not merely a fiery Radical of the most advanced kind but a self-declared republican, who had been known severely to criticize the ruling family. Chamberlain was the King of Birmingham rather than its Mayor, and he held sway over an immense following in the surrounding countryside. Joseph Chamberlain was, in fact, a rather sinister figure in the land in the year 1874. It was anticipated that their reception by the citizens of Birmingham and by the huge crowds which were said to be flocking in from the country out of curiosity rather than loyalty might be uncomfortable or even insulting. Every Birmingham policeman was in the streets, in case of trouble, when their special train drew into the terminus.

Their passage through the streets to the Town Hall, with the pennants of their Lancer escort fluttering in the wind, was a new and picturesque sight to the morose multitudes of the locality. Many a hat stayed on many a head as they trotted by, the acclamations expressed little joy and were not loud enough to hide occasional boos and jeers. But it was plain from the talk among the crowds—there was said to be over 700,000 people in the streets—that the Princess, who had bowed and smiled most winningly and with the utmost grace the whole way to the Town Hall, had made her mark on the spectators.

The Corporation was rich and generous and the reception was magnificent, but it promised to be cool. To appreciate fully the delicate situation, it must be understood that this reception had been literally forced upon Birmingham Corporation by the Prince himself. It was a case of Daniel in the lion's den: the first of those occasions upon which he deliberately set out to visit people and places who he believed might be unwilling to see him, and that Alix would be an asset to him in such circumstances he did not doubt.

It was known that the Prince if roused had a sharp temper, and there were some at the elaborate luncheon who watched for a quarrel to break out between the royal guest and "Red" Chamberlain, as he was sometimes called. Both were noted for plain speaking; but quarreling was the last thing Bertie contemplated. He did not, perhaps, prosper greatly with Chamberlain—he would be more skilled at this kind of work in after years—but the two were friendly and respectful. On the other side of Chamberlain sat the Princess of

Wales, and, since she was being constantly observed, it could not go unnoticed that Chamberlain appeared very much taken with her. By the time Chamberlain rose to make his speech there seemed to the watchers to be something lamblike about the lion of Birmingham. He appeared to be smiling to himself contentedly.

Some measure of the manner in which Chamberlain was seen by his contemporaries can be gathered from the profound sensation he made by the utterance of one simple phrase. "Here in England," he declared, in proposing the royal toast, "the throne is recognized and respected as the symbol of all constituted authority and settled government." It was even suggested that Chamberlain had thought up these words at luncheon as he chatted with the Princess of Wales, and that he subsequently altered the whole tone of his speech.

Perhaps the worthies of Birmingham had expected their Mayor to be frigidly polite, since there was a lady guest, but they had at least looked for a ringing and rugged note of independence. The entire Press of England hailed Joseph Chamberlain's words with mockery and wonder. "The lovely Princess won the heart of the Radical city as she bowed right and left with her grave, sweet smile" seemed to be the basic idea upon which they built their accounts of the remarkable visit.

The Times summed things up:

"We have heard and chronicled a great many Mayors' speeches," it pronounced, "but we do not know that we ever heard or chronicled speeches made before royal personages by Mayors, whether they were Tories, or Whigs, or Liberals, or Radicals, couched in such a tone at once of courteous homage and gentlemanly feeling, which were so perfectly becoming and so much the right thing in every way as that of Mr. Chamberlain."

Punch published a celebrated cartoon, *A Brummagem Lion,* in which Joseph Chamberlain, with a lion's mane, paws and tail, kneels before the Princess of Wales with a look of supreme satisfaction while she clips his claws. In the background the Prince of Wales smiles behind his hand.

This was the end of Joseph Chamberlain's republicanism, almost the end of his Radicalism. Before long he would be in Parliament in the Liberal interest, serving his party and his country with steadfast zeal, and rather further in the future would be the time when he would appear as a frequent and welcome caller at Marlborough House.

It had been conjectured at Birmingham that after this turncoat action of their firebrand Mayor they would reject him forever; but in practice things went the other way. It was Chamberlain who carried Birmingham with him. And it had seemed almost as if the miraculous conversion of their Mayor in the Town Hall had there and then by some subtle means affected the crowds outside the building; for the return journey of the royal pair was greeted with a roar of cheering, and most of this seemed to be directed toward the beautiful Princess of Wales.

Chapter 18

STARS AND CLOWNS AT MARLBOROUGH HOUSE

IT WAS ON AN EVENING in June 1875 that the Prince of Wales came late to a supper party after the opera given by Sir Allen Young, the Arctic explorer, a rich bachelor. Among the ten guests of Sir Allen was a young woman whose beauty was such that at first it struck people speechless, and she was shortly to become the most blazing star of the Marlborough House set. Since her sudden appearance in London in the previous year she had become the sensation of society and the artistic world; and the Prince of Wales, having heard his youngest brother Leopold raving about this gem of indescribable beauty, had come to Sir Allen's party out of curiosity, knowing she was to be there.

She was Mrs. Lily Langtry, the bride of a rich and happy-go-lucky young Irish yachtsman. Her father was the Dean of Jersey. Lily Langtry had every gift of nature: tall, a superb figure, a mass of rich golden hair, blue eyes so intensely beautiful that they were probably vaguely hypnotic, a perfect color and complexion and truly Grecian features. She was lively and highly intelligent. Soon all the shops would be full of her picture, she would with a nonchalant effortlessness outrival all the "professional beauties," people would climb on park chairs and even fight with umbrellas and sticks to see her pass. And there would be plenty of opportunities for ordinary mortals to see her, for when Marlborough House was open she was regularly to be seen riding in Rotten Row with the Prince and Princess of Wales, and sometimes alone with the Prince and his party in the fashionable hour, the late afternoon.

143

Thus began the famous attachment between the Prince of Wales and the most beautiful young married woman in London society, who later, as the result of a then unforeseen domestic upheaval, was to convert herself almost overnight into a glittering star of the stage, an astute actor-manageress and subsequently into one of the most sensational figures of the theatre in London and the United States.

Perhaps it was due to the sporting tastes of her royal admirer that she used much of the wealth she quickly amassed from her theatrical ventures to make herself the leading lady racehorse owner and horse fancier of Britain, an elegant and colorful ornament of every notable turf event and a dazzling and familiar feature of the Prince of Wales's racing coterie.

For Edward, Prince of Wales, Lily Langtry would exercise a fascination which he would express in social and public life with a naïve lack of concealment, puzzling and engrossing to his contemporaries. There were, perhaps, few who knew the truths about the relationship between the Prince of Wales and Mrs. Langtry, but thousands would soon think that they did so. Lily, apart from her bewildering loveliness, was of a vivacious, free and easy disposition, as is often the case where a single sister with many brothers is left to bring herself up in a motherless family, and inevitably she appeared fast in that age of repression. The pair were destined to become the ribald jest of every London club and the subject of urgent whispers in the boudoirs of Mayfair.

The nation, which was supposed to be so puritanically minded, adopted them as the principals in a sinful and mysterious romance, weaving a kind of erotic unwritten literature about them which has echoes even till the present day. Whatever may or may not have taken place behind locked doors in London flats or the guest chambers of famous country mansions—the multitudinous bands of baronial flunkeys and demure, rustling ladies' maids were ardent secret-mongers who often had no need to lie about the habits of their blue-blooded employers—it must be borne in mind that from this decade onward till the close of the Victorian reign the British people watched the endless public activities of the Prince and Princess of Wales against a murky and intriguing background supplied in their imaginations by their Wales-Langtry complex.

But if Marlborough House acquired a brilliant recruit in this year, it also lost a familiar figure whose going inevitably harmed the reputation of his innocent friends. In June, Colonel Valentine Baker, late commanding officer of the Prince's regiment, the 10th Hussars, then a staff officer at Aldershot and a frequent guest of Marlborough House, was arrested for an assault on a young woman in a moving railway carriage outside Woking.

Baker may have been the victim of an imaginative hysteric—his victim was found clinging to the footboard—but he was sentenced to a year's imprisonment as a first-class demeanant. His imprisonment was a farce, as quite clearly his own circle regarded his action less gravely than would probably be the case today. But the Queen insisted on cashiering him, against the strong representations of his friends, which meant that Baker, a "purchase" officer, lost the privilege of selling his rank to another aspiring candidate. The lower three-quarters of the nation were shocked, and the rest deprecated the clumsiness of the man of fashion. Valentine Baker had to go into voluntary exile, which he did in the service of Turkey and Egypt. But Marlborough House never abandoned a friend: it was made known to him that he would still be received when he visited the country. At a later date both the Prince of Wales and the Duke of Cambridge, the commander in chief, would take part in a fruitless effort to have Valentine Baker restored to the Army List.

During this summer the Queen and Alix figured in an impromptu and picturesque little incident, which is preserved in a peculiar publication, the only obituary pamphlet put out at the death of John Brown. The pamphlet, a mere hasty newspaper-cutting compilation of a journalistic hack, revealing little of Brown but much of royal activities, is occasionally interesting on the latter score.

"After having lunched at Marlborough House it entered Her Majesty's august head to suggest to the Princess of Wales that they should take a drive in some unusual quarter," says the writer, H. L. Williams, who naturally depicts his hero Mr. Brown as being in attendance, and doubtless correctly. "This (the unusual quarter) was to see Mr. Spurgeon's Tabernacle over the water. Immediately the whim was put in operation and soon they reached the 'Elephant and Castle.' On going further south an unexpected block appeared, the Walworth road being 'up.' An extensive work in connection with the lower sewage was in progress.

The coachman, to his infinite disgust, was compelled to make his way through narrow streets, hedged with miserable two-storey buildings, to reach a broad thoroughfare. Out of all the windows unkempt heads of children appeared, and women rushed to the doors from the family washing. The boys accompanied the vehicle, a perfect rarity in such passages, with many a flip-flap and Catherine wheel. Luckily the men were from home at that hour in the afternoon. The ladies smiled and laughed at last at the horrified expression of the rubicund coachman and the footman, whilst the laugh was shared heartily by the usually grim-faced man in the Scotch cap. Then the equipage luckily blundered out upon Camberwell Green."

In October of 1875 Bertie departed on his Indian visit, which was to occupy nine months. Alix remained at home. The Indian visit was Disraeli's doing. The Queen accepted his views that the loyalty of India to the Crown ever since the Mutiny had been of a very indolent character, but was most reluctant to believe that the appearance of her eldest son might stir up the enthusiasm of the Indians. She not only appeared to think the Prince of Wales would challenge the supreme dignity of the Governor-General, but that it would *tire* him too much. Mr. Disraeli prevailed. Dizzy had, in fact, a more colorful project up his sleeve, but he held his peace, and saw the Prince depart, confident that his genial and easy manner would have its effect upon the powerful princes and rajahs.

Bertie on his way out stayed two days with George of Greece at Athens. He did not find his troubled brother-in-law any more optimistic concerning Hellenic affairs than he had been in the past. Bertie was able to write to Alix that her brother had welcomed the invitation he had brought that George, with Olga and the family, should be their guests at Marlborough House in the following summer. Bertie had assured King George that he would see that he had an opportunity of revealing all the Grecian problems to Mr. Disraeli, a prospect which seemed to much brighten the outlook of the disillusioned monarch.

It was while in India that Bertie was one morning bewildered, enraged and humiliated to be casually informed by local officials that by Act of Parliament his mother had become Empress of India. He shared this totally unexpected news with every bearer, every syce, every sweeper, every merchant in the bazaars. He felt a perfect fool. For once his mother had gone too far. To his indignant letters she sent an unqualified apology. It did seem that in this case Disraeli had blundered, perhaps through his anxiety to keep his plan secret and a fear that the Prince might not keep a firm check on his tongue. The wily statesman, a friend of Marlborough House and an admirer of Prince Hal, knew how to appease his angry young friend. He informed him that he had just bought the Suez Canal shares for Britain, and the recipient who had inspected the wonderful canal and had prophesied how valuable it might be to the country was delighted. But when Dizzy went on to declare as a special titbit that now the Prince and Princess of Wales could have themselves addressed as "Imperial Highness," Bertie blushed with diffident shame. He was not going to have that at any price. He was insulted. It sounded like *opéra bouffe.*

Bertie arrived home from India in July 1876, and the London season had missed him. But great preparations were in hand in honor of his triumphant return. And it *was* triumphant, for the impact of his personality had cleared the murky air in British India much more effectively than Her Majesty's grand Proclamation. The tone of the Indian newspapers showed that beyond dispute.

Alix was radiant when on shipboard in Portsmouth Harbor she met "hubby" again, for so she usually referred to him among her friends. It was a well-known characteristic of hers that she could never see Bertie depart even for a few days during the earlier half of their married life, or seldom greet him on return, without clinging and dissolving into tears; and since these farewells and reunions generally took place on station platforms before hundreds of sympathizing eyes, the occasions, although enjoyed by a sentimental public, were somewhat embarrassing to the dignity of the Prince of Wales.

Of the ceremonies of welcome, the brilliant dinner party given by the Prime Minister, Mr. Disraeli, at No. 10 Downing Street, drew the most public attention. It was a blue-blooded affair, as might be expected of Dizzy—nothing stuffy and parliamentary about it to bore the Princess—and tiaras and diamonds flashed in the lamplight from the windows of the crested carriages as they swept into the dim narrow street off Whitehall.

The fantastical Dizzy had made a huge success with the Queen by calling her his "Faerie," a kind of male attention of which she had never had much in her life: he was now ready to enchant the Princess of Wales, with whom as yet he had not made much headway. This, however, was more difficult for him. She honestly preferred the Gladstone steam roller to the Disraeli ballet. Nevertheless, when Dizzy advanced to her in the gorgeously embellished gloominess of 10 Downing Street and overburdened her arms with his ample rose and orchid bouquet, which he himself has described as "bright, sweet and pendulous and studded with butterflies and humming birds," her rapturous reception of his delicacy, though perhaps it honestly surprised him, must have seemed to him a fitting gesture to such a courtier as himself. For the Princess of Wales unfixed the largest and brightest of his butterflies and pinned it in her hair, where he could admire it ecstatically as she sat by his side throughout dinner.

Probably the Princess of Wales had not time to be bored with blandishments that evening, for she was so very earnestly cultivating Mr. Disraeli. George and Olga were due shortly from Athens, and if anybody could help poor George that man was Benjamin Disraeli, the acknowledged wizard of Near Eastern affairs.

The first task of the Prince of Wales was to introduce his sad brother-in-law of Greece to the life of a London man of fashion, while Alix entertained Queen Olga and the children. One of the favorite visiting places of the Prince and Princess of Wales when they had notable visitors to entertain was the Crystal Palace at night, when the great firework displays were given by the Brocks. But even the magnificent display put on for King George with a gigantic set piece showing the Parthenon in colored fire and the words "Long Life to King George of Greece" would scarcely have stirred his depressed spirits if Bertie had not been taking him to see Mr. Disraeli on the morrow.

Alix was deeply distressed by the worn features of her once gay brother, and she attributed the baldness already appearing over his brow to his troubles; but perhaps George looked no more haggard than she had expected after the woeful tone his letters had taken all through that year. As early as March she had written to a friend, "I grieve to think what a hard task my poor brother has before him, and all that he has gone through these twelve years." To George, Grecian affairs seemed now quite desperate, and not unnaturally, perhaps, his forceful young Russian wife was seeking to bring him into the Russian anti-Turkish bloc, a measure much acclaimed by the fiery Greeks but which George saw miserably as the surest means of cutting himself off from the power he always looked to—Britain. At the moment the Greeks, with no army worth the name and no military stores, were calling upon their King to lead them in an armed seizure of Crete, Thessaly and Epirus against all the might of the Ottoman Empire. They believed that by such bold initiative they would find Russia behind them. That was why George wished to seek out Mr. Disraeli.

King George, with his brother-in-law sitting by him, poured out his troubles before Disraeli, who listened long and patiently. But Dizzy, unlike Gladstone, the great classicist, was not Hellenically minded. He saw Greece—with Turkey—simply as the barriers between Russia and India. He solemnly cautioned King George at all costs—it might cost him his throne!—to reject a Russian entanglement, and then he might hope—and here things became vague—for the help of England.

King George departed almost as dolefully as he had come, and though by the courtesy of the Queen he was now a Knight of the universally coveted Order of the Garter, the inspiration of the chivalric Order seemed to have little effect on his overtaxed spirits. Marlborough House, meanwhile, set itself to cultivate Mr. Disraeli very delicately in the interests of brother George; and Dizzy, who was by no means impervious to the strange spell of the Princess of Wales, was not entirely unwilling to be cajoled. A letter of his written two years later to the Prince of Wales bears witness to his zeal in her cause:

"I did something for Greece yesterday, it was very difficult but by no means to be despised. It was all done for her Royal Highness's sake. I thought of Marlborough House all the time, and

after many efforts it was not decided till the last moment."
(6 July, '78.)

He had secured Greece a slightly better frontier with Turkey, but
how long the Turks would observe the new arrangement remained
in doubt.

Before King George left for home Alix had promised to spend
two months with him at Athens in the following spring, and when
the time came she was escorted to Naples by Bertie and there took
boat alone. She arrived primed with messages from Bertie and Disraeli to keep himself out of the Russians' clutches, which presumably
she had to deliver when Olga was out of hearing. To give added
weight to those messages of hers, Bertie sent George a telegram—
at Disraeli's suggestion—most "urgently" stressing the same advice.

Nothing did George so much good as hours spent in the company
of his sister. During the busy London stay he had not seen her alone
as often as he would have liked, but now he had a real chance of
refreshing his spirits, as he frequently would in the years ahead, for
she would often join him at Athens. After the solemn pomp of England it was all comic opera to her, and she loved it. Only Alix could
make George a boy again. The best story ever told about the two of
them comes from the late E. F. Benson. A young Englishman who
was allowed to walk in the Palace gardens at Athens was sitting
peacefully in a rose pergola when he was disturbed by the hurried
and noisy approach of human beings. A moment later a tall man
ran round the corner kicking a lady's hat before him. Hard on his
heels, yelling and laughing, followed a tall and very beautiful
woman. They stopped and smiled sheepishly at the stranger. The
footballer was the King of Greece, and his sister, the Princess of
Wales, ruefully plucked the remains of her hat out of the dust. "So
rude of you, George!" said she. "I can never wear this again." The
King, evidently thinking some explanation was required, addressed
the Englishman. "Look," he appealed, calling his attention to the
hat. "It was a very ugly hat—what do you think? I don't like it, so
I pulled it off and kicked it!"

The London season of 1876 had flagged a little without the zestful
leadership which the Prince of Wales gave, but the 1877 season was
as brilliant as ever. We have some intimate glimpses of the Waleses

and their life at this period from Lily Langtry, who was now, by virtue of being invited to the little Sunday dinner parties, considered to be one of the most favored members of the Marlborough House set.

The Princess of Wales was at that time, says Lily Langtry in her memoirs, so fascinating "that one could not take one's eyes from her," and her words are borne out by the eulogies of many others. Her kindness was a byword and Mrs. Langtry gives a good example of it. Immediately after one of the Sunday dinner parties Lily was seized with violent pains. She was in great distress, but it was not etiquette to leave the royal presence. Charlotte Knollys noticed her and told the Princess of Wales, who at once urged her to go home. Lily had scarcely got into bed when Sir Francis Laking, the Household physician, arrived, sent upon the order of the Princess, who felt that her food must have poisoned the guest.

> ". . . next afternoon I was feeling better," says Lily, "and was lying on the sofa in my drawing-room about tea-time, when the butler suddenly announced Her Royal Highness, who entered followed by her inseparable secretary Miss Knollys.
>
> "The honor of the unexpected visit brought me at once to my feet, ill though I felt, but the Princess insisted on my lying down again, while she made herself tea. . . . She always used a specially manufactured violet scent and I recall exclaiming on the delicious perfume, and her solicitous answer that she feared possibly it was too strong for me."

In Rotten Row the Prince of Wales's party, picked out by the red brow bands on the royal mounts, was always one of the London sights; but when in the smart cavalcade there appeared side by side the two most beautiful women in the land, the Princess of Wales and Mrs. Langtry, the new sensation, people returned from the park well satisfied with their sight-seeing.

It was at a May Drawing Room that Lily Langtry was presented to the Queen by the Marchioness of Conyngham, one of the Ladies of the Household. Bouquets were then in fashion at Drawing Rooms, and evidently the style of gown to be worn by Mrs. Langtry was known at Marlborough House, for she records that before leaving for the Palace "an immense bouquet of Marechal Ney roses" was delivered from the Prince of Wales, which matched the imitation Marechal Ney roses on her gown and train.

It was usual at Drawing Rooms for the Queen to give up receiving after half an hour or so, and to delegate her office to the Princess of Wales, but much to the general surprise she was still at her post when Lily Langtry, very late in the line, reached her. The Lord Chamberlain did not require to look at her card, but simply said, "Mrs. Langtry comes next, Your Majesty."

That night at the ball at Marlborough House, Lily tells us of the Prince of Wales "chaffing" her because of the enormous feathers she had worn, and agreeing with her that she had certainly dressed on the safe side after his mother's order that ladies were to discontinue wearing "miniature" feathers, which were, of course, so much easier to keep in place. During the royal quadrille the reason for the Queen's remaining to the end of the Drawing Room was revealed to Lily. Her Majesty had declared that she intended to see Mrs. Langtry, and had waited solely for that end, expressing much irritation at the length of time she was delayed.

Another rising star at Marlborough House in the late 'seventies, who in his own inimitable way shared the honors with Mrs. Langtry, was a young naval lieutenant, Lord Charles Beresford, who had been with the Prince of Wales in India. Lord Charles, a small impish Irishman, had a career before him, thanks perhaps to royal interest, but he certainly did nothing to smooth the way for himself. He said what he thought and did as he felt inclined. To Alix, Charles Beresford was always "my Little Rascal." That was an age of practical jokers, and the Little Rascal was well suited to shine in it.

Beresford, while staying in the country near London, was once invited by letter to dine at Marlborough House. He wired back: "Can't possibly. Lie follows by post." He stole a cock from a farm-yard, doped it, and placed it under the bed of a pompous guest at Sandringham. With the dawn the cock recovered, but having its legs tied it could only greet the rising sun from under the bed, and a footman roused by frantic bell-ringing was amazed when required by an indignant guest to remove a cockerel from the room.

Lily Langtry tells of an occasion during Cowes Week when the

Prince and Princess of Wales, with herself among their party, visited *H.M.S. Thunderer,* the small vessel commanded by Lord Charles in the roads. The cabins were below the water and oxygen was artificially fed to them through air shafts. Beresford led the royal party down to his cabin and then shut off the oxygen supply. With faces turning a ripe scarlet, momentarily growing more uncomfortable, they regarded one another in puzzled dismay. "We began to go through the sensation which must be experienced by a fish out of water," says Lily.

But the best of all the stories about the Little Rascal concerns a dinner party at Marlborough House. Through the good offices of the Prince of Wales, Beresford had received the C.B.E. The dinner was an important occasion, and Lord Charles was asked in a tone of some irritation why he was not wearing his award.

"I am wearing it, your Royal Highness!" came the answer.

He was asked to explain himself. Beresford turned his back, bent over, threw up his coat tails, and glittering on the seat of his trousers was the C.B.E.

Mrs. Langtry was naturally one of the ornaments of Cowes Week and on the famous lawns of the headquarters of the Royal Yacht Squadron, and she was frequently a guest of the Prince and Princess aboard the royal yacht *Osborne.* The presence of the Waleses at Cowes had now created a situation where the whole of society tried to pack into the overstrained and prospering village for one week, accepting, if they had no yacht, the most primitive lodgings.

Perhaps the most entertaining story Mrs. Langtry recounts of Cowes is of a shore occasion. She attended a spiritualistic séance at the cottage of Mrs. Cust on the front. The Prince and Princess of Wales were there and also the gay young Prince Imperial, who always came to Cowes with his mother, the still beautiful Eugénie. The Gallic high spirits of the Imperial Pretender almost rivaled the Irish ingenuity of Beresford, and he was a great favorite in the royal circle.

Spiritualism—taken more or less seriously—was a craze, following perhaps the example of the Queen, who seems to have been a stern and ardent disciple; but this séance was an amateurish affair with a circle of clasped hands in the darkness, where people hopefully waited for some table-turning or spirit-rapping.

That night they got more than they expected. The furniture started to dance. Things upset all around them. Lily Langtry knew the reason. Her neighbor the Prince Imperial had slipped out of the circle. The turbulent spirit was going too far for Mrs. Cust. Lights revealed the culprit. The Prince Imperial was locked out of the room.

The room was an upstairs one, and they now settled down to a more profound study of the spiritual world. It was perhaps a quarter of an hour later when everybody in the darkened room began to feel uneasy. Strange things were happening. Something inexplicable was in the room with them. Here and there came a soft rustle, a scarcely audible pattering. Their cheeks tingled as if brushed by the lightest feather. They could not believe it. They did not believe it. Somebody struck a match.

There was the Prince Imperial in stockinged feet with a large bag of flour, and there was the Prince of Wales blanketed in whiteness and the whole circle liberally besprinkled. Louis Napoleon had climbed up the creeper and slipped unnoticed through the window.

Mrs. Langtry tells us also of the Prince of Wales and the Prince Imperial hoisting a live donkey up through the window of a guest-room at Mrs. Cust's cottage and placing the beast in bed, though she cannot understand how they kept it there.

She records how she bought Prince Eddy (family name for the Duke of Clarence), who was a youthful admirer of hers, a trinket from the fashionable jewelers in the High Street on the eve of the departure of the two brothers on their world tour in the *Bacchante*. Next morning Prince Eddy cheerfully assured her, "I've had to take off Grandmother's locket (the Queen's) from my watch chain to make room for yours!"

There are two stories coming from the middle 'seventies concerning the Wales boys and their encounters with the redoubtable John Brown. Eddy and George had heard enough in the family circle to make them lose no love over Mr. John Brown. Brown, for his part, chose to ignore the boys when they were at Windsor or Balmoral, just as he did his best to ignore their father.

But the spirit of practical joking then prevalent had caught up Eddy and George. The ponderous Scot moved about with a pomp and circumstance which might easily be unsettled. One autumn evening, when the family was staying with Grandmamma at Windsor, Eddy and George tied a string across the foot of the staircase in Clarence Tower, where Brown was lodged. Twilight was falling and the lamps had not been lit. They could not resist lurking in the gloom for Brown to descend from his apartments.

Brown tumbled headlong over the string with a storm of curses. But it was not so dim that he failed to see the Wales boys in flight. Brown thundered after them with flying kilts. He seized them and belabored them furiously for all to see outside the Wales apartments.

Fortunately the Prince of Wales was not inside, but the news soon reached him. They thought he was going to have a brainstorm. He was about to rush out and assault Brown himself. Considering the relative sizes of the two men, this might have been difficult: nor might Mr. Brown in his indignation have hesitated at the Prince of Wales. The Queen declared that Bertie's tantrum was "nonsense": they had deserved what they got. Bertie persisted that he was personally insulted, and demanded the whereabouts of Brown. Alix and everybody in the room, perceiving the danger of the Prince in such a mood encountering Brown, set to persuading him to have his annoyance tended to Brown by a third party and an apology demanded. Reluctantly he agreed to this. An apology reached the Prince and Princess, but in what terms Brown had actually expressed it to the third party is not related.

It was perhaps after this event that the rumored incident of the Prince of Wales and his friends tipping a prizefighter to teach Brown a lesson took place. At about this time Brown took to his bed after some kind of "accident," but some, remembering that whisky had once caused Brown to fall flat on his face when following the Queen on a public visitation, attributed the cause to this.

A second Brown adventure involving Eddy and George happened only a few days later. This time it was a mistake, and might have had a more serious ending, but the climax was comical. Not dismayed by their misadventure with John Brown, the princes decided to try their practical joke on somebody better-humored.

Once again when darkness was falling at Windsor they had out their ball of string. They tied it across the open doorway of the room they were in and rang the bell for the footman of the corridor.

This man was a friend of theirs and would enjoy the joke with them.

The princes listened anxiously. Somebody was approaching the doorway. Mr. Brown appeared, bearing a message from the Queen.

Brown crashed over the string, upsetting the paraffin lamp, and the carpet went up in a blaze. By the time the flames were stamped out a little crowd was in the room, and Brown, possibly more sober than on the previous occasion, was in possession of his equanimity.

"Under the table wid ye!" he commanded the frightened princes with ferocious dignity—"till I fetch Her Majesty."

This was a punishment which he had seen the Queen inflict, and Eddy and George meekly obeyed. Brown strode grimly out and presently reappeared with the Queen and their parents. This time the Waleses were speechless and humiliated. It was Brown's round. Grandmamma was about to exhibit one of her flashes of cold rage which could be so terrifying to everybody in the Presence. In tense silence she ordered out her grandsons.

George appeared first. He was stark naked, with his clothes neatly folded over his arm and his boots hung round his neck. Sheepish and defiant, he glared at them. Brown, always an admirer of spirit, led the laughter and the boys escaped unpunished and almost unscolded.

During a New Year family party at Windsor one of the most epic events in the Brown saga was enacted. The Queen, wishing for Mr. Brown, sent a young maid to the Clarence Tower to summon him. The girl returned to the royal company with a scared look. She said that Mr. Brown was unwell, and the Queen accepted this and made no comment.

The story of what had actually happened came from the servants' hall via a housemaid, who told the Princess of Wales's dresser, and so to the Waleses.

After much knocking at the chamber door in Clarence the girl had been commanded to enter. Brown lay stretched under the bedclothes. The maid announced that the Queen wanted him. Brown, face aflame, whiskers bristling, shot upright in the bed. He was clothed to his jacket.

"She'll no be seeing me the day," he roared. "She knows damn well I'm fu' (full drunk)!"

At that, the great man had subsided under the bedclothes.

Eddy and George had left home for the first time in May 1877, when with their tutor, the Reverend J. N. Dalton, they joined the naval cadet training ship *Britannia* at Dartmouth. They were to be subject to the normal discipline of the ship, which was strict, even harsh by modern training ship standards. The move to the *Britannia* had been against the Queen's wishes. She wanted the boys to go to Wellington College, the new public school founded by Prince Albert not long before his death. Bertie, however, said that his sons would profit more from a naval training, and Alix, though she knew that Eddy and George would have a rougher time on the *Britannia,* remembered that brother George of Greece had once been a naval cadet and perhaps was the better for it in facing his troubles. She supported her husband, and the Queen gave way.

Her Majesty was, nevertheless, very much put out in the following May when she wrote to her son saying that she intended to have Eddy and George to stay with her at Balmoral for her birthday. The reply came back that unhappily that would be impossible, as they could not be allowed to interrupt their naval studies.

In 1879 George and Eddy were ready to take to the sea, and in September, escorted by their parents, they boarded *H.M.S. Bacchante* for the first part of their two-year cruise round the world. Dalton, the tutor, accompanied them, and this first part of the tour was to confine them to visits on the West India station. They would be home in nine months, and then re-embark on the *Bacchante* for the more ambitious portion of the tour. The boys were excited, their father seemed pleased and proud, but it was observed that their mother appeared very doleful.

In the meanwhile, early in the year the Zulu War had broken out: a remote affair to most people at home, which could be settled in the end by the Regular Army, whose job it was, whatever bloody casualties were caused by bungling at the outset. But for Bertie and Alix it had struck a tragic personal note.

The Prince Imperial, to whom they were both much attached, had completed his training at the R.M.A., Woolwich. Immediately war broke out, Louis Napoleon volunteered to serve with the Royal Artillery as a token of his gratitude for the hospitality of England. Both the Queen and her eldest son were delighted, but Mr. Disraeli saw grave complications. The French royalists would be indignant at the Prince Imperial's being allowed to risk himself, and the republicans jealous at the royal and official acclamations which would shower on the French Pretender.

Argument between the Throne and the Prime Minister grew heated. In the end royalty won, to the extent that the Prince Imperial should be allowed to go to the front as a "spectator," not a combatant. When somebody shortly afterward spoke to Dizzy of the royal family's triumph, he remarked sardonically: "I hope the French government will be as joyful! In my mind nothing could be more injudicious than the whole affair."

The Prince Imperial, "spectator" though he might officially be, was sent to war like a hero by his distinguished friends; and, as Mr. Disraeli doubtless foresaw, the gallant Frenchman quickly proved himself a most enterprising "spectator" at the front. The soldiers were all too ready to let this pleasant young prince have his way.

At last, in June, the Prince Imperial rode out on a forward reconnaissance with some irregular horse. They were ambushed in long grass. Each man for himself, the party galloped off. On the ground lay the Prince Imperial, wounded. Later they found the body riddled with assegai wounds.

Britain was aghast. The Queen was speechless with horror and rage. The Prince declared openly that the Army was disgraced forever: the Prince Imperial had been "wantonly sacrificed." Even French republicans were disgusted at this desertion of one of their countrymen.

The Queen ordered a battleship, *H.M.S. Orontes,* to bring the body home. The Prince of Wales declared that the Army, which had betrayed their guest, must accord full military honors to the corpse.

Then Bertie and Alix hastened to Chislehurst to comfort the afflicted mother and, indeed, to apologize for the behavior of the British Army. The Queen reached Chislehurst shortly after them. The rumpus was copiously reported in the continental newspapers. Disraeli grew more and more uneasy. Who would grudge the gallant Frenchman his last honors if only he had not been French Pretender? He saw that the royal family by their outcry daily made the republican government more jealous and bitter.

The Prince of Wales headed a committee to raise a public statue. The Queen thought this should be in Westminster Abbey. She informed the Prime Minister. To Mr. Disraeli's relief the Commons condemned this plan. The statue of the Prince Imperial, which the Government would most willingly have done without, was executed by Victor Hohenlohe, the cousin and boyhood friend of the Prince of Wales, and was eventually deposited in the honorable seclusion of the R.M.A., Woolwich. Disraeli watched the end of the tragic affair with cynical satisfaction.

Part Four

FULL GLORY

Chapter 19

ALIX AND THE ELEPHANT MAN

*U*P TO THE MIDDLE of the nineteenth century, hospitals had been considered unfit places for a lady of breeding to enter, and by many as unfit for any kind of human being. With the return of Miss Florence Nightingale from the Crimea the amazing influence, wielded from a long sickbed, of this powerful personality brought gradually a remarkable reformation. There was much to be done, but by the end of the 'sixties wards were no longer stables, which sickened, horrified or morally shocked all but the toughest.

It thus came about that the first royal personage to be actively interested in hospitals was the Princess of Wales, and no royal personage since her time seems to have brought to hospitals quite the same personal touch or entered them with the same spirit of obstinate and benevolent interference as did she. Perhaps such an attitude is no longer needed. Alix never met the redoubtable Miss Nightingale, but the two had something in common, and at least one famous cure which saved the lives of thousands was introduced into England solely through her unflagging persistence in defiance of something very near professional scorn and snubs.

In the London Hospital there is a Finsen lamp which has cured hundreds of the terrible disease of lupus. It was the gift of the Princess of Wales, the first of its kind to arrive from Denmark. Above it the committee have engraved three words: *"Nothing like perseverance."* This is the monument to her greatest battle.

It is said that Alix first took an interest in hospitals after her agonizing rheumatic sickness of '67. She felt that others were entitled to some of the immense care lavished upon herself at that time. The first hospital she entered was Bart's, and she was soon seen at many others. All over the country are to be found Alexandra wards and Alexandra wings; but it was not long before she had adopted the London Hospital in the East End as her own.

The Princess of Wales became president of the committee, and her presidency was not an honorary and absent one with duties delegated to a vice official. She used to arrive at the London without warning with Charlotte Knollys, or sometimes, especially if she was visiting the men's wards, with the faithful Dighton Probyn towering behind her. She made herself tea in the matron's room while she discussed the affairs of the hospital. She asked embarrassing questions at times, which caused things to be put right in case she asked others later. Her manner was vague, but she had a way of suddenly coming to the point with a sharp abrupt sentence, distinctly foreign sounding, in her slightly husky tones. She asked for the difficult cases and visited them, wandering through the wards with no train of dignitaries in her wake to intimidate patients. She approached beds here and there and sat talking with the inmates. If a patient seemed lonely and unvisited she sent flowers and other gifts. She never forgot a face on a second visit, and even remembered names. She knew all the young probationer nurses and heard about their troubles. Everybody loved her. Even the medical staff, who thought her interfering, were charmed and amused by the Beloved Lady.

But of all the legends concerning her at the London the most interesting is the story of John Merrick, the Elephant Man. That incident happened in 1886.

One morning in that year railway passengers at Liverpool Street Station who entered the general waiting room were seen to slip out again with horrified faces. Eventually the staff were informed that huddled in the darkest corner of the waiting room was a human monster of the most horrible description, who appeared to be ill. Some women had fainted at what they had seen and several men had become physically sick.

This creature had a kind of trunk of flesh like an elephant and he was incoherent with terror and distress, which made him the more frightful. In his pocket was a card with "Sir Frederick Treves" written on it, and Sir Frederick was the big name at the London. Sir Frederick Treves was informed and hurried to Liverpool Street. At sight of him the monster cried with delight and began to talk in a hoarse but sane manner.

Two years before, this monster, John Merrick, had been brought to him for examination. It was the most advanced case of *elephantiasis* he had ever seen. Since then the unhappy Merrick had been carried around the continental fair grounds till he ceased to pay. His proprietor put him aboard a cargo boat bound for London Docks with the card, a little money, but no food, and he had not dared buy any.

Merrick could not be left to the streets. Sir Frederick brought him to the London. His arrival caused a sensation. He could not be left with the other patients. A young nurse who was sent to his room dropped her tray and fled in terror. Experienced sisters approached him only with an effort. Even the doctors found themselves shuddering and trying to hide their disgust. All news about the London went to the Princess of Wales. She arrived in the matron's room and said she had come to visit the Elephant Man, the name by which Merrick was referred to in the hospital. The case, she was told, was too frightful for her to look at, but he was quite comfortable. She stood up, exclaiming, "I go!" and went.

She shook hands with Merrick, she sat by his bed and her smile was as sweet for him as it was for everybody else. She talked to him as if it were her job to welcome new patients. She left Merrick with the impression that perhaps he was not so much unlike other people.

The Princess of Wales came to chat with Merrick regularly, and such simple and unaffected attention from so exalted a lady, and one whom he knew to be the most beautiful in the land, altered the whole outlook of Merrick upon his terrible life. He was, she perceived, a man of great courage, and worth her attentions.

When Christmas time came Merrick received cards, gifts and a signed photograph from the Princess of Wales. He clutched the photograph and wept, rocking himself to and fro on his bed in his emotion. When they came to clean his room he would have nobody touch the photograph. It was sacred. It was, in fact, the only thing of golden happiness in a life of bitter sadness. The brief and clumsy note of thanks written to the Princess of Wales, beginning "My

Dear Princess" and finishing with "Yours sincerely, John Merrick," may still exist. It may almost be said that the Elephant Man in his last days was a normal-thinking human being who had forgotten the appalling measure of his affliction.

But the good deeds of Alix were not confined to hospital wards. At Sandringham her touch was individualistic. An old Sandringham inhabitant has said, "I remember how the Princess of Wales always knew of the sick cottagers, and sometimes after visiting them she would return after ten or eleven o'clock on a winter's night with soup and other delicacies and medicines."

Her vagueness made her charities of rather a haphazard description, and difficult for her long-suffering staff to control. She had a long pension list of old or invalid people, which she might add to without any notice to her secretary and be indignant when the person was overlooked. It was her joke that as soon as enfeebled persons came on her pension list they miraculously recovered and lived forever to draw her pension.

The strenuous efforts of Charlotte Knollys to protect her from begging letter-writers often failed. Hundreds of begging letters used to arrive for the Princess, and she would pick one here and there and become interested. On one such letter from a man in allegedly pitiful circumstances she penciled a note, "Give him £10." Charlotte Knollys, suspicious of the letter-writer, caused enquiries to be made. Presently she triumphantly informed her mistress that the letter-writer was a notorious rogue, who had actually had his letter smuggled out of prison.

"Never mind," was the answer. "Send him the £10. He'll need it when he gets out!"

On another occasion Miss Knollys thought that £5 was altogether too generous a present for a certain applicant. She had penciled her opinion across the letter and left it on the royal desk. The letter returned to the secretary. It had been amended. The £5 had been crossed out and £10 had been scribbled over it.

But in other respects the Beloved Lady would not be put upon. She did as she liked, not as others suggested. A personal friend of hers, a lady of standing in her county, wanted her to visit a country bazaar in the autumn. Early in the summer, therefore, she sent the Princess of Wales a beautiful old miniature, which though highly attractive to the recipient, who collected miniatures, was perhaps not much valued by the family. At the end of the letter accompanying the gift casual reference to the autumn bazaar was made, with the hope that Her Royal Highness would honor the occasion. The personal friend found the miniature returned next morning. Alix's letter was quite polite, and the kindness of the gift was appreciated, but, she explained, "my birthday is not until the 1st of December, so I do not think I should accept it now." She visited the bazaar.

One good story concerning the vagueness of Alix, though it has nothing to do with good works, may not inappropriately be introduced at this point. She always laughed at this unfortunate incident herself. She was reputed at dinner parties and suchlike occasions to be a good listener. In fact, even before the days of her deafness, she often had only the haziest idea of what her neighbor was talking about. Her mind was straying, but she was skillful in throwing in remarks which hid this fact. It was not the custom of the Waleses to observe in their homes that painful royal rite by which guests spoke only when they were addressed. Once at a dinner at Marlborough House, Alix sat between a man who was an enthusiast on carnations and a man who bred dachshunds as a hobby.

She first began a conversation with her neighbor who bred dachshunds. Then she turned her attention to the carnation lover, and heard about his carnations. Although she put in an occasional word to encourage the speaker, she was soon not listening, and was suddenly awakened by the dachshund expert on her other side joining in the talk on carnations. This puzzled her slightly, and then momentarily her attention was diverted to another part of the table.

After that she realized that she did not know which neighbor loved carnations and which dachshunds; but perhaps it did not matter very much. She turned to the dachshund breeder, and he seized the opportunity to renew the interesting talk on his dogs. She did not hear him after a few moments, beyond knowing that he was praising something—carnations doubtless—and she thought it time to put in a word.

"Yes," said she brightly, "that kind are nice, but personally I like best of all the old-fashioned fat pink ones, which smell so lovely."

This was the Alix of the 'eighties, and her ways were known and loved. Bertie, or "Teddy" as he was known to the world at large, also had a great following, though some at sight of the many cartoons displaying their Prince of Wales with the look of a plump middle-aged rip with tip-tilted hat or yachting cap were genuinely shocked. But shocking as he may have been at a distance, everyone who had heard "Teddy" make one of his splendidly apt speeches, or had personal experience of his immense courtesy and gentleness, his open friendliness and his interest in everybody, great or humble, was his staunch supporter. Ladies of all ages who had the good fortune to meet him found him most understanding and attractive.

"Teddy" was doing more good in the cause of royalty than he was doing harm, because he was humanizing them to the common people. He was the perfect set-off to his mother, who, about to lose dear Mr. Brown to the eternal shades, was on her way to an effortless assumption of that fabulous goddesslike Queenhood with which the Victorians mantled her from her Jubilee till her death.

This was also the period when another side of the Prince of Wales was becoming plain to the leading men of the country; his diplomatic skill, which appeared to be of an unusually high order, his willingness to use this in the interests of the government in power, his accumulating knowledge and wisdom in foreign affairs, which were becoming his hobby, and his wise and commonly judicious judgment of human beings.

Both Gladstone and Disraeli, the rival stars of Toryism and Liberalism, held the highest opinions of his abilities, and blamed his shortcomings largely on the intractable attitude of the Queen. Both statesmen were glad to inform him on the affairs of the moment. The doors of Marlborough House and Sandringham were open to each of them and to their wives. Gladstone, who had known Bertie since a lad, maintained a fatherly attitude toward him, and if the Prince of Wales seemed to have acquired a rudimentary knowledge of classical problems, Mr. Gladstone and not Gibbs, the tutor, was responsible. For Gladstone loved to talk of his classics anywhere and at any time to anyone, even to the fascinating and intelligent "Skittles."

Disraeli, the deeper man of the two statesmen, found his Prince Hal amusing, with a shrewdness worthy of his own. When Alix was told by Lady Ailsbury that Lord Beaconsfield (Disraeli) had praised her husband in the highest terms, speaking of his "well-used opportunities of conversing with the two masters of the destinies of Europe," she knew how to appreciate the importance of such a valuation and appeared to be deeply delighted. She believed opinions of that kind might help to kill the criticism of which she was too sadly aware. For she was, indeed, developing a hatred for gossip and scandalmongering second only to her loathing of things Teutonic, and it would soon be well known that with the Princess of Wales you must talk of things, not people, or she might snub you and avoid you ever after. In the latter years of her life this disgust of slanderous rumor, so common in her circle, grew into a passionate obsession. Framed over her bed hung a card printed with the Ninth Commandment—"Thou shalt not bear false witness."

Bertie was now approaching middle age—he was thirty-eight at the turn of the decade—and as he grew in years he was acquiring with increasing flesh a certain pomposity which so easily comes to a man much deferred to and admired in a wide circle of his own. He was eager to learn facts from others, but his opinions were unshakably those of the Prince of Wales. He valued himself the more for being crushed in the matter of his birthright. Criticism, though he might secretly think it not unjustified, enraged him and sometimes genuinely hurt him. He was above it. On the threshold of the 'eighties his circle knew that, if you wished to keep the close friendship of the Prince of Wales, you must never overstep the mark with a familiarity, however innocent. Nobody minded this childishness in "Teddy." If he was rude, irritated or impatient, he would soon recover himself if you took no notice. "Teddy" was a lovable man, but he was becoming rather spoiled.

There was, however, one characteristic of Bertie which must sometimes have given pain both to his wife, his friends and to those who faithfully waited upon him. This was on rare occasions an exhibition of cold rage which might become truly terrifying. A minor manifestation of this underground fire could be perceived by the discerning if he was too brusquely contradicted, and might become much more obvious if he thought himself unjustifiably crossed in any way. They may have suspected that scenes of an epic character sometimes occurred in the private apartments of Sandringham and Marlborough House between a wife so unshakably obstinate and careless and a husband so precise and used to omnipotency.

One extraordinary tale has been told of the temper of the Prince of Wales, and it is so unusual that it may be true. He was at dinner at some country house party, and an unhappy footman in serving the royal guest splashed a little creamed spinach on his shirt front. The guests watched with horrified eyes while the Prince of Wales thrust his hand into the dish of spinach and, flaming with rage, rubbed a handful of spinach in circles all over his starched front. He darted to his feet, muttering, "May as well make a complete job of it!" and in a petrified hush strode from the dining room. He reappeared later in the evening in a perfectly unruffled temper.

$\mathcal{C}$hapter 20

ARCHBISHOP—PRAY FOR MARLBOROUGH HOUSE

$\mathcal{E}$ARLY IN MAY 1880 Eddy and George returned from the West Indies, and their mother was able to have her sons with her for just over two months. They rejoined the *Bacchante* on July 19. Perhaps Eddy was a little sad to leave his mother, but the obvious eagerness of the boys to be gone to the sights of Australia, Japan, India, the Holy Land, Egypt and Greece seems to have been rather distressing to Alix.

At the outset the second tour appeared as if it were not going according to plan. News had reached the Waleses that the little fleet which accompanied the *Bacchante* had reached the Falkland Islands on their way to Australia, when an Admiralty order must have come to Alix, at least, as a sharp blow. The first Boer War had broken out at the Cape. The *Bacchante*'s squadron was ordered to proceed immediately to South Africa, and to land a Naval Brigade with guns to proceed on active land service under the local commander in chief. Midshipmen of the Princes' age would be marching with this shore party, and it was generally assumed that the Princes would go with them. The country was thrilled at this prospect. Their father was eager for it, saying nothing could do them more good, and they should certainly go. He would very much have liked to have gone himself. Alix entirely agreed that it would be the right thing for Eddy and George to take part, and probably only Charlotte Knollys knew her true feelings. But for the Queen, there can be no doubt that Eddy and George would have returned to the Cape. Her Majesty's letter to Alix on the occasion makes things plain.

"My darling Alix,

"I am very sorry Bertie should have been sore about the boys; but I think he must have forgotten the *arrangements* and *conditions* and *instructions* respecting their going to sea. I, and even Bertie and you, only consented to their *both* going to sea for their *education* and *moral training.* This being the case—the *Bacchante* going to the Cape, which was done in a hurry without one consultation with me (I disapproved)—and feeling how valuable these two *young* lives are to the *whole nation,* I felt *bound* to protect them against useless and unnecessary exposure in a cruel *Civil War*—for so it is, the Boers being my subjects, and it being a rule that Princes of the Royal Family *ought not* to be mixed in it. In any other war, should in time there be one (when Georgie be older) and his ship be *obliged necessarily* to take part in it, I would quite agree with Bertie. Pray show this to him, as I am sure he and everyone would agree in this being the *right course."*

Thus, the *Bacchante* was instructed to sail on alone to Australia. It was perhaps as well that Eddy and George did not take part in the "Civil War," since so far as their country was concerned it was short, disastrous and ignominious, ending with the rout, massacre and cowardly surrender at Majuba Hill and Gladstone's patched peace, which made many Britons hang their heads.

In October 1880 nephew Willy of Germany was in England. He was twenty-one and had engaged himself to Augusta Victoria, "Dona," the daughter of the exiled Frederick of Augustenburg, the Schleswig-Holstein pretender, who had been foiled by the schemes of Bismarck. Willy had come to stay with "Dona's" uncle, Prince Christian, who had married Princess Helena and lived at Cumberland Lodge, Windsor. He received an invitation from Uncle and Aunt Wales to stay at Sandringham for his uncle's birthday.

When Willy arrived at Sandringham, Bertie, and Alix presently, had to admit with puzzled discomfort that Willy had changed since the confirmation. Bertie was genial and avuncular. But there was no denying that Willy was on guard against his uncle. The suite and guests were startled to hear the young German prince "take up" the words of the Prince of Wales in a way which they knew would have stirred a deep underground eruption had it come from another. To Aunt Alix the manner of Willy was fluctuating and uncertain. Strangers to him, who were at Sandringham, thought him a "puppy."

The truth was that Willy was fresh from his military training under arrogant Junker officers. He was practicing the Junker swagger, which was entirely in tune with his own crippled nature; he had learned to worship military conquest, to despise the English military officer, of whom he considered his uncle a sleek and fatuous specimen. He came to them, also, fresh from the Berlin Foreign Office under Bismarck and his son Herbert. Bismarckian tutelage had exposed to him his mother as the *Engländerin* who sought to direct Germany in accordance with letters received from her mother Queen Victoria and her brother the Prince of Wales. It had, moreover, roused in his warped mentality a resistance to his mother's meddling and moralizing with himself, a scorn at her preachings about England, and a fury that she had driven his father the Crown Prince out of the old German ways. Willy was beginning to hate his strong-willed and voluble mother, and with her her English relations; all except grandmother Queen Victoria, whom he could never hate. He was before the threshold of the nightmare years of hyena loathing and love for England, which brought him at last in babbling impotent despair to the War of 1914.

At Sandringham that November of 1880 came the first tangible sign. Two days before his uncle's birthday Willy, without warning, without giving any reason, ordered his luggage to be packed, and departed from Sandringham.

It was such extraordinary behavior that his uncle did not take it seriously. The Prince of Wales was bubbling with geniality when he attended his nephew's wedding in the Berlin Schloss in the following February. But the absence of the Princess of Wales from the Berlin ceremony, for which there was no satisfactory excuse offered, was believed, at least in England, to be the direct result of her nephew's rudeness in the previous autumn.

Bertie had barely reached home after the German wedding than dreadful news arrived from Russia on March 14. Czar Alexander II when returning from a review to the Winter Palace had been blown to pieces by a bomb thrown under his carriage.

Dagmar was now Czarina of Russia. Since the previous day when the horrible assassination had taken place she had been Empress Marie Fedorovna. It was only with slow and shocked realization that Alix understood her dearest sister was really Empress of Russia.

It is a heavy task to find oneself suddenly to be sovereign of any country. It was a grim, dire and dreaded infliction indeed to assume the Imperial Crown of Russia in the latter half of the nineteenth century, and none knew this better than the ruling Romanoffs. In friends and kinsmen it was a matter for commiseration. In the helpless victim it called for courage of steel, nerves of ice and a strong measure of fatalism.

On March 16 Lord Granville, the Foreign Secretary, received a note from the Prince of Wales. "I feel firmly convinced that we *ought* to go to St. Petersburg. Everyone I have spoken to expects that I am going." We need not doubt that "everyone" approached him with that cheerfully expectant air which people do adopt when somebody else is about to embark on some risky mission. Granville also believed the Waleses should go; but he doubted what the Queen might say. Alfred, Duke of Edinburgh, Bertie's brother and the husband of the new Czar's sister, had reached St. Petersburg the day after Bertie had written to Granville. He telegraphed home that the Czar and Czarina very much wished for the presence of the Princess of Wales. Alix felt she must go to her sister in this time of trouble. The danger to royal persons in the Russian capital was well known. The police were known to have traitors in their ranks, and even the secret police were said to harbor a network of conspirators. It is not surprising that the Queen hesitated on this occasion; yet her ministers were so strongly of the opinion that this was an occasion when her son might use his gifts to bring about a better understanding between England and Russia that she gave her consent.

Bertie and Alix left London on March 21 and reached the snow-covered Russian capital four days later. Alix would bring with her only one lady in waiting, Charlotte Knollys; for she was the only unmarried one with no close dependents. The faithful Dighton Probyn also accompanied them, and he was to spend much of his time wiring to the Queen that another quiet day had passed, that the Prince and Princess were safe and heavily guarded. From the moment they reached St. Petersburg they were, in fact, little better than prisoners. They were taken to the Anitchkoff Palace, and the head of the secret police informed them that provided they never appeared in public near the Czar and Czarina he believed he could promise them their safety.

St. Petersburg was a city of terror and suspicion, and in the snowy streets where the endless gloomy processions of obsequies seemed to drag their untidy way to and fro for day after day, the onlookers watched tensely, starting back at an unfamiliar sound. How far the Nihilists were prepared to go was revealed only later.

At last the slow, fantastic obsequies were finished, and Alexander and Dagmar were brought from the Winter Palace to join Bertie and Alix at the Anitchkoff. Alexander III, handsome and amiable, whose giant bulk belied his weak resolve, seemed truly comforted by the cheerful company of the Prince of Wales. He wrote to Queen Victoria to tell her so. Dagmar—Marie Fedorovna—the resolute partner of this couple, was destined to be a hard Traditionalist for a daughter of freedom-loving Denmark. One day she would be blamed for the Russian Revolution. Yet, perhaps, with the wavering Alexander, her ways were forced upon her.

At the Anitchkoff in a private ceremony Bertie invested Alexander III with the insignia of the Garter. Alix was filled with dismay to observe the life which Dagmar and her husband were now doomed to live. No wonder it seemed hard to bring a smile to the lips of the grim giant whose destiny had made him Czar of all the Russias. At home, Alix might go shopping whenever she pleased, and almost unescorted. But at the Anitchkoff, as a letter of Bertie's informed his mother, Alexander and Dagmar had only a narrow backyard "worse than a London slum" in which they could safely take exercise in the open air. Even in their Black Sea villa at Livadia they would need an army to guard them, and then their safety was far from assured. The only freedom in their lives would be the Christmas visits to Denmark to the family parties at Fredensborg.

Bertie and the Duke of Edinburgh departed in a train bristling with armed men on March 31, and a sigh of relief went up from all those who knew the real state of affairs when the Russian snows lay behind them. The leading men in the government were well pleased with the Prince's efforts both with the new Czar and leading Russian statesmen. All reports went to show that by his personality alone, since he went empty-handed, he had changed the entire outlook in Anglo-Russian relations. Alix stayed on for another week with Dagmar and Charlotte Knollys, and Dighton Probyn remained with her. She did not confine herself to the Anitchkoff, and it was said that the people in the streets seemed delighted that she had come among them.

Several conspiracies were exposed by the secret police while the Prince and Princess of Wales were still in Russia. A house was discovered stored with peasant caps, each fitted with a bomb, which cheering enthusiasts were intended to hurl toward passing royalty. But nothing better illustrates the dangers of Russia and the ruthless ingenuity of the Nihilists than the plot of Boganowitsh, the contractor, discovered prior to the Coronation a few months after their departure. Boganowitsh held the contract to install an extensive electric light circuit in the Winter Palace. As royalty entered, the lights of the circuit were to flash up. At the same time Boganowitsh's bombs, wired into the circuit, were to be exploded by the current.

The season of 1881 had one unique sensation for the Marlborough House set. One of its most colorful members, the idol of society and the ornament of every picture-shop window, made her debut on the London stage. Stage people were then only on the fringe of high life. Their origins and respectability were uncertain. They were the only artists who rarely found their way into society. Henry Irving was marching to glory at the Lyceum, well launched on his ardent campaign to make the stage an honored profession, and in twelve more months the impact of Irving, armed with the friendship of the Prince of Wales, would smash down all barriers. But in 1881 the appearance of Mrs. Langtry at the Haymarket was an event in the Marlborough House circle.

Lily Langtry and her improvident Irish husband in their efforts to vie with the wealth of the landed aristocracy had ruined themselves. Abandoned by her husband, Mrs. Langtry retired to Jersey; but with the 'eighties she was back in London apartments, and soon she was once again the guest in half the great houses in the land.

Mrs. Langtry was frank. She did not know what she was going to do, but she knew that in order to stay among her friends she would have to do something for a living. Some people suggested flower-market gardening, others fashionable dressmaking. Mrs. Henry Labouchère, who was an ex-actress, wife of the celebrated Radical M.P., supplied the answer. She set to work to train the Jersey Lily for the London stage.

Mrs. Langtry took the stage at the Haymarket, at a benefit matinee for the Theatrical Fund, playing Kate Hardcastle in *She Stoops to Conquer,* with a supporting cast of famous actors and actresses. The promise of her appearance drew the Prince and Princess of Wales to the royal box and packed the house with blue-blooded families. But at rehearsals the Bancrofts, the lessees of the Haymarket, had been so impressed by Mrs. Langtry that they had offered her the leading part in *Ours,* the celebrated Crimean melodrama which they were reviving in the New Year. This performance by one of their set took on added interest for the spectators by the knowledge that this might herald the start of a tremendous stage career.

Thus, by accident almost, the Jersey Lily embarked on a course which brought her the frenzied adulation of British and American audiences, and eventually made her the leading lady on the British Turf and one of the most celebrated sporting companions of the Prince of Wales.

A stage career to some extent cut Mrs. Langtry off from society by the hours which it imposed upon her. But her five o'clock week-day dinners were often little salons, where the Prince of Wales, Mr. Gladstone, Whistler, Lady Lonsdale, the Earl of Warwick, "Harty-Tarty" Hartington (8th Duke of Devonshire), Millais and Oscar Wilde, to name but a few of a notable company, were at times to be met with, and where curious foreign royalty, such as King Leopold of Belgium, the Empress of Austria and the ill-starred Crown Prince Rudolph of Austria, later to be involved in the Mayerling tragedy, made their calls on the Jersey Lily.

It is not without interest, Mrs. Langtry tells us herself, that many of the best objects in her Norfolk Street house had reappeared at her new apartments, despite the brokers' men who had done their best to ravage Norfolk Street. She reveals the reason. At Norfolk Street, before her flight, many exalted friends had left the house, after calling to sympathize, carrying off her most cherished goods hidden under their coats or mantles. Others had bought her possessions and now returned them. Even an "unlucky" stuffed peacock was once again a feature of the Langtry establishment.

On August 4, 1881, news came that *H.M.S. Bacchante* was off St. Albans Head. The Princes' tour was ended. Next day Bertie and Alix went to sea in a corvette to greet the *Bacchante*. As the corvette drew near they recognized the two midshipmen on duty at the head of the gangway. They were Eddy and George. Their mother noted with delight as they reached the deck that "Eddy had shot up to be taller than his father." This achievement of the eldest son was perhaps less pleasing to the Prince of Wales. But he, in any case, was more interested in the robust and livelier George.

The month of February 1882 was destined, thanks to the Prince and Princess of Wales, to be an epochal month in the history of the stage, for in that month Henry Irving and fifteen of the leading London actors were commanded to dine with the Prince and Princess of Wales at Marlborough House. Respectability had reached the profession at last. Squire Bancroft, the senior actor-manager, as was fitting, sat in honor on the right hand of the Prince of Wales; but all the guests knew that the man who had really brought this about, the man who was the lion of the Prince and Princess, was forty-four-year-old Henry Irving, the strange mystic of the Lyceum. Perhaps such an odd figure had never stood at the door of Marlborough House as the lean and lanky genius with the dark burning eyes and the monstrous shining top hat with its broad curly brim perched over a mop of shoulder-length hair. The Prince and Princess always appeared at the Lyceum at a new Irving production; and before that evening was out Henry Irving had learned that perhaps his royal hosts would like to sup with him in his celebrated Beefsteak Room, which he had established to entertain his friends in the back of the Lyceum.

In June came the military outbreak of Arabi Pasha at Alexandria, the massacre of Europeans and the bombardment of Alexandria by the British fleet. The Canal had to be secured and the lives of foreigners in Egypt made safe against the frantic natives. An expeditionary force was ordered to Egypt, and judging by the threats of Arabi they would certainly see active service. The Guards Brigade was under orders and the Prince of Wales was their colonel in chief. At last this was Bertie's chance, and Alix did not discourage him from seizing it. He informed the Queen and the Duke of Cambridge, the commander in chief, that he would proceed to Egypt with his regiments. It was no good. Contrary to the healthy custom of Continental armies, the next-in-the-British-succession did not take the field. This time the Queen had the backing of all her ministers. The appointment of his young brother, the Duke of Connaught, to command the Guards Brigade was secretly a bitter humiliation to him. But on this occasion the Queen did write a full explanation to her eldest son in an appreciative and understanding vein.

Yet June did provide one little incident of light relief, which gave Bertie and Alix something to laugh about at an otherwise tedious official visitation. They went to Leicester for Alix to plant an oak tree in the newly opened Abbey Park, and were received with the pomp and lavishness then usual on such occasions. The unforeseen happening so painful to the city fathers is best described in the words of the *Illustrated London News* correspondent in the issue of June 10:

"There was but one incident of a slightly disagreeable character: a tipsy fellow thrust himself close up to the carriage of their Royal Highnesses, and insisted upon asking the Princess to shake hands with him. He was instantly hustled away, and consigned to the police, who next day brought him before the Mayor and magistrates: they inflicted a sentence of twenty-one days' imprisonment. But when the Prince and Princess read of this in the daily newspaper they graciously telegraphed to the Mayor, begging that the foolish man should be forgiven and he was accordingly released."

The correspondent does not make it perfectly clear if the "foolish man" actually reached the hand of the Princess, or whether he was hustled off with outstretched arm, but if he did touch her we may assume that Alix greeted him with cheerful equanimity.

It was early in 1883 that Edward White Benson, obedient to the Queen's invitation, left the See of Truro to become Archbishop of Canterbury. At twenty-nine he had been chosen by Prince Albert as headmaster of his new public school, Wellington College, and since those days the Queen was in the habit of ending her letters to him "ever yours affectionately." Archbishop Benson held broad views. Of a distinguished family himself, he knew everyone, and doubtless he held his own opinions about the manner of living of certain influential sections of society and the possible inspiration for ill these might give to the young in all strata.

But the new Archbishop must have felt it almost an unfair decree of Providence that in the very first months of his difficult archiepiscopate he should be called upon to tackle one of the most delicate problems that he could envisage.

Archbishop Benson received a letter from Lady Tavistock asking if she might bring to Lambeth a small party of ladies to discuss with him a confidential matter pertaining to his high office. He recognized this as a request to receive a deputation—his first as Archbishop—and since nearly all the ladies wishing to interview him bore titles he admitted to himself that this was the last direction from which he would have expected such an advance.

The ladies who presented themselves at Lambeth with Lady Tavistock were the Duchess of Leeds, the Marchionesses of Bristol and Ailsa, the Countesses of Aberdeen, Zetland, Haddington and Stanhope, Ladies Mount-Temple, Muncaster, Harriet Ashley, Welby-Gregory, Mrs. Lowther and Mrs. Reginald Talbot. Most of them were on the young side and he knew them for the more earnest members of their class.

The late E. F. Benson, the celebrated son of Archbishop Benson, has clearly recorded the object of this aristocratic deputation.

"With the best and highest of motives," says he, "they had come to ask my father if he could do nothing to stop the moral rot, which, they affirmed, was ruining London. Girls newly 'come out', they said, of high tone and upright intentions, were speedily corrupted by it, and what they had been brought up to regard as evil they soon regarded as natural and inevitable; young married women had no standard of morality at all, and the centre of the mischief was the Marlborough House set. They wanted my father to start a sort of moral mission for women of their class and to hold devotional meetings for them at Lambeth. . . ."

The meetings were the simplest part of the ladies' suggestion. But they also wanted him to interview the Prince of Wales, with whom he was well acquainted, and point out to him that he was not giving at all the right kind of lead to those around him. "He will listen to nobody but you," they solemnly declared. Thirdly, they wished the Archbishop to invite the Princess of Wales to attend these religious meetings. "Nobody else was so smart—even the Queen would not be so good!"

The third request seemed to make the second impossible. If the Prince was rebuked by the Archbishop and his wife was then recruited as a patron of the Lambeth prayer meeting it would look like asking the Princess to take part against her husband. Edward White Benson believed that such direct approach often worked the opposite way to that intended. He assured the deputation he would give the whole matter careful thought and would shortly tell them his plans.

His final decision was that he would start the prayer meetings at Lambeth immediately—a short service followed by an informal address—and that he would continue this series year after year. He would also invite the Princess of Wales to attend, fully explaining to her the general object of the meetings. But he did not consider himself justified in going directly to the Prince, since he could offer him no reason for doing so except a lot of uncircumstantiated gossip.

The Archbishop's invitation to Alix to attend the meetings in Lambeth Chapel may perhaps have given her pain. Carefully phrased as this doubtless was, it had to disclose the purpose of the gatherings, and she could scarcely have failed to see a finger pointing toward Marlborough House. She replied that she would very much like to attend and she believed such meetings might do much good if conducted by such an eminent public figure as the Archbishop. But there was no previous example of royalty coming to anything of quite this sort. She was going to consult Her Majesty before she would give an answer.

The Queen, who had once declared that "there was no Lent" in her younger days, was a devotionally orthodox but not an imaginatively religious woman and appeared to be really angry at her daughter-in-law's suggestion—quite speechless. At last she exclaimed, "I can't understand why princesses should want to go to Lambeth meetings." Then she paused for further thought. "It's all sacerdotal," she declared. "I can't think what it's all about!" There was no getting round that. The Queen's mind was honestly perplexed. She disapproved. The Princess of Wales was unable to come to the Lambeth meetings; but she wished them well. The Archbishop's meetings did, indeed, prosper in the sense that Lambeth Chapel was packed to the doors by fashionable ladies of all ages for many years to come; but though the Lambeth influence may have preserved certain individuals from behaving in a worse manner than they might otherwise have done, no notable change appeared in the ways of aristocratic society, and there would be further occasions when Archbishop Benson would be troubled by the name of the Prince of Wales.

In February, Bertie arrived in Berlin to be the guest of Vicky and Fritz during their silver wedding celebrations. Alix had declined their invitation. The silver wedding festivities of the Crown Prince and Princess were very magnificent and traditionally Prussian, and the affability of the Prince of Wales was highly appreciated in Berlin, where the family of the *Engländerin* were always watched with a secret suspicion. Even nephew Willy was full of friendliness to his uncle after being presented with a full Highland costume of Royal Stuart tartan. In this he strode about in great delight at the fancy dress balls and aroused in Berlin ballrooms exactly that kind of sensation which suited his nature. So pleased was he that he had himself photographed for the benefit of his friends. It may be many Continental friends were impressed by the portrait of the statuesque young Berlin Highlander, whose mustache tips were already turning upward, and may even have admired the enigmatic words he had written below in ink on each portrait, *"I bide my time";* but Willy's Highland picture did not receive an honored place at Marlborough House or Sandringham.

March of that year brought an event which alerted the entire nation, and not least the Prince and Princess of Wales. On the morning of the 28th the newspapers announced that Mr. John Brown had died suddenly of erysipelas in his room in the Clarence Tower at Windsor.

It is scarcely an exaggeration to say that a kind of fearful hush fell in the land, like that which had fallen at the death of the great Consort. Neither man had been loved, but the shock of their deaths registered on the public for exactly the same reason in each case: the blind devotion, the almost total reliance, which the Queen was understood to rest first upon the one, then on the other. This time the Queen could not fall into the arms of her family for commiseration. Even the Prime Minister, Mr. Gladstone, who had suffered much offense from the late Brown, thought it fitting to write the Queen a suitable letter of sorrow; but he clumsily spoilt it by the expressed hope that she would find *another* to take his place. Indeed, the royal family found it hardest of all to sorrow with their mother in her loss.

Bertie was silent, and would have remained so if Alix had not persuaded him to change his mind. He was triumphant, and declared his satisfaction to his circle, and Alix must have sighed with relief; for too often John Brown had been an acid irritant which had burned into the tranquillity of her domestic hearth. To Bertie, the great usurper, the footman who had held the place in the affections, and probably in the confidence, of his mother which he should have held, was gone: the sodden flunky who had besmirched the Throne and befooled the Queen with spiritualistic claptrap could no more bar him from the Royal Closet. Bertie flamed with a vicious jealousy against this Scotsman such as he never knew for any other in his life, not even for the Emperor William II.

But if Bertie rejoiced, the death of Brown quickly brought a grave embarrassment to the Waleses: one totally unforeseen and truly of an appalling description for the difficulties it presented. Scarcely had the Queen with her friend the ex-Empress Eugénie—another admirer of Brown—laid their wreaths on the coffin in Clarence Tower, than Her Majesty declared that she was about to write the life of John Brown for publication. As an author she had been much encouraged by the reception of her two volumes of *Life in the Highlands.*

Members of the Government, everybody about the Throne, heard of the determination of the Queen with incredulous dismay. In matters of State the Queen after arduous toil could usually be coaxed or inveigled out of her set opinions; in personal matters she was an ogress. But this was impossible, and, moreover, her *Life in the Highlands,* with its constant naïve references to the comforts and activities of "dear good Brown," gave a sinister indication of how a full-length biography of her personal footman written by her own hand would appear to the public and to foreigners. The Queen had been latterly gaining popularity and high respect as she made more frequent public appearances. The "Mrs. Brown" days were long dead, but if this happened she might soon become the "Widow Brown," and all would be lost.

Mr. Gladstone, the Prime Minister, the person whose advice should have held greatest weight with the Sovereign, was the least suited to approach her with success on this delicate theme. She hated him, and made no secret of it, and had fought so obstinately to keep him from office that she had almost stirred up a grave constitutional crisis. The ponderous advice of Gladstone would only set the Queen in her determination. It was well-nigh hopeless for Bertie to approach, since his mother perfectly understood his feelings toward Brown. It was a bewildering and excessively painful task even for "darling Alix" to venture. Great courtiers shuddered at the prospect of going to the Queen on such a mission, and ladies of the Household were as reluctant.

A veil is drawn over the details of what followed. Everyone who mattered is supposed to have broached the matter to the Queen in their own manner, stressing more or less diffidently the injudiciousness of her intention. She was not indignant, only puzzled and injured; and, unmoved, pursued her work on the life of Brown. At last a quite unimportant person outside the Court was prevailed upon to battle with the Queen. He was Dean Stanley of Windsor. She admired his sermons, and he had the added advantage of having married her ex-favorite lady in waiting. Stanley was more than an hour in the Closet. He had no comment to make when he came out. Her Majesty required time for reflection. No more was heard of the Life of John Brown.

It was on May 8, 1883, that Henry Irving was empowered to carry out a project which he had looked forward to ever since he had dined at Marlborough House in the previous year. As an after-theater host the now almost fabulous actor with his Beefsteak Room was famous. Even the great Gladstone, prior to a beefsteak supper, had once mingled with the supers on the stage during the *Corsican Brothers,* and had been delighted to be recognized and cheered by a Lyceum audience. Now Irving had been informed that the Prince and Princess of Wales would like to sup with him after the performance of *Much Ado About Nothing*. The Beefsteak Room had been suggested, but the apartment was scarcely ambitious enough. Supper for fifty guests was ordered to be set out on the stage by Gunter's the instant the last curtain fell at the Lyceum, and the army of stagehands whom Irving always employed were enjoined, instead of going home after removing his monumental scenery, to embellish the Lyceum stage with several hundred pounds' worth of decorations.

Irving and Ellen Terry received the royal guests in the Beefsteak Room, while the sceneshifters, less careful than during performance, caused the crowded stage to rumble and clatter. The supper guests were the leading members of the Lyceum cast, other prominent stage personalities, the American Ambassador and a number of stage-struck men of title. Though in appearance the stage supper party suggested a ceremonial occasion, the spirit at the table was lighthearted and without restraint, giving the Prince of Wales and Henry Irving, the two best impromptu speakers in the kingdom, a brilliant opportunity to outrival each other.

As the middle 'eighties approached, the family gatherings in Denmark at Fredensborg Palace were becoming very lively occasions. Alix nearly always came to the summer parties as well as the winter ones, and in the summer Bertie sometimes put in an appearance for a few days between his other Continental engagements. For, with so many nephews and nieces on hand, the tone of life in King Christian's palace was excessively noisy and undisciplined, lacking that air of settled dignity and those openings for earnest discussion which the Prince of Wales was coming to prefer.

Even his brother-in-law, "dear Sacha," Czar of All the Russias (Alexander III), whom he knew to be so grim, autocratic and unapproachable in St. Petersburg, irritated him at Fredensborg, where like a vast elephantine boy the Czar plunged about with the young people, squirting them with garden hoses and delighted to be drenched himself. Alix loved every minute of these caperings.

At this time these rowdy reunions might consist of King George and Queen Olga of Greece with their four boys and three girls ranging from sixteen to two, the Waleses and their family, aged fifteen to twenty, Czar Alexander and Dagmar with their four children, the seven children of Crown Prince Frederick and Louise of Denmark, and Thyra with her husband the Duke of Cumberland, with their four eldest. Ernest of Cumberland, the exiled King of Hanover, a brother-in-law much liked by Alix for his downright undignified ways—he so hated evening dress that he changed into his old leather shorts and Tyrolean jacket after dinner—was the very antithesis of Bertie, and disturbed him accordingly. There was probably Waldemar with his French Orléanist bride, the only Catholic of the family, and various elderly aunts and uncles on the Glucksburg side, all very lively and talkative for their years. It was a "babel," as the Prince of Wales so often declared in his letters home.

The late Prince Nicholas of Greece, father of the present Duchess of Kent, the favorite Greek nephew of Aunt Alix, as his daughter Marina was later her favorite grandniece, has left on record some amusingly typical pictures of the Princess of Wales in Copenhagen in those days.

One morning they all decided to visit the Copenhagen Zoo. The entrance of this excited company of royalty to the monkey house without any ceremony or noticeable police protection naturally drew a vast crowd. The monkey house was packed to the doors with curious spectators and people surged outside. Dagmar, who as the fabulous Czarina of Russia was a figure of especial wonder to the Danes, happened to be wearing a new straw hat piled with imitation cherries. With the Princess of Wales she approached very close to the bars of a cage. The two beautiful sisters were, so to speak, the apex of a great circle of attentive people.

A small monkey thrust its hand through the bars and firmly gripped the cherries. The hat, attached by an elastic band round the back hair, jerked toward the delighted monkey; but the elastic band held firm. Clutching at the brim, Dagmar backed away, crying hysterically to her sister for help. Alix, equally hysterical, pulled at Dagmar, and a frenzied seesaw tug-of-war began in front of the cage. The circle of royalties tumbled against one another in convulsions of weeping delight; while the Czarina and the Princess screamed for aid, the commoners in shocked amazement waited motionless in the background in dutiful silence.

There was a day at Fredensborg when Nicholas and his brother George summoned Aunt Alix and the Czarina to their bedroom, thrust them hastily into dressing gowns, pushed top hats on their heads, and stretched the astonished visitors under the bedclothes with orders not to move. The boys hurried to old King Christian, who was always encouraging them to collect curiosities. They assured him that they had some very strange curiosities in their room which they thought he should see. In all seriousness the royal patriarch arose, praising his grandsons for their perseverance in the fascinating hobby he had recommended, and proceeded with several elderly guests toward the bedroom.

The King stopped in the doorway, glaring in amazement at the two top-hatted strangers in the beds, and fumbling for his spectacles. Momentarily he seemed to believe that these had invaded the bedroom after his grandsons had left it. So happy-go-lucky was the routine of the royal palace that this was not, in fact, quite impossible.

Such were the lighthearted ways in the home of Alix's Danish parents—a striking contrast to the life which crept about Bertie's mother at Windsor.

The season of 1884 brought to Marlborough House a fresh personality, who, in his time, would be a figure of significance in the Wales family. He was a lean, swarthy man with dark glowing eyes, elegant in his gait and dress, but so ugly and so blue about the chin that they would soon nickname him the "Blue Monkey." He was Luis Marquis de Soveral, who had arrived in London to be Portuguese Secretary of Legation.

Luis de Soveral never spoke to a woman but he won her heart. Men of the Anglo-Saxon breed were, perhaps, bewildered by him; but his popularity with the ladies soon made him one of the most frequently met guests in high life, in town or country, and the "Blue Monkey" would hold his honored place in society till long after the century had ended. At last, this strongly marked Latin would be more English than the English, except in appearance and in a measure of poised and suave wisdom which earned him a unique place for a foreigner in Edwardian days as a power—and a respected and unresented power—behind the Throne. Before that time the "Blue" Marquis would have graduated to the Portuguese ambassadorship, have lost his post in the Portuguese revolution, and, rather than accept employment from his republican government, have chosen to stay as a private person at the side of his close friend

King Edward VII. Soveral used to be puzzled by the lighthearted attitude which his royal friend seemed to adopt toward his various unofficial diplomatic feats in Europe, for he could not understand the difficulties and frustrations put in the way of the Prince of Wales by his mother. It was Soveral who once said wonderingly to him in front of several hearers, *"Vous êtes un grand diplomate, un homme d'état remarquable et vous l'ignorez!"*

From the first, Bertie took to this clever Portuguese, since he had all the colorful Continental qualities which so appealed to him, and Alix found the Marquis as amusing and attentive as did other women. It was said of Bertie that, although some of his friends might be questionable, his judgment of men was so true that he never chose a near friend who was not sound, and since in the endless memoirs of late Victorian and Edwardian days the "Blue Monkey" so constantly strolls out of the pages with a cool smile, which always seems to be welcome, it may be assumed that in his Portuguese friend he chose well.

In September an interesting, although perhaps not overwelcome, guest at Abergeldie—at least to Alix—came over from Balmoral to make an enthusiastic stay. This was Herbert Bismarck, son of a mighty father, and intended to succeed the ageing man of blood and iron in the guidance of the greater Germany he had created. This for Herbert Bismarck was the end of two years spent in Britain: a period at Balmoral with the Queen and a visit to the Prince of Wales at Abergeldie. Herbert was no lover of England: he had played his part at the Berlin Foreign Office in corrupting Prince William against his English mother and against the people of her island. He had spent two years in a round of England's best houses and in earnestly cultivating her leading men. For a spy, planted by his father to learn the ways of those whom he saw as the most dangerous and underhand people in Europe, Herbert Bismarck had been well received.

Herbert, with that duality of thinking so characteristic of the German, was during this Scottish sojourn at the same time enjoying a richly sentimental delight in the picturesque life of Abergeldie and sounding his royal host with a persistent smile of cunning animosity. He departed to write in florid terms of his "beautiful memories of Abergeldie" to the man whom he had decided was becoming, and shortly would be, a sinister and unfathomable power in European politics.

There had been at Balmoral in September another guest, whom the Queen quite unexpectedly seems to have found more uncongenial than Herbert Bismarck. This was her Lord Lieutenant for Ireland, Lord Spencer. The reason for Her Majesty's sudden distaste was the earnestness with which Lord Spencer set out to persuade her that a full ceremonial visit and tour of the Prince and Princess of Wales through Ireland would be of the greatest benefit in the unhappy state of affairs then existing.

Who could blame the Queen for her reluctance this time? Only two years before, Lord Frederick Cavendish, Chief Secretary for Ireland, and Mr. Burke, Permanent Secretary, had been savagely murdered in daylight in Phoenix Park in sight of Viceregal Lodge. Already fatal dynamite explosions had been caused by Fenians in London, and the police expected more to come. Ambushings, brutal assaults and house-burnings directed against the authorities were common in the bad parts of Ireland. Fenian threats by letter had been reaching Marlborough House and Sandringham for some time. In that January the Fenians had threatened to kill the Prince of Wales during his Bristol visit, and an armed desperado had been taken in lodgings at Clifton. Ireland, except when in open rebellion, had never looked more dangerous.

No wonder the Queen would have liked to avoid Lord Spencer. But she knew he was right. Romance and sentiment may act like magic on the warm hearts of the Irish. She had seen that herself with darling Albert years ago. She knew Bertie was good with the very worst kind of people, and Alix always won everybody with a smile. Their appearance at such a time might have wonderful results on the Irish. She presently found that the Government were divided about an Irish visit. All agreed that it might have the effect on the Irish which Lord Spencer promised, but many shrank from the extreme hazards: a viewpoint which fiery Irish members in the House gleefully assured them was amply justified.

But the final consensus of Government opinion submitted to the Queen in the late autumn seemed to be that Lord Spencer, whose office was an exceedingly troublesome and expensive one, ought to have his wishes met in the matter if with his knowledge of local conditions he was convinced that a royal visit ought to take place, and would promise a reasonable measure of safety for the Prince and Princess. Lord Spencer, having himself braved the Irish for several years, was hardened, and this last he optimistically declared he could do. Spencer was a personal friend of Bertie, and thus the project became known in the earliest stages to the people who were to undertake it. Only one thing could now have given the Queen an excuse to shelve the Irish visit: if she had discovered that Bertie and Alix were reluctant to embark upon such a very risky expedition for such a problematical object. But they were not; they openly proclaimed that they would most certainly go on an Irish tour, and they would take Prince Eddy with them.

Eddy had his twenty-first birthday at Sandringham on January 7, 1885, and as part of the elaborate celebrations in which the whole estate were invited to take part, Sanger's Circus, then in the height of its flamboyant glory and performing in the country, was commanded to come into Sandringham grounds, where a full performance with elephants and camels took place. Eddy was now a subaltern in his father's regiment, the 10th Hussars. A tall, gentle, rather vague young man, with much of his mother and some of the nervous earnestness of his grandfather Prince Albert apparent in him, Eddy obviously lacked stamina, which sometimes worried or irritated his robust father, of whom perhaps he was rather afraid. His beautiful mother was still everything to him.

The news of the coming Irish visit was now getting abroad. From Ireland came howls of rage and insult. Ferocious Nationalists promised their friends that their chance had come at last. The Fenians of Ireland and the U.S.A. publicly offered a reward of £2000 for the body of the Prince of Wales dead or alive. The meager amount was in itself an insult, though it might well bring results in the poverty-stricken land. The Queen was indignant and terrified. From the attempts made on her own life she knew such things were not always idle threats. She was inclined to blame the Government and Lord Spencer, who must be entirely responsible for anything that happened. She also, becoming practical, insisted that the Government must pay for everything. In January a Fenian attempt to blow up the House of Lords was discovered, and a further stock of explosive was unearthed just in time to save the Tower being blown skyward. An explosion in the Commons killed several persons.

But before they could go to Ireland a visit had to be made to Berlin. Alix found that preparations for the Irish visit gave her an excuse to avoid Berlin. In early March Bertie arrived in Berlin to attend the eighty-eighth birthday of the Emperor. His nephew seemed to him surly rather than cordial, and ready to avoid his company.

The Prince of Wales had visited Germany alone in the previous June to stay with his eldest sister. Prince William on this occasion, although his uncle was then unaware of it, had pretended to find in the transactions of the Prince of Wales an operation of machiavellian craft. Shortly after his uncle's departure in 1884 Willy had gone to Russia to stay with his cousin Czar Alexander III. What the German Prince said to the Czar while he was his guest has never been disclosed; but it was on his return that William began that series of abusive letters against his uncle which were only disclosed with the breaking open of the Russian Imperial archives after the 1918 Revolution.

The Prince of Wales, William assured the Czar, was, from his own certain knowledge, "the most formidable foe of Russia," whose anti-Russian intrigues in Germany, carried on through the Crown Princess, was still yielding "extraordinary fruits, which will continue to multiply under the hands of my mother and the Queen of England." Czar Alexander, who liked the Prince of Wales and who felt the close bond between Dagmar and Alix, did not seem to take the exaggerated tone of the letters too seriously. Nevertheless, he thought it worth while to file these venomous letters, which were always written in English. Just before the arrival of the Prince of Wales for the eighty-eighth birthday celebrations William had written to the Czar,

"we shall have the Prince of Wales here in a few days. I am not delighted by this unexpected apparition because—excuse me, he is Your brother-in-law—owing to his false and intriguing nature he will undoubtedly attempt in one way or another to push the Bulgarian business—may Allah send them to Hell, as the Turks would say—or to do a little political intriguing with the ladies."

It may be that Alix was already aware of the general nature of the abuse reaching the Czar from her German nephew, through the constant letters of her sister the Czarina, and may have revealed this to her husband; but it was only after the birthday visit that the Prince of Wales began to speak with some anxiety of his nephew, and this was partly on account of things which Vicky had told him about her son while he was in Germany.

It was in the early morning of April 7 that the Channel Squadron, escorting the royal yacht *Osborne,* anchored at Kingstown. Perhaps nerves were at stretch in the royal carriage when it began to pass through Dublin streets, but the thunderous cheers of the Dubliners, which drowned the boos and hoots, must soon have restored their confidence. The Lord Mayor of Dublin had publicly announced that he would haul down the Union Jack over the Mansion House as the royal visitors entered his city. But there was the flag fluttering bravely over the Mansion House as they approached it, and there was the Lord Mayor waiting to receive them. He was positively guilty and apologetic.

Nothing had been officially scheduled for that afternoon. But the Ballsbridge agricultural show was on; they decided to go. The mounted escort was ordered out. The Prince canceled it. They told him the police had not been warned for street duty. He said that did not matter.

They drove out into the streets en route for Ballsbridge. Struck with astonishment, the Dubliners watched the unguarded carriage pass among them. Then they cheered themselves hoarse: even the ardent Nationalists. At Ballsbridge the drink booths did better than for many years. People flocked about them, many of them drunk. The smile of the Princess of Wales did all that could be expected of it.

That night many of the most brightly illuminated shop windows were smashed by bricks. Some scenes of angry riot were dealt with by the police. It was nothing. While this went forward Bertie sat in Viceregal Lodge cheerfully writing to a friend, "You will, I am sure, be glad to hear we met with a very enthusiastic reception here today, and I confess I was surprised at the enthusiasm displayed after all that I had heard."

The Prince of Wales held a packed levee at the Castle. The Princess held a packed Drawing Room. The Prince was made a Doctor of Law at the University. The Princess was made a Doctor of Music. Her photograph in cap and gown appeared in the shop windows. People rushed to buy it. The Dublin students, famous for rabble demonstrations, wanted to unharness their horses and drag the carriage. Poor artisans in the slum districts ran with amazement to greet a royal carriage which suddenly arrived among them. The escort had stayed at home. Almost hugged in the arms of ragged Irish, they inspected the hovels shortly to be condemned and replaced by the new Government Housing Commission.

The Lord Lieutenant proudly reported to the Queen upon a welcome which had been "most genuine and hearty from all classes of the community." But even while the Queen was reading Lord Spencer's letter she had before her the intelligence reports sent from other parts of Ireland. A very grave situation might develop in Cork and the district when the royal party arrived. The provincial Nationalists, enraged by the disgusting display of the Dubliners, had sworn that they would make up for it. There were among them some very dangerous characters, who might not be contented with insulting demonstrations. Whole countrysides were preparing themselves. And the English newspapers were industriously adding fuel to the flames by crying to the housetops the glorious reception which the Irish were giving to the Prince and Princess. The Queen was informed of all the danger spots on the tour. With a map of Ireland before her she wrote out a cable to Lord Stanhope ordering changes of route. The worst places could easily be missed. All would be well.

Somebody blundered: the time for departure on tour had come. No cable had arrived. Amid the applause of the Dubliners, Bertie and Alix with their son boarded their special train and started along the original route.

They were some miles short of Mallow when a new phenomenon appeared beside the line. Groups of people were waving black flags painted with the skull and crossbones. Stones began to fly at the windows. Fists were shaken in the air. The rumbling of the train was obviously drowning the curses and howls of infuriated peasantry. There were even some with their black flags who tried to run level with the royal train in crowded jaunting cars or on donkeys.

The train drew to a standstill in Mallow. A roar as of wild beasts greeted them. The platform and the road outside were black with a mob brandishing the skull and crossbones. It was a strange reception committee which they smiled upon as they prepared to descend: three Nationalist M.P.s in old billycock hats and with faces of thunder, two full-size empty coffins, backed by a crowd which suggested the French Revolution. Suddenly the mass quivered. It surged forward. Armed Irish Constabulary hurled themselves in the way. Whether the mob meant to wreck the train, to capture the Prince and Princess or to tear them in pieces, was never known, since most of them did not know themselves. While battle raged on Mallow platform the royal train steamed from the station. Mallow was hopeless.

Through a hostile countryside they came to Cork. Cork was known as "rebel" Cork: it was supposed to be the inspiration of all these things. They were to drive through the streets of Cork. Cheers were heard at Cork. But the insults and curses often drowned them. There was at one point on their route a young Hussar officer whose men were keeping the way. He had been the little boy whose warts had been cured by the Princess of Wales. He had a special reason for adoring this goddess. When, therefore, in Patrick Street, the royal carriage drew opposite, and the Princess bowing with her sweetest smile was cursed and spat at by the people behind him, while a miniature coffin sailed past him and almost struck his Princess in the face, blind fury seized him. His action was almost as savage as the worst Irish. He slapped down his hand on the rump of his thoroughbred charger. Instantly it lashed out backward. The insults fell on a new target. Though scattered and overturned, the furious Irish escaped unhurt, and Alix heard her champion triumphantly declare his deed shortly afterward. Cork offered nothing worse than insults, to which they gave back smiles. They probably left behind them respect in the hearts of many who had cursed them. Authority heaved a sigh of earnest relief as the royal train steamed away to a well-earned rest by the lakes of Killarney. The peace of Killarney fortified them against the savages who flocked up in force to receive them in their hazardous progress through Tralee and Limerick on the return to Dublin. They had been cool and unshaken to the end; and though it seems difficult to believe that such an experience did not leave them with nerves unscathed, Alix, who often afterwards recalled "the Irish visit," used to speak as if she had enjoyed it. Perhaps the vociferous loyalty of Northern Ireland, which they experienced in generous measure before they left, seemed a tame exhibition after the earlier excitement.

"Candidly, I am inclined to think our visit has been a success, much more so than I honestly expected," ran the modest letter of the Prince of Wales to Mr. Gladstone, who had written on behalf of the Government to thank them for the task they had carried out with such courageous resolution.

Yet the Alix who could come through such an experience with cool equanimity, even apparently with a kind of enjoyment, and who would calmly face death itself in the years ahead, was a creature of hysterical emotions in the small things of life, quickly moving from tears to laughter and back again.

Her favorite nephew Nicholas of Greece told of an occasion in his boyhood, in the rose garden at Fredensborg during a family gathering in the summer, when the Princess of Wales totally abandoned her dignity.

She was carrying a tray with milk and biscuits to her mother, who had been ill and was resting among her roses, and behind the Princess came trotting her beloved Pekinese from whom she would never be separated. The rose garden was full of nephews and nieces, so that Queen Louise was not perhaps having a very peaceful time. Suddenly Constantine, Nicholas' elder brother, whirled down the path on his bicycle. His machine passed straight over the howling Pekinese.

Aunt Alix, hurling the tray from her to the ground, burst into tears, and clutching her pet to her breast danced to and fro in an agony of terror.

"He has killed my dog!—he has killed my dog!" she wailed, and people outside the rose garden could hear her cries mingled with the yelps of the indignant and uninjured Pekinese. When it was absurd any longer to proclaim his death, she frenziedly displayed her dog in all directions to show his fearful injuries. Her limp, never entirely absent, grew more marked in moments of emotion. She was inclined to totter. Her young relatives thought the scene decidedly ridiculous.

At last Nicholas, who prided himself on his mimicry, gave his aunt an imitation of herself. She stopped, broke into peals of merriment, and soon, as Nicholas persisted in his exhibition, she was swaying and weeping with laughter at herself. She was so delighted that when her nephew ceased she asked him to begin all over again. Even years afterward, when he was a grown man, she would call upon him to re-enact this drama.

Chapter 21

THE WORST SNUB OF HER LIFE

W HEN IN JUBILEE YEAR, 1887, the committee responsible for the ceremonial arrangements decided that extra color would be added to the ceremonies if Her Majesty for the first time since her widowhood should be seen in the Abbey in her Robes of State, it was generally agreed on the spot that the putting into practice of this plan might present difficulties. The opinion turned out to be correct.

The Queen indignantly repulsed every suggestion that she should don the dreaded Robes of State. Yet the idea undoubtedly was a good one. Even the Prime Minister admitted it was hopeless to go further with Her Majesty on the subject. Somebody pointed out that the Prince of Wales had not yet taken up the matter with his mother. Bertie was quite certain he would not be listened to, and frankly told them so. But there remained her Royal Highness: could the Princess of Wales help them? The Queen was supposed to have never refused anything to her daughter-in-law. The Prince thought his wife might do something.

Alix went to see the Queen. She was not long in the Royal Closet. She came out looking pink and crushed.

"I have just had the worst snub of my life," she said with a smile.

In 1887 Queen Victoria sat on a pedestal amid Olympian mists; but it is difficult to find any tangible reasons why she had reached it in the minds of her people. Whether or not her health had justified her, she had neglected them. She had even defied them. Statesmen, commanders in chief, men of affairs, knew that there were many reasons for thinking her a great Queen. The people had not even a sensational Press to stimulate them. She was Empress of India, and that had probably helped her; the story of the soft-footed Indian servants who now always crept devotedly about her had helped her; the cool and silent state she gave to her guests to save her own energy had helped her with its awful legend; but most of all, perhaps, the hunger of later Victorians to raise to themselves such an idol had helped her.

In all the pageant of plumes and color and steel which wound endlessly through the packed streets of London on June 21, Jubilee Day, where an Empire for the first time was on the march, there was one rider who seems to have arrested the dazzled crowd more than all the rest, almost more than the Queen herself. Advancing behind the royal carriage at the head of the foreign princes came a giant Wagnerian figure on a high-stepping black charger. Sunlight flashed from his brazen helm crowned by a large brazen eaglet, it glistened in the gold of his spreading beard and lighted the white purity of his uniform. All eyes followed this superb warrior who seemed to have ridden out of the mists of Germanic myth. It was Crown Prince Frederick William—he who must soon be Emperor of Germany, husband of Victoria the Princess Royal, and father of Prince William. The roaring cheers for the royal carriage bearing the Queen and his wife died as if in awe at this sight. He passed, and the cheers renewed in volume. People watched the back of the tall white figure in wondering admiration and let the other foreigners sweep by. They told each other how strange and sad his face had looked. Some said the vision of the still white horseman who gazed unflinchingly ahead was positively uncanny—as if he were a phantom from another world.

It was almost the truth. This guest of Marlborough House was balancing on the edge of his grave. The little hoarse sound that spurted from the quivering lips of this burly soldier, who spoke only when addressed, struck with horrified bewilderment those who heard it.

This was the tragic prelude to a dismal and sordid transaction into which his English brother and sister-in-law at Marlborough House were to be unwillingly dragged by circumstances. George and Olga of Greece and the gay and worldly young Crown Prince Rudolph of

Austria were also at Marlborough House, and the family party, which might have been so amusing, was sadly damped by the obvious suffering of Fritz. Everybody agreed he was the best of the Germans—the only true Liberal. Alix even believed that when he came to the Imperial throne Schleswig and Holstein would be returned to Denmark. But now they followed his painful speechlessness with baffled dismay. Fritz, unknown to himself or others, had cancer of the throat. He was to spend three months in England seeking a cure for the mysterious complaint, and then to take refuge with his wife in a Riviera villa.

It was unfortunate, since it did no good, that, in view of coming events, Bertie in the following spring went over from Cannes to the Villa Zirio at San Remo to visit his sister and the invalid Crown Prince. Thereby the Prince of Wales identified himself and his family in German minds with the "English party." The Crown Princess, who always knew best what she must do, had infuriated Germans by engaging an English throat specialist, Mackenzie, who firmly declared that the complaint was *not* cancer.

In Berlin, terrible things were happening. Prince William, inspired by Bismarck and Herbert, was proclaiming that his father was unfit to succeed, that the announcement that the Crown Prince had cancer was only being hidden by an English plot so that his mother could thereby drag his dying father to the Throne and make herself Empress to please the London gang. On the only occasion that Prince William himself appeared at Villa Zirio he openly insulted his mother on the doorstep, and he left his enfeebled father complaining that he had been treated as if he were already dead. That the Crown Princess in a last desperate hope brought herself to believe in Mackenzie's diagnosis cannot be doubted; but the old Emperor was clearly dying and the family skies loomed black with storm clouds. Thus stood affairs in the early spring of 1888.

Then on March 9 the eighty-nine-year-old Emperor died. The dying Frederick William was Emperor, and was brought to Berlin for the dreadful Hundred Days' reign.

March 9 was the eve of the Silver Wedding anniversary of Bertie and Alix. It was actually in the morning of their Silver Wedding Day that Madame Albani, the famous singer, received a brief letter from the Princess of Wales, which is very characteristic of the writer.

"My dear Mme. Albani," she wrote. "The Queen is going to dine with us on our silver wedding day, and it would be very kind if you would come in the evening at 10 o'clock and sing one little song, as you know what an admirer she is of your lovely voice. Yours very sincerely, Alexandra. (10-3-88.)"

The Queen has a Silver Wedding Day entry in her journal:

"Found all the family assembled at Marlborough House, Alix looking lovely in grey and white, more like a bride just married than a silver wedding one of twenty-five years."

The sober gray and white tones of Alix's costume were a token of the German Emperor's death on the previous day. But it was her only observance of that event. She would not accompany Bertie next morning to the Berlin funeral. She would not even attend the memorial service in London. The dead Emperor was the thief who stole Schleswig-Holstein.

The youthful appearance of Alix, which was noticed by the Queen, was becoming one of her notable features, and would presently be a thing for astonishment. She was forty-four.

It was in the autumn of this year that a diplomat, writing from Austria, tells of having seen the Princess of Wales and her three daughters at Gmunden, Hanover.

"She looked so young," says he, "and they dressed so much alike that at a little afternoon dance at the (ex) Queen of Hanover's (her sister Thyra), the unsophisticated Austrian officers, who had been invited from a neighbouring town, were always asking the mother to dance, imagining she was one of her daughters."

It must have been at about this time that young Margot Asquith, one of the most lively and celebrated debutantes of her day—she had even smoked cigars to the end—was gazing into a photographer's window in the West End when she unexpectedly found herself meeting the Princess of Wales for the first time.

Margot Asquith's impressions are interesting, for she was no sycophant. The Prince of Wales she already knew, and she was one of those bright and attractive young women of her day whom he liked to talk to at dinners, dances and race-meetings. Margot was so "original," as the Prince himself assured her, and in her memoirs she confesses that though "quite unconscious of it at the time," she was "told afterwards that people were beginning to criticize her."

On that afternoon in the West End, a footman came beside Margot and touched his hat. Behind in a carriage sat the Duchess of Manchester. "Jump in, dear child!" she invited.

"I got into her carriage," says Margot, "and we drove round Hyde Park, after which I followed her upstairs to her boudoir in Great Stanhope Street. In the middle of tea the Princess of Wales came in to see the Duchess. She ran in unannounced and kissed her hostess.

"My heart beat when I looked at her. She had more real beauty, both of line and expression, and more dignity than anyone I had ever seen; and I can never forget that first meeting."

Shortly after six o'clock on the morning of June 15 Emperor Frederick William lay dead at Potsdam. The news reached Bertie and Alix at Ascot. This time Alix would go to Berlin: from all she had heard poor Vicky would need her friends to stand by her.

Alix was right. The instant his father was dead William had slipped from the chamber. The new Emperor had orders to issue. All, even his mother, were to be prisoners. Potsdam, since the previous evening, had been quartered with strange soldiery like a hostile place. William believed, or pretended to believe, that State papers had for weeks been smuggled to London, that greater quantities would now vanish. "No one, including doctors, to carry on any correspondence with outside. . . . If anyone attempts to leave the Palace he will be arrested!" Von Doehme gives the extraordinary picture of a palace turning into a prison.

"Divisions of training battalions approached the Palace at the double; round all the terraces was a regular system of guards with guns loaded. Major von Natzmer sat ready mounted, and the moment death was announced he galloped round the Palace giving orders. Suddenly the Hussars appeared at a trot; divisions established themselves at all the gates of the Park; the Palace was, in a military sense, hermetically sealed."

Even Eulenburg, William's bosom friend, was shocked. "In the dead man's room . . . no ceremonial . . . no service . . . no thought of the religious aspect. . . ."

The coffined corpse was almost jostled along to the chapel. There, after passing through the inquisitive rings of soldiery, Bertie and Alix early on the 17th stood in the chapel while it was hastily decorated amid shouts and clatter, and according to Emil Ludwig "the coffin stood among the hammering workmen like a tool-chest."

Next day, with Bertie in German uniform, they attended the funeral, where, says Eulenburg, "the troops were undignified, the clergy were laughing and chattering. Field Marshal Blumenthal, with the Standard over his shoulder, reeling about, talking . . . it was horrible." As for the German public, they saw nothing. But for the bombastic proclamations of the new Emperor, which were startling all Europe, they could scarcely realize the old Emperor was dead.

Bertie and Alix were lodged at Charlottenburg Palace, and each day they drove through the guarded environs of Potsdam to sit with the desolate and bewildered Vicky. Alix up to that time had been apt to hold a little aloof from her sister-in-law. She whom the Germans had found too English, Alix had thought too German. But now, in this hour of Vicky's terrible trouble, the two women drew close together, and remained firm friends to the end of the Empress's life. Vicky was dominating, rather clever for Alix perhaps, but after all she had always been Bertie's favorite sister.

It was then that Bertie and Alix first heard Empress Frederick utter that sharp exclamation, "Willy is *mad!*" She would cry that out even before strangers in the years to come. To Bertie it had been a humiliating shock to perceive that his Imperial nephew saw him now as an inferior. William patronized him, and his sneers at his mother and his dead father filled his uncle with scarcely stifled rage. When Herbert Bismarck called his dead brother-in-law "an incubus" —"an ineffectual visionary"—"a dumb man unfit to rule," it became known that the Prince of Wales had lost control. Emperor William, hearing a highly colored version of his uncle's explosive words, and determined to enforce the dignity of his Imperial status, held it against him for future occasions.

Bertie and Alix returned to London on June 23, and only a fortnight later the Queen heard with incredulous amazement that her grandson, the new German Emperor, was arranging to make full State visits to the Czar of Russia and Emperor Francis Josef of Austria-Hungary in August and September. The Queen still regarded William as a child. As such she wrote to him in tones of scolding disapproval. William replied that his boyhood was past. Mourning must be ignored in the interests of Peace and of Germany. "We Emperors must stand together!" he explained. He also informed his startled grandmother that Uncle Bertie was interfering in the affairs of his mother, and was unfairly misrepresenting his own intentions towards her.

In August, when Bertie was at Homburg, his nephew the Emperor was not far distant at Frankfurt-on-Oder, where he unveiled a statue to a hero of the 1870 war. It was the occasion for a stirring speech. Everybody knew that one passage of this was straightly aimed at his uncle the Prince of Wales and his Aunt Alix, who were reputed to have been in collusion with his father in a scheme to return Schleswig-Holstein to Denmark. "There are people," cried the Emperor, glaring about him as he stood on the plinth of the statue, "who have the audacity to maintain that my father was willing to part with what he gained on the battlefield. . . . We cannot tolerate, even for a single moment, such an insult to his memory. . . . We would rather sacrifice our forty-two millions of inhabitants on the field of battle than surrender a single stone!"

The thrust went home in Homburg. But it was nothing to the mortification which poor Uncle Bertie was about to suffer. In September he was to pay a month's social visit to Emperor Francis Josef and go shooting with his friend Crown Prince Rudolph. He wrote to his nephew declaring how delightful it would be to meet him in Vienna during the State visit. As soon as he knew the date he would make arrangements to be in the capital. He got no reply.

He arrived in Vienna full of good will, dressed rather ridiculously for his figure in the gold frogging, scarlet breeches and tasseled Hessian boots of the Austrian Hussars of which he was honorary colonel. His remark in the carriage to the Austrian Emperor and his son regarding his pleasure at meeting his Imperial nephew in Vienna was listened to with embarrassment. It was hesitantly explained to him that the German Emperor had insisted that no other royalty should be in Vienna during his State visit. This was regretfully confirmed by the British Ambassador, who had it from the German Ambassador. The Emperor had declared that he would not meet his English uncle.

The dilemma of the Prince of Wales was pitiful: he cast about desperately for some means of saving face. He could not really believe it. He had never in his life suffered such a barefaced slight, and now he was forty-six and ill-equipped to bear it. By a roundabout channel he had the information conveyed to his nephew at German maneuvers through the British military attaché that the Prince of Wales was greatly looking forward to meeting his nephew at the Vienna railway station. He would be in Prussian uniform for the occasion. The German Emperor, who had always been friendly with the British military attaché, cut him dead from that hour.

There soon remained no doubt: the Prince of Wales would have to be absent from Vienna when his nephew arrived, and his friend Crown Prince Rudolph thought it would be more dignified if he were out of Austria altogether. On the eve of the German State visit, Bertie left to stay with the King and Queen of Rumania. He returned to Vienna the day after his nephew's departure to rejoin for a few days his apologetic hosts. Not only was his humiliation known all over Europe, but the Continental newspapers were hinting that the German Emperor had made his stipulation because his uncle meant to spy and interfere in his conferences with the Austrian Emperor.

In November the Empress Frederick came to England for her first stay as a widow. It was the Queen's desire that the country should show sympathy with the unhappy plight of her eldest daughter. She sent Bertie across to Flushing to meet his sister. William, as was to be expected, not only regarded his mother's visit with the deepest suspicion, but would like to have prevented it. Vicky stayed first with her mother at Windsor, and in the following January joined Bertie and Alix at Sandringham.

In February Europe was shocked by news of the mysterious deaths of Crown Prince Rudolph of Austria and his notorious mistress in the lonely hunting lodge at Mayerling. Murder or suicide—none knew; but soon grim rumors of a dual murder of the most horrible and sadistic kind were widespread. Rudolph's reputation was very bad: the Queen had always received him coldly, and the staunch friendship of the Prince of Wales and, to a lesser extent, his wife, for the worst man in Europe had filled her with impatience. The sordid tragedy, distant as it was, did no good to the Prince's public reputation, more especially as he had just returned from a shooting expedition with Rudolph.

In April the Queen came to Sandringham. Clocks returned to the proper time, and a silence seemed to enshroud the house, while turbaned Indians fluttered wraithlike in the shadows about her still figure. Henry Irving with Ellen Terry arrived to perform his most famous piece of macaberie, *The Bells,* and the trial scene from *The Merchant of Venice,* in the bowling alley.

It was at about this time that Emperor William announced that he was coming to Cowes Week; and it was characteristic of the Queen that she was surprised when her eldest son declared his categoric refusal to meet his nephew. He would not attend the Week at all. This wild-eyed recalcitrance Uncle Bertie was persuaded to drop after strenuous efforts by sympathetic relatives and friends. It was the beginning of that dramatic Cowes comedy which played itself out in the 'nineties, and there has its place.

On July 27 their eldest daughter Louise was married to the Duke of Fife in Buckingham Palace Chapel. Louise was her father's favorite; but he gladly saw her go, for Fife, a man much older than the bride, was his friend.

"I think it was a very pretty sight," wrote the bride's father to a friend, "and the departure of the happy couple from Marlborough House gardens in an open carriage and four—amidst the showers of rice and a dense concourse of people—very effective."

They were in Athens in October for the marriage of George's eldest son, Constantine. Athens on the threshold of the 'nineties was little changed. The lively bugler still darted from the palace portico at the slightest excuse. Kifissia Square rotted in the golden sunlight, as rugged, as neglected as ever. But a grimy steam tram now ran down to the seaside, which the royal family found very convenient. George was balder, more patriarchal. Only forty-five, he was a family—indeed a national—autocrat, stern with the bitter wisdom of experience, but always patiently available to his subjects. None but Alix seemed now able to stir in him the laughter of his boyhood.

Part Five

REIGN IN TWILIGHT

Chapter 22

'TWIXT THE BOSS AND THE PEACOCK

E. F. BENSON, son of the Archbishop, has left an account of the most "desperate *gaffe*" he ever made in his life, and the Princess of Wales plays a leading part on "that dismal occasion." It was 1890, and he had been asked to a dance in Portman Square. He was one of those young men whom hostesses then snapped up for their dances, and he had never visited the house before. The London squares were not so brilliantly lighted as they are today. He gave the driver of his hansom the correct instructions and woke from a dream to discover the vehicle halted in the square where a red carpet ran across the pavement and up some steps.

In the empty hall he was received in some state and brought up to the first floor. But, ceremonious as his lonely progress was, it was not enough unduly to surprise so fashionable a youth of his time. He knew that his hostess was ill and that her daughter was to officiate for her. He had never met the daughter, but presumed her to be the elegant young woman who greeted him in an open doorway. He rather prided himself on the effusive and graceful manner in which he presented himself to hostesses. Just behind her stood the Princess of Wales. Since he saw the Princess of Wales at many parties that did not in the least dismay him.

The Princess smiled at him and began to chat. She had recently returned from Greece and happened to know that he, too, had been holidaying there. Their conversation on Greek conditions promised to be a long and pleasant one. He was once or twice mildly surprised when the Princess turned and threw an aside in a rather familiar tone to the young lady by the door.

"But by degrees," says Benson, "this pleasant little talk began to wear the aspect of a nightmare, for looking round the room I perceived that I was the only person in it who was not of royal birth. There was a galaxy of princes and princesses, but not even an earl or a marquis to bridge the bottomless gulf which lay between them and me."

His cabby had dropped him at the house of Louise, the newly married Duchess of Fife, who was giving a family party. The reason for his penetrating to the upper regions without suspicion from the footmen was because one or two carefully chosen and somewhat important non-royalties had been invited to "look in" later in the evening.

One of the major irritants for the Waleses in the first half of the 'nineties were the summer visits of the Emperor William to Cowes. Both Bertie and Alix looked forward to their yachting holiday as one of the best parts of the year. The change which took place in the atmosphere of the Solent when the All Highest was present was inevitably felt more by his Uncle Bertie, who fell into the position of host, than by his Aunt Alix; but indirectly she suffered much from the ill-tempers of Bertie and from the almost apoplectic sense of outrage which sometimes seized him when he talked about his Imperial nephew. And it used to seem as if Bertie never would stop talking about him. It went on all through the year till the next dreadful visit came around. This Cowes episode started with the summer of 1889 and, with the exception of 1891, continued till 1895. The comedy is best dealt with in one piece, for those few weeks during a space of six years seem to shadow the whole period.

The Emperor first appeared in his flamboyant white and gilt steam yacht, the *Hohenzollern,* in the Solent in 1889. With him came twelve German warships. His affability to his uncle, if it maintained a measure of Imperial patronage, at least made it possible for his host to demonstrate good nature in return. If he could not entirely forgive his nephew, he had smothered the fires more

effectively than others believed possible after what he had suffered.
The Emperor was, in fact, in joyful mood, for by the Queen's desire
he was to receive from her at Osborne House a commission as
honorary Admiral of the British Navy. "Fancy wearing the same
uniform as Nelson!" he chortled. "It is enough to make me quite
giddy!" His new honor seemed to him an encouragement to criticize the British warships drawn up in the Solent for his inspection.
It was the Emperor's first assay at unwanted advice, and he was
generous, while his uncle listened in pained surprise.

Each night there were dinner parties aboard the *Hohenzollern,*
at Osborne House, aboard the *Osborne,* and once at the Royal Yacht
Club, where the Emperor was proposed by his uncle for membership in the Royal Yacht Squadron. Perhaps Uncle Bertie suffered
vague qualms as he made his proposal; yet that first year's visit of
the Kaiser gave little inkling of what was to come. It was in the
next year when Emperor William appeared in the character of
British yachtsman, as ready to run the Royal Yacht Squadron as he
was to reorganize the British Navy, that the trouble started. His
Uncle Bertie, who was Commodore of the Royal Yacht Squadron,
had been the King of Cowes for years.

The *Hohenzollern* reached Cowes on August 4, 1890. It was the
day upon which Great Britain officially ceded Helgoland to Germany in exchange for territory in East Africa. The Emperor stood
jubilantly at his gangway in the uniform of a British admiral to
receive the Prince of Wales. The transition to yachting rig soon took
place and the Emperor was ready to enjoy himself. Members of the
Emperor's suite aboard the *Hohenzollern* have left some interesting
records of the events which followed; for they scarcely observed
their Imperial master with affection.

Ludwig, the eminent German biographer, says,

"during these eighteen midsummer weeks (the total period when
the Emperor was at Cowes), in the precarious intimacy of life
on board, the antipathy of the two men (uncle and nephew)
developed into an enmity which was to affect the history of the
world."

Von Eckhardstein, invariably in attendance, noted that William treated his uncle "partly as a *quantité négligeable,* partly as the victim of his schoolboy pranks, conversational and otherwise."

These Imperial pranks, so far as his staff were concerned, included such puerilities as making elderly generals and admirals do physical training before the crew on the deck of the *Hohenzollern,* when the Emperor might dart forward to tip up some straining veteran with howls of delight. Play of this kind applied to his uncle, nearing a stout and dignified fifty, was not cheerfully accepted.

Soon the Prince of Wales was known to be calling his nephew "the Boss of Cowes"; nor was he too careful of his words in the presence of the German suite. "The Emperor's interest in ships is all very well," he was overheard to murmur on one occasion, "but when one sees him taking a hand in everything with that paralyzed arm of his, as he's doing just now on deck, one can't help being afraid he'll do himself some damage." Sometimes the offended uncle was vehement, sometimes plaintive. "The Regatta used to be my favorite relaxation," he muttered, "but since the Emperor has been in command here, it's nothing but a nuisance. Most likely I shan't come at all next year!"

William was gifted with a vivid imagination, and at last he found the perfect description of his uncle—so apt that when it reached the person to whom it was applied it made a deep wound. "He is an old peacock!" said William. As enmity between uncle and nephew grew more open, though it always had to stay just below the surface, so William's attentions to his Aunt Alix grew more abrupt. She made no effort to hide her dislike of her swaggering nephew, though she had to see a good deal of him.

Once Uncle Bertie snubbed his nephew for some more than usual overbearingness in the Royal Yacht Enclosure. To punish the presumption of the Commodore, the nephew entered his yacht the *Meteor I* for the Queen's Cup—the only challenger to the Prince of Wales's *Britannia*—and, at the last moment, canceled his entry, forcing the *Britannia* to sail the course alone. His boast that he had done so, which was soon widely broadcast, was considered the nearest he could approach to a direct affront to his uncle without falling foul of his royal grandmother, whom he always treated with an earnestly devotional respect.

Each year, as Commodore of the Squadron, the Prince of Wales and his Imperial guest delivered generous good-will speeches at one another: the uncle grave and faintly sardonic, the Emperor with a wolfish grin. Once at a dinner-party on the *Osborne* with his uncle and aunt, a report was brought in to the Prince of Wales concerning the dangerous Russian situation on the Indian frontier. A similar report from the German Embassy was handed to the Emperor at the same time. The Emperor, realizing that he and his host were reading of the same event, suddenly burst out laughing, slapped his uncle on the back, and shouted, "Well—now you can go to India and show whether you're any good as a soldier—at last!"

A withering silence followed this sally. William had hit his uncle's tenderest spot. He subsequently carried further this line of insult by declaring that "the Prince of Wales is the only 'Crown Prince' in Europe who has not seen active service!"

Once, thanks to nephew William, his Aunt Alix had to watch her husband being scolded like a schoolboy before a large company at Osborne House. There was to be a race round the Isle of Wight between the *Britannia* and the *Meteor I*. The race started, but the wind suddenly dropped. The two great yachts lay becalmed. Time passed. No wind blew up, and Uncle Bertie, mindful that he and the Emperor were to dine that evening with the Queen at Osborne House, signaled, "Suggest postponement of race owing to Queen's dinner." The reply flashed, "Race must be fought out no matter when we finish." The Imperial guest had to be complied with: the race *was* fought out.

At 10 p.m. the Prince of Wales and the Emperor, having hastily dressed, entered the long pillared Osborne drawing room. Dinner was long over, and a "Queen's dinner" and its aftermath when there were guests was a solemn affair of undertones, which almost seemed to have a religious flavor about it. Any breakdown in the stage management deeply disturbed the equanimity of the presiding goddess.

There is a story that while the Emperor swaggered up to his grandmother in the seat of isolation, which she always adopted on such occasions, the Prince of Wales was seen hovering behind one of the white pillars and wiping the nervous perspiration off his brow. This may be a gross exaggeration; but there were plenty of eyewitnesses to the crushing reception he received when he advanced to bow before his mother. It was a moment which would have pleased the late Mr. Brown, and doubtless nephew William, who was standing beside Grandmamma, was not unamused.

But though William was generally sympathetically treated by his grandmother, she was not blind to his ways, or to the irritation he might cause to others. She once referred to him as "an impetuous and conceited youth"—he was thirty-seven—when seeking to mollify her ruffled eldest son.

It has been said that in the contest between William and Uncle Bertie it was the uncle who got in the last *word* and the nephew the last *act*. Uncle Bertie had for some time appeared to be anxious to say something truly scathing about his nephew, but, failing inspiration, had inclined to be glowering and silent. At last, with an air of triumph, he hit the nail squarely on the head. "My nephew," he declared, "is the most brilliant failure in history!" To contemporaries it was a perfect description of the bewildering German Emperor. Whether William ever heard this, as he learned of much else that was said of him by his uncle from the lips of his own mischief-loving suite, is not known. But the nephew achieved the last *act*. The Emperor never came to Cowes after 1895; but as soon as he reached home in that year he sent an order to the builders of the Prince of Wales's yacht *Britannia* to construct the *Meteor II*. This was to be greatly superior to the *Britannia*. Though William had shaken off himself the bitter spray of Cowes forever, the *Meteor II* was to appear in the succeeding years with her German crew to knock the *Britannia* out of the running, and to remind the Commodore of the happy days gone by.

During this decade it became clear that the Princess of Wales was no longer content to nurse her anti-Prussian feelings in the discretion of silence. Doubtless the visits of nephew Willy had some hand in this development.

Whenever Prussia became a topic in a conversation—and Prussia was much in the news in those years—people with startled embarrassment listened to the Princess of Wales, who never abused anybody, declaiming her views on "the dirty, filthy, beastly Prussians!"

When George, while Duke of York, wrote during a visit to Berlin to tell of some honorary rank in the German services bestowed upon him, at which he seemed rather elated, she sent her son the crushing reply that she would "sooner be dead at the bottom of the sea than see him in a Prussian uniform."

The first years of the 'nineties for the Waleses were to be a time both of public trouble and family affliction.

The public trouble was the Tranby Croft case, which came to court with the Prince of Wales summoned as a witness for the defense in June 1891. The Tranby Croft affair was said to have caused a fiercer outcry than anything that had gone before. It was, to say the least of it, very bad luck for the Prince of Wales; but it is probable that if a similar case were to occur today involving a high royal personage, that person would be as surely singled out as the scapegoat as happened in 1891.

The court case was an echo of an event in the previous September at a house party given by Mr. and Mrs. A. Wilson at Tranby Croft, near Hull, for the St. Leger meeting. At the request of the Prince of Wales, after dinner they played baccarat, which was his favorite game. The son of the house thought he detected Sir William Gordon-Cumming, Lieutenant-Colonel of the Scots Guards, cheating by surreptitiously withdrawing or adding to his stakes after studying the cards in his hand. He revealed what he had seen to four others later that night. All five watched the Colonel on the next night. All were convinced that he was cheating. They told the Prince of Wales and a certain General Owen Williams.

Gordon-Cumming was summoned before a kind of committee, headed by the Prince, and it was perhaps the Prince of Wales's idea that the most gentlemanly way of dealing with an unsavory problem was to offer Gordon-Cumming the choice of being publicly exposed or of signing a paper declaring he would never play cards again for money. After vehement denials the accused man chose the latter alternative. This, though well meant, was clearly unfair, for the Colonel might still have been innocent and signed the paper out of desperation. Everybody in the house was sworn to secrecy, and the Tranby Croft party broke up. The paper was filed in a sealed envelope at Marlborough House.

Not only had the Prince of Wales now involved himself in this risky affair as deeply as was possible, but as an officer on the Army

List he had transgressed the Queen's Regulations by failing to disclose the dishonorable conduct of a brother officer. Thus he made himself liable to a court-martial by identifying himself with the offence.

Only a few months had elapsed when Gordon-Cumming received an anonymous letter from abroad. Somebody in the Tranby Croft party must have broken the promise. In a fury of reckless indignation the Colonel brought an action in the High Court against the original five who had accused him before the Prince of Wales. His contention was that he was innocent and had been forced to sign the paper.

Nobody on either side in the court appeared in anything but a shabby light. The Prince of Wales stumbled under examination in the witness box. Somebody among the defendants had broken a solemn promise. All had acted in a questionable manner when seen in the public viewpoint. The military authorities were disturbed; for might not the Prince of Wales's example be bad for other officers?

Gordon-Cumming had damned himself, for he lost his case; but the defendants scarcely won theirs with honor. But what lay behind all this? It was "Marlborough House"—the royal gambling den—where the damnable document had been concealed in the secret files till the Law had dragged it out to show to the righteous of the nation. Who was responsible for the gambling craze which was sweeping and corrupting and ruining the country? It was the Prince of Wales, a vicious gambler from his youth, who never traveled without his luggage being stuffed with gambling counters for huge amounts and stamped with the three royal feathers!

The Times, in its leader, declared that it was a pity that the Prince of Wales had not signed the same document as Gordon-Cumming, and thereby put an end to his own gambling activities. The *Review of Reviews* calculated elaborately the number of prayers which must have been offered up at church services for the Prince of Wales in his lifetime. Here, said they, is the answer to prayer—the Tranby Croft case. The national Press went mad and the provincial newspapers followed it.

Continental papers, always fond of telling wild stories about the Prince of Wales, were amused. The whole of Europe was able to discuss a garbled version of the Tranby Croft scandal. Many foreigners must have thought it was the Prince of Wales who had been found out cheating.

The Tranby Croft case caused very deep distress at Marlborough House. Archbishop Benson, much perturbed himself and devoutly wishing the Prince of Wales did not gamble, received a summons to Marlborough House. He was staggered and white with anger when the Prince, equally enraged, told him that he believed that he was at the bottom of the savage campaign against him and asked him what he could do to control the forces he had let loose. The Prince declared to the Archbishop that he never had been "a gambler." People said he "always carried gambling counters with him as a Turk carried his prayer carpet," he complained bitterly. The truth was that you could not play baccarat and many other games without counters, and the reason why he carried them was to keep people from playing high stakes. His were only marked from 5s. to £10, and the kind of people he always played with could easily afford such sums.

The Archbishop's assurance that he had played no part in encouraging the public outcry, nor expressed an opinion to anybody, was accepted; as also were his private views on gambling. They parted friends, but the Prince was evidently unmoved by Benson's outlook on gambling in so far as his own participation in it might influence the country. He had become perhaps rather tyrannical with his hosts about "cards" at the many house parties he attended: cards after dinner were a habit with him, which the advancing years made it most difficult to drop, and with cigar in mouth and brandy beside him he intended cheerfully to pursue his way to the end. But there were never again any suggestions made of big money changing hands at the royal table. The War Office found it convenient to forget the Prince of Wales's ignorance of the Queen's Regulations, especially as the matter did not seem to perturb Her Majesty.

Chapter 23

SORROW WHICH NOTHING CAN LESSEN

IT MAY BE THAT the Tranby Croft scandal, and the ruffled feelings it aroused at Marlborough House, were partly responsible for high words and disagreements which came between husband and wife late that summer; but some kind of falling out there certainly was. It became known that the Princess of Wales was not returning to Sandringham after her visit to Copenhagen. She was going to Russia with her two unmarried daughters to stay at the Imperial villa of Livadia on the Black Sea.

Her husband reached Sandringham alone. He had never done that before. He did not know when she was returning; but it would not be for a long time. He was plainly upset and restless. For the first time since they were married she would not be at home for his birthday. It was, moreover, his fiftieth birthday, which depressed him very much. He had his usual shooting parties, but something seemed to be lacking. People were rather sorry for the Prince. Also, game was bad that year, and hardly anybody, including himself, seemed to be able to shoot straight. That added to his misery. Fire broke out at Sandringham. It looked at one moment as if the place was going to be burned down in Alix's absence, and perhaps he felt that would be almost a justification. But the best part of the house was saved, though he seemed almost to blame his wife that the fire had broken out at all. Some of their most cherished and oldest possessions were destroyed, and that made him moodily sentimental.

Then his birthday arrived, and he wrote a doleful report of the day to Livadia. He had doubtless curtailed the celebrations as far as possible out of self-pity. Even the visit to Sandringham that evening of the leading actors of the country, who presented him with an inscribed gold cigar box on behalf of the profession for which his influence had done so much, and the amusing theatrical supper party which followed and which normally would have greatly pleased him, failed to rouse his spirits.

Finally, he was worried about George, who was on leave, and had just returned from a stay with Eddy's regiment at the Curragh. He grew so perturbed about George that he broke up the house party. George was going into a high fever. He thought he had seen the symptoms before. Fevers had been the traditional terror of the royal family ever since the death of the Consort. He was frightened, and perhaps he began to feel a kind of blind fear of Sandringham, where he himself had so nearly met his end. He brought George from the country to Marlborough House. His illness was declared to be enteric fever. A cable flashed across Europe to Livadia.

Traveling day and night for six days Alix with the girls reached London. By that time George had passed the crisis, and his father appeared to be more in need of care. But Bertie soon brightened now that the family was reunited and Alix, however justified her grim departure had seemed, was able to rest with a sigh of relief and chide herself for ever going away.

If any coolness remained in the household which returned to Sandringham it was soon dispelled by a letter received in early December from Mary of Teck at Luton Hoo. Eddy, who had obtained leave from the Curragh, had joined the house party at Luton Hoo given by the Falbes, the Danish Minister and his wife. Princess May of Teck (the future Queen Mary) was there with her mother, and quite unexpectedly the Duke of Clarence had asked May to marry him. May had been known to Eddy and George since their earliest days. She had accepted Eddy's proposal.

Delight reigned at Sandringham, though the matter could scarcely be mentioned above a whisper in case somebody on the staff overheard. Eddy had still to reach Windsor to plead for the Royal Assent of Grandmamma. It was scarcely conceivable that she would not be as pleased as they were, but she would be very angry if she discovered that somebody knew about it before she did. Grandmamma was most happy to give her consent. May was clever, very well educated, and was believed to be more interested in helping her mother in the many charitable organizations she directed than in balls and other amusements, which lighter sides of royal life the Queen was persuaded had been receiving too much publicity. May should do very well, she averred. Alix was especially joyous over the engagement, because although it was perfectly true that May's father was an Austrian—much better than a German, of course— yet he had long been entirely Anglicized, and it meant that at least one of her boys was going to be saved from having to marry some princess "imported" straight from Germany.

The house party which assembled at Sandringham for the New Year, 1892, included, naturally, Princess May and her mother. George was so far recovered and was so delighted at having just received his promotion to naval commander that he intended to play a full part in the festivities. The Duke of Clarence had not himself been very well since before Christmas, when he had gone with his father in a bitingly raw and damp day to attend the funeral of Prince Hohenlohe, the Prince of Wales's boyhood companion and cousin, at Sunningdale. Eddy was not strong, and particularly susceptible to damp and cold. His mother knew that well, and she had not wanted him to go and stand about at Sunningdale. But it was his father's contention that a cavalry subaltern could not afford to coddle himself like an old woman; so Eddy had accompanied him to the funeral.

There was a sharp epidemic of influenza abroad that winter, and although nobody in the assembling house party was aware that they had brought it with them to Sandringham, the letter of May's mother, Mary of Teck, to her friend Miss Thesiger on January 9 portrays a stricken household.

"We came here last Monday, and but for that *cruel plague* 'influenza' should have had a delightful time, for we are a huge family party with only the addition of a few guns. On Tuesday Victoria and Admiral Stephenson succumbed; Thursday Count Mensdorff hurried back to London to lay up there, and that afternoon poor dear Eddy had to take to his bed, and, though up in his sitting room yesterday, his birthday, was too seedy and wretched to come down. Such a bitter disappointment! May, too, cannot shake off the very severe cold she has had all last week, and has had to stay indoors most of the time to nurse her cough, which is very troublesome. . . . George is quite convalescent, and dined with us yesterday for the first time."

Here is a report from a house party which gathered in high spirits and is breaking up in disaster, but there is no foreboding of tragedy. Thirty-six hours later Mary of Teck sent a letter to Lady Salisbury to put off a visit she was to make to Hatfield. That morning the newspapers had begun to show anxiety about the Duke of Clarence.

". . . I hope and believe," she wrote, "dear Eddy is doing as well as can be expected at this stage of this fearful illness. I cannot conceal from you that we are very anxious and must continue so, until the crisis is over and the inflammation has begun to subside. His strength is very fairly maintained; the night was a tolerable one . . . with youth on his side and God's blessing, I trust we may soon see him on the road to recovery. . . . As at present arranged we stay on here until Wednesday or so; but, of course, everything depends on the progress the dear patient (*a most exemplary one,* the Doctors say!) makes. May is wonderfully good and calm, but it is terribly trying for her. . . ."

Three days later the Duke of Clarence lay dead. It was an appalling shock. It was almost beyond belief. In a daze Alix herself performed the last offices for Eddy. Alone with the dead, she prayed by the bedside. All those at Sandringham knew the measure of her ghastly loss. They stood aside inadequate. Her intense quietness, her frightening restraint, called for a deeper spiritual aid than they could offer. Her kindness in her affliction left them with a heartbreaking sense of guilt.

Eddy had been her sheet anchor. There had been much in her life which she had not cared about at all. She was Princess of Wales, and had to do what others expected of her. And the older she got, though she might look like a carefree young woman, she cared less about some of those things. But she had faced it all, and done it very well—she knew that—while she had Eddy to be with her from time to time. Now there was no Eddy—nothing really—but she had to go on; and the Queen was getting old, and she knew what that meant for her, perhaps before very long. The future offered nothing to her except service. Perhaps, for some time, the past had not offered very much either.

From that time Alix, deep down inside her, hardened, tightened, grew brittle a little, tense, was bewildering sometimes. Only occasionally would she display this transformation, and people whose equanimity was not disturbed by it would think it funny, as outwardly it sometimes was; but the seed of it lay in her tragic loss.

She would have liked the funeral to be in Sandringham church— her funeral in the church she loved. But she knew that could not be: they would have to take Eddy from her. There would be crashing guns at Windsor, and bored military processions trailing toward St. George's Chapel. She would have to share the last sight of Eddy with a crowd of strangers. They let her have a memorial service in Sandringham church, and that was the true funeral.

Two of her children grew closer to her than before: George, because he had always wanted that place, and Victoria, who became her mother's close friend and companion. Two years later Alix wrote to her friend Lady Granby, who had just lost her son under rather similar circumstances, and her letter reflects at least something of her feelings about Eddy.

"I was so touched that you should have turned to me who has had to bear the same despairing sorrow which nothing on earth can ever lessen or change, which must be borne with patience and submission to the will of God. Our only consolation is that they are safe in the keeping of our Heavenly Father and waiting for us there, and that they were spared all the world's pain and sorrow. And pray God these dear ones may have links to draw us up to Him and Eternal Life."

She rarely spoke of Eddy after those first days, when she would unburden herself in quiet tones to the Queen and to all those friends whom she believed in part understood things. But from that time onward she bore one visible token to Eddy. She never again was seen dressed in anything but neutral shades, though up to that time she had always been so colorful.

Although the ageing Queen was distressed by the death of her grandson, she does not give the impression of being deeply moved.

"Poor darling Alix . . . ," runs an entry in her journal, "looks the picture of grief and misery and he very ill; dear Alix looked lovelier than ever in her deep mourning and a long black veil, with a point, on her head."

This was noted down after the funeral, which the Queen, who was at Osborne, did not attend. This, however, was against her own wish, because in view of the wintry weather Alix had urged her not to run the risk. Perhaps Eddy had not been of a tough enough mold to satisfy his grandmother, who by this time, by imperceptible stages, had grown very tough herself; perhaps he did not seem to her of the fiber of which kings are made, and that his premature death had saved him from a life which to him might have proved troublesome and unhappy. The nation sorrowed with the Prince and Princess of Wales in their loss; but very little was known of the Duke of Clarence except that he was not strong, so that in the country mourning was of an impersonal kind, and this fact must have made the mother feel all the more deeply that Eddy's loss was a thing almost sacred to herself.

Bertie and Alix went down to Eastbourne for several weeks of complete seclusion. Their friend Harty-Tarty, now Duke of Devonshire, had lent them his rather flamboyant seaside villa. There were some who thought the Princess of Wales was going to be seriously ill. But by the time they left Eastbourne, although she looked sad and said little, the "slight youthful figure" of Alix moved with its old buoyancy. Bertie took her to Cap Martin for a month. It must have seemed strange to Bertie to be on the Riviera and not to enter a casino or to appear at any of those places where the veteran cosmopolitans usually gathered. They went for long drives and walked on the *plage* and scarcely spoke to anybody. One morning Bertie when alone came face to face with one of his old acquaintances. The man in question may have been a cynical type and perhaps did not know the Prince of Wales very well. He remarked that he feared his Royal Highness must find life a trifle "dull" after his usual round of activities on the Riviera. The remark was received coldly.

"What on earth does that matter," answered the Prince, "if only in any way it does the Princess any good." He continued on his way and did not wait for any further conversation.

Then came the Golden Jubilee of the King and Queen of Denmark. The Queen could hardly be expected to have been sympathetic toward this at any time, because her dislike for Queen Louise, whom she scarcely ever saw, had increased rather than mellowed with the years. The idea of her grief-stricken daughter-in-law hurrying off to join her father and mother in the rejoicings in Denmark struck her as deeply shocking. It was most un-English and quite out of the family tradition. But Alix was determined to go. She and Bertie arrived in Copenhagen. They did not appear at any of the festivities or at any entertainments other than small family ones. She returned happier and more settled.

Prince George, now that his brother was dead, was a figure of importance in the land, and the Queen recognized this on her birthday, May 8, 1892, by creating him Duke of York. It was at the end of April in the following year that Bertie and Alix while abroad received news for which they were totally unprepared. George, who was staying with his sister, the Duchess of Fife, at Sheen Lodge, had asked May of Teck to marry him. They were perfectly astonished, but very delighted. Once everybody had got over their surprise there was universal agreement that George could not possibly have made a better choice. George would have great responsibilities one day and May, who was known to be historically minded, serious in her views and highly intelligent, would be the right wife to support him.

The wedding of George and May took place at the Chapel Royal, St. James's, on July 6. George, because of his naval duties, which he took very seriously, was not as yet well known to the public; but May, whose mother the Duchess of Teck had ever since her Cambridge days been one of the most popular royalties in the country, was a figure of great interest, and huge crowds were out to see the street processions. The wedding had one unusual feature for a royal wedding: something went wrong.

The Queen with the Duchess of Teck and her son-in-law the Grand Duke of Hesse-Darmstadt traveled from Buckingham Palace via St. James's Street to the Chapel. All the other royalties were to approach by St. James's Park. The plan was that all the royalties should be gathered at the Chapel entrance to receive Her Majesty, who was to enter just before the ceremony began. Somebody had failed to discover that the Queen's approach route was the shorter one. Her Majesty's starting time was set too early.

Many of the ordinary guests had not as yet claimed their seats in the Chapel when an usher at the door saw with horrified embarrassment that the Queen was approaching. His first instinct was to turn and run. But the Queen looked faintly amused and he stood his ground. The Duchess of Teck took control. She instructed the usher to escort the Queen and the Grand Duke to the retiring-room, always prepared for the Sovereign on such occasions, and herself with Miss Thesiger behind her advanced up the corridor to the Chapel. They were on the threshold of the Chapel when Miss Thesiger felt somebody tug at her dress from behind. She turned indignantly. There was the Queen on the arm of the Grand Duke.

"I'm going in first," she announced.

The Chapel was in some confusion with people settling themselves in their seats, and the advance of the Queen to the front without a dignified escort was observed with incredulity. The Queen was contentedly seated in her place and regarding with interest the new arrivals when, with a scurrying at the door, the Lord Chamberlain and the great officers of the household seemed to burst into the Chapel. They stood staring at the Queen with consternation. Her Majesty, quite unperturbed that she had discomfited her loyal courtiers by her breach of etiquette, nodded graciously to them across the Chapel, and for the first time in many years it was said that her blue eyes looked mischievous.

One of the Marlborough House guests at this wedding was Dagmar's eldest son, the Czarevitch Nicholas, whose appearance aroused unusual interest because he was the image of his cousin the bridegroom. In temperament poor "Nicky" was soon to prove himself a lesser man. With him the pleasures of life had almost run out, for very shortly he was to become the last Czar of the Russias. "Nicky" was at that time engaged to Princess Alix of Hesse, the daughter of the Queen's daughter Alice, who had died of diphtheria while nursing her children when stricken with that malady. The next Czar of Russia, therefore, like the Emperor of Germany, was soon to be another devoted worshiper of the great Queen, although he lacked that bittersweet quality in his adoration which was the characteristic of William. Soon "Nicky" would be so enchanted with things English that he would borrow his wife's relationship to the Queen and always call her Grandmamma. The freedom of life in England quite enthralled the young Czarevitch, and he made a very good impression on his uncle and aunt at Marlborough House. Quite soon he would be addressing them as "dearest Uncle Bertie and dearest Aunt Alix" and sending them his "tenderest love."

King Christian of Denmark and Queen Louise were also at the wedding of their grandson, and perhaps the Queen did not much exert herself to make the opposite grandparents feel anything but poor relations at the feast. On the day of their arrival, the eve of the wedding, the Queen held a great evening reception at the Palace, and Louise may have felt that she could not face her after the rigors of the journey. She announced that she was "too tired," and was the only important guest who did not appear. At the wedding luncheon, however, when Louise, as a Sovereign consort, had to be placed by the Queen—a disposition regarded with no little anxiety—everything, in the universal opinion, went like clockwork.

In July 1894 Alix and her two daughters were in St. Petersburg. Her niece, Grand Duchess Zenia, her sister's eldest daughter, was to be married to Grand Duke Alexander Michaelovitch, whose father was one of those rather theatrical Russian aristocrats much seen in the company of the Prince of Wales on the Continent. Bertie himself was unable to come; but it was not long before his presence was required in Russia.

While Alix was in St. Petersburg he had heard from her that Czar Alexander looked shockingly drawn and hollow-cheeked. They had always liked this immense, affable man, and now they were doubtless grateful to him for not taking the blandishments of Emperor William too seriously. Poor Alexander spoke little during Alix's stay, though he always seemed pleased with her company. He was only forty-nine, but the huge frame was unhealthily flabby and he walked with his stick like a man in a daze.

In September news came from Dagmar that Alexander was seriously ill. At the end of that month the doctors urged the Czar's removal to the Black Sea villa at Livadia. Four weeks elapsed and then came further news from Dagmar that she believed her husband's case was hopeless. He had not long to live. She was in deep distress. She said it would be a comfort to her and to Alexander if Bertie and Alix would come to them at Livadia.

They left London on October 30, and on November 3 they reached Livadia. Alexander was dead, and "Nicky"—Nicholas II—had been proclaimed in his stead. Bertie traveled with the funeral train from Livadia to St. Petersburg. Once they had passed out of the Riviera-like sunlight of Livadia, bitterly cold winds howled around the dismal train crawling over the flatlands under overcast skies, while beside the tracks in groups, mile after mile, the weeping peasants knelt, crooning dirges. Alix stayed to bring the widowed Czarina back to St. Petersburg.

"I am so glad," ran a letter of Bertie's, "we came out tho' alas too late to find dear Sacha alive. Alix has been the greatest possible comfort to Minnie and I don't know what she would have done without her sister: she is calm, dignified and resigned to her irreparable loss. Nicky's devotion, love and tenderness toward her are beyond praise. A dearer, nicer and simpler boy does not exist, but I do not envy him the terribly responsible and arduous position he is now called upon to fulfil.

"Every day we attend a Service in the Church of the Fortress and the Family mostly twice a day. The funeral is now fixed for the 29th and the wedding probably on the 28th as it must be before the great Russian fast, otherwise it cannot take place till January. It is essential that it should take place for Nicky's and Alicky's sake and more for the sake of the country, who look upon it as a necessity that their Sovereign should be married. They are the most devoted couple and Alicky acquits herself of a most difficult position most admirably."

The Prince of Wales, who had just passed the strangest birthday of his life—his fifty-third—in a groaning funeral train almost Oriental in its macabre fantasy, stood beside the new Czar when the obsequies began on November 11 in the Archangel Church in the Kremlin at Moscow, and accompanied the cortège to St. Petersburg, where on November 19 the corpse was laid in the Imperial vault in the fortress cathedral of St. Peter and Paul. At St. Petersburg, Prince George had joined his parents, and if it had been that the design of all these things was favorably to dispose the ever-suspicious Russians toward Britain, it seemed that the appearance of the Duke of York beside his father gave the final touch to their satisfaction.

On the day of the wedding the Prince of Wales on behalf of the Queen made the young Czar an honorary Colonel of the Scots Greys, and the Czar in return created the Prince a Colonel of the 27th Kieff Imperial Dragoons.

The Prince of Wales and Prince George departed amid cordial acclamations on December 2. They stopped on the way home at Berlin, as the Prince of Wales wished to call on the new Chancellor, Prince von Hohenlohe. Emperor William, having emerged paladin-like from his tutorial stage under Bismarck, had decided that his pilot was too masterful, and had consequently dropped him over the ship's side. To the visitors von Hohenlohe seemed to be an improvement: he was small, gentle, and seemingly wise, which last attribute was clearly much needed in Emperor William's Germany. Unhappily, Hohenlohe's gentleness was the characteristic which had chiefly recommended itself to William. He meant to have his own way. They drove out to Friedrichshof to visit Empress Frederick, still by no means free of embarrassments which her eldest son was ready to put in her way. His suspicion that in her widowhood she was contriving to be an English agent was strong.

It was not perhaps surprising, therefore, that the Emperor William should arrive at Friedrichshof while they were with his mother. His manner was polite but coldly injured rather than pleasant, especially when his uncle, scenting the cause of his dolefulness, mischievously enlarged on the immense cordiality of the Russians toward himself; for the truth was that William now thought that the arch-intriguer and spy of Europe was deep in a new design to form an Anglo-Russian alliance against Germany. Nor, judging by the eulogies on the successful Russian visit which greeted the Prince of Wales from Governmental circles on his arrival in London, was the German Emperor entirely astray in his ideas. A visit, which at the outset had been intended solely on the grounds of humanity and family friendship, had, before the end, because of his uncle's remarkable flair for diplomacy, developed a strong political flavor.

Alix, while these events were going forward, had remained in Russia, where she was to be with her widowed sister for two months.

From this time onward Russia was very much on the minds of British statesmen, and it was realized that in a country where the ruler was a complete autocrat, subject to nobody except perhaps petticoat government from his nearest kin, the close and affectionate tie with England's royal family was a factor of immense importance. It was in the summer of 1896 that the Queen was persuaded to invite the young Czar and Czarina and their baby daughter for a September stay at Balmoral. It was to be a family affair.

Bertie learned of this in August when he was taking his usual cure at Homburg. Knowing his nephew Nicky and, indeed, the imaginative quality of the Muscovite temperament, he believed that some plentiful splashes of scarlet and steel, a skirl of many bagpipes and a generous display of kilts, a deferential attendance from the greatest in the land, would better advance the Anglophile enthusiasm of the chief guest than the peace of an evening in Balmoral's tartan drawing room. He urged this on his mother and she, being more prone to listen to him than in the past, entirely agreed with him and gave the necessary orders.

Thus when, on September 22, the Imperial yacht *Standart* berthed at Leith, the Prince of Wales as a Kieff Dragoon, the Duke of Connaught in the Scots Guards uniform, Lord Rosebery the county Lord Lieutenant, and the Lord Provost of Edinburgh, came aboard to greet the Czar and Czarina. Highland guards of honor waited at Leith, at Aberdeen and at Ballater, and even Balmoral produced a highly furbished body of Volunteers. Lord Salisbury, the Prime Minister, waited at the portal, and within the hall the Queen and Aunt Alix.

Nicky was delighted. He was able to wear his Scots Greys uniform for the first time. Most of the guests at Balmoral were military, "as Russians, like Austrians and Germans, think so much more of military rank than that of a civilian, however great . . ." During the fortnight's stay of Nicky and Alicky, Balmoral rendered that stirring Highland display which was expected of it; but Nicky, unlike his cousin the German Emperor, did not, perhaps to his regret, acquire the right to wear a kilt.

Doubtless certain significant trends in the affairs of the Romanoff family were already understood at Balmoral through the medium of the constant letters which Alix received from her sister, the Dowager Empress; but the chance of intimate personal contact which this visit offered must have made things even plainer to so shrewd a judge of humanity as their Uncle Bertie.

Nicky was a weak young man. He was subject to two powerful opposite strains. His mother, the Dowager Empress, to whom, as his father before him, he was very much subject, was a Dane. Therefore she was an anti-German. Her affection for her sister the Princess of Wales made her an earnest Anglophile. His wife Alicky, whose English mother had been dead since her childhood, was strong in her German sentiments.

Thus two parties were in a state of embryonic formation in Russia: the English party of the Dowager Empress and the German party encouraged by the young Czarina, and there were many German wives in high places in Russia to support her. Alexander III used to call his wife "the Angel of Russia." That amiable giant had, indeed, been as weak as his son, and Dagmar with her forcible character had done much to make his lot easier. Now she intended to do the same with her son Nicky. She would rule Russia for Nicky as she had ruled it for Alexander. It was an attitude which suited her English relations, since it was the ambition of her widowhood to achieve a solid Anglo-Russian alliance.

For a clever woman, however, the colorful Dagmar, or Empress Marie Fedorovna, as she was known to the Russians, was short-sighted in her manner to her lonely young German daughter-in-law. With a faintly scornful neglect the mother left out the wife from councils which she held with her son, forgetting that the wife in her turn could ascertain the nature of those councils and even hinder them from the privacy of the conjugal bed.

Alicky spoke little Russian, she moved without friends in bewildered dumbness through the scenes of hollow, exotic glitter which were daily enacted in the sealed palaces, giving girl-child after girl-child to a Tartar race which demanded sons. Some gentle sympathy might have stirred in Alicky her English blood. She was left to fall back on the Germans. There came a time when the young wife with bitter humor showed her husband a sketch she had made of himself as a baby with bib and tucker, seated in a high chair and being fed with a spoon by the Dowager Empress.

Thus it was that the favorite sister of the Princess of Wales, while working for an entirely different end, was even then preparing the ground in Russia for the notorious German party and for their evil high priest, the monk Rasputin, which in the end played so sinister a part in the downfall of Imperial Russia. Meanwhile another Sovereign, glancing about him with eyes full of wolfish cunning and suspicion, was knocking on the door of the Romanoffs. This was Emperor William of Germany. While upstairs in the gorgeous perfumed secrecy of Muscovite palaces the Dowager Empress and the Empress played shuttlecock with the puzzled Nicky, in London and in Berlin, Uncle Bertie and Cousin William, each writing in their own characteristic way, abused one another and cajoled the attentive Czar.

It was not at all to the taste of the German Emperor that Czar Nicholas upon leaving Balmoral was by his own request met by a French fleet, and under its escort sailed across the Channel to pay a State visit to the French Republic. That visit was doubtless well approved of by "the true Parisian, the Frenchman at heart," the Prince of Wales; but at the time it meant little to Britain, for in 1896 Britain was on anything but cordial terms with the French, and in that quarter there seemed no prospect of a break in the clouds.

It was in 1895 that Prince Nicholas of Greece made his first visit to England as the guest of his Aunt Alix, and he has left some interesting impressions of Marlborough House and Balmoral at that time.

He had been staying at Fredensborg, where the Princess of Wales was also a guest, and she took her favorite nephew home with her in the royal yacht *Victoria and Albert*. Since the Queen never used the vessel, this had become the yacht of the Prince and Princess of Wales. Nicholas had never before entered a room that truly belonged to his aunt. He regarded her cabin with astonishment. It was packed with oddments like an antique shop. He knocked over relics as he moved about, and was greeted with frenzied admonitions to "take care!"

"How can you travel with all these things?" he exclaimed.

"They are all the thoughts of my friends. I can't do without them," she explained.

When Nicholas entered his aunt's rooms at Marlborough House, it was even worse: chairs of all periods, little tables crammed with ornaments, books jumbled everywhere, photographs propped up by priceless *objets d'art,* the walls quite hidden under ill-assorted pieces. It was bewildering even to a person of that era of bric-a-brac. He had to walk through it all crab-fashion. The rooms must have been the despair of servants, and seeing the Princess of Wales's writing desk he realized what a patient and able woman Charlotte Knollys must be. He presumed Aunt Alix never actually attempted to write at her desk. Even her bedroom was so loaded with gilt-topped gift bottles and incongruous souvenirs that it must have presented a great problem to her. "I defy anyone to give anything like an approximate inventory of the things," was his verdict.

In her homes Aunt Alix was never seen without a number of little dogs at her heels, and these sat round to be fed at all meals except dinner. Nicholas observed that many of the pictures scattered all over the house were very bad, and imagined these could have been bought only because the Waleses wanted to encourage the artists. Although in the daytime meals took place with all the suite in the big downstairs dining room looking out over the garden, in the evening he dined with his uncle and aunt in a small upstairs room beside her boudoir. It was really the Princess's private dining room, and it was crowded with furniture. Footmen caught their feet and bruised their legs as they struggled around the table. Uncle Bertie, so talkative abroad, was silent in his home, and let the lively conversation of his wife flow over his head. The Prince of Wales, a most genial and thoughtful host to his nephew, and amiable to the people around him when everything went well, would flash with annoyance at the smallest hitch—as, for instance, when contrary to his express wish he could not find a pad of paper and a sharpened pencil in every room of the house which he entered. Nothing angered Uncle Bertie more surely than this deficiency; but whatever his complaint, Aunt Alix continued in unruffled and bubbling enjoyment of life.

They took Nicholas down to Sandringham for the autumn shooting parties. Like others before him, he felt the atmosphere of "homeliness and comfort" at Sandringham. He noticed that it was all rather out of date, and, of course, all his aunt's apartments were as overburdened with souvenirs, valuables and rubbish as elsewhere. The great feature of the house was the hall, the central meeting place and the invariable room for afternoon tea. He was doubtless introduced by his aunt to her little green parrot in his cage at the back of the hall; the bird had been taught, before one of the Queen's visits, to give "Three cheers for Her Majesty!" in pauses of the conversation.

The Sandringham establishment, Nicholas notes, was run with great efficiency, as, indeed, it required to be, for an unending procession of guests of the most contrasting description were arriving and leaving all the time. Probably this was owing to the close co-operation of the Prince of Wales with Charlotte Knollys. Charlotte Knollys was hailed just as Charlotte, the family intimate, and everybody pursued her for everything. Aunt Alix, although anything but methodical, was always bustling and attentive for the comfort of her guests, and if anything was amiss—outside her own rooms—she was the first to observe and to insist indignantly that it should be put right instantly.

On the day of his arrival Nicholas was led by his aunt up to a small bedroom which appeared to be prepared for a guest. Then he noticed that a bunch of wilted flowers lay in the middle of the pillow. She just said, "Here he died"—no more, and then went over and replaced the faded blooms with a fresh bunch in her hand. They stood gazing in silence around the neat room, where nothing had been disturbed since his cousin Eddy died there in the New Year of 1892.

Nicholas stayed on at Sandringham over Christmas, and attended the servants' ball in the servants' dining room. The dance music was churned out by a hand organ and, one by one, male guests and members of the suite took their turn at the handle. Aunt Alix danced the first quadrille with the head butler, and Uncle Bertie danced with the housekeeper.

At home a change had come in high life by the middle 'nineties. In the previous decades people had spoken of the Marlborough House set as if it was a circle with its headquarters in a private house in London. But with the 'nineties the mellowing Marlborough

House set had spread itself. It was more truly the country house set. Including in its sweep as it did most of the great ruling families of the British countryside, or some prominent branches of them, it was a significant feature of the times. It may be, as a celebrated blue-blooded lady novelist of Edwardian life has suggested, that some of those house parties, generally of married people, were conducted on generously broad-minded principles, in which bedrooms were a no-man's-land for the enterprising adventurer; but the importance of those aristocratic house parties in history lies in another direction. People in those houses, perhaps scarcely conscious of it themselves, were gathering their strength, waiting in the twilight of a reign for the era of power which lay in the future.

That short but in many ways glorious reign which followed upon the death of Queen Victoria has been called the reign of country house government.

There were men who had long been in the circle and men who were just beginning to move toward the circle—men of great wisdom and worldly understanding, whom some by the old standards might call peculiar—who up to that time had been welcomed for their purely social qualities, but who would shortly find themselves, while holding no parliamentary office, to be men of great power and influence in the land.

There were the fabulous Rothschilds, who in their generations had been in the circle since the beginning. There was Ernest Cassel (afterward Sir Ernest, Privy Councillor), who, emerging from the glory of his mansion, Moulton Paddocks, upon the national race-courses, was soon entertaining the premier royal racehorse owner. He was first publicly acknowledged as a royal intimate when the Prince of Wales appeared at his daughter's wedding in 1901, to become subsequently godfather to Cassel's first granddaughter, now Lady Louis Mountbatten.

There was Dr. Felix Semon (Sir Felix), Cassel's German friend, who became King Edward VII's confidential physician, another of those shrewd cosmopolitans who, falling under the spell of the Prince of Wales, took British nationality to please the master to whose interests he grew devoted.

There was Soveral, the "Blue Monkey," popping up everywhere with his simian grin, feared, always respected, hated, much adored, now Portuguese Ambassador. Cassel and Soveral, so opposite in temperaments, would soon be recognized as the two most intimate, loyal and useful friends of the new Throne in that coming period when constitutional monarchy probably wielded more personal power than ever before or since.

The suave Soveral and the forthright Cassel, each saluting the qualities of the other, cherished a friendly jealousy. When the Prince asked the "Blue Monkey" if he had seen Oscar Wilde's *The Importance of Being Earnest,* the answer snapped in his face, "No, Sir, but I have seen the Importance of Being *Ernest Cassel!"*

There was the tall aristocrat, Reginald Viscount Esher: the typical Etonian, amazingly clever, totally without ambition, who took pride in refusing high offices and honors. He became Secretary of the Office of Works at forty-three in 1895, and administered it with cool and broad-humored triumph through the active period of the Diamond Jubilee and the great palace changeover at the death of the Queen and the Coronation. Dutifully, philosophically, almost with elegant boredom, Esher assumed the role of national sage and odd-job man with cheerful energy, which earned him a place more onerous and scarcely less intimate with his Sovereign than that of Cassel's and Soveral's.

There was Mrs. Langtry, who, in the intervals of her arduous business as a highly successful actor-manageress of international fame, appeared before the sporting population as the leading lady racehorse owner of the country; and there on the famous racecourses she might be observed to tower over the Prince of Wales in earnest confidence. Still a formidably beautiful figure and a picturesque guest at many of the great houses, celebrated as much now for her business acumen as for her mellowing Junoesque loveliness, she was the honored woman friend. Ability and enterprise interested the Prince perhaps even more than beauty, and so high was his opinion of this remarkable woman that in the coming reign King Edward was sometimes seen to take the arm of Lady de Bathe, for so she became in 1899, on the promenades of the Riviera.

But as the Marlborough House set spread countryward, it also did something that was startlingly new. During the season it began to abandon its glistening, immaculate dinner tables, sagging under the weight of their flowery monumental epergnes and candelabra, and to dine instead before the dazzled public gaze in London hotels and restaurants.

With the turn of the 'nineties, Cesar Ritz with his famous chef Escoffier, and Johann Strauss with his lilting waltzes, had opened their campaign at the wondrous new Savoy in the Strand. Their Sunday evening dinners became a part of the London season after the Prince and Princess of Wales and the Duke of Clarence, like royalties of bygone days, had unconcernedly eaten their dinners there before the eyes of an entranced assembly. Royalty had often been seen on its best behavior toying with knife and fork at public functions, but this was altogether more intimately fascinating. Savoy Sunday evenings, with fashionable people come to associate themselves with royalty and common people gathered to regale themselves in the company of both, were the new craze.

Other hotels and the smart restaurants called in the decorators and inspected their kitchen and table staffs. German, Hungarian and Viennese orchestras flocked to London and the florists delivered big orders. Royalty appeared at some of these places, and the smart people followed. It was in 1896 that a lady was first seen to smoke a cigarette at the dinner table at the Savoy, and she followed the first cigarette with a chain of many others. She was not a royal lady: she was the Duchesse de Clermont Tonnerre, one of those French royalist friends of the Prince of Wales. Cigarettes were, however, smoked by ladies at Marlborough House, including the royal hostess, even when distinguished churchmen were included in the company. The new reign was to bring many changes: ladies who drove cars, ladies who drank generously and smoked in any company, ladies who scorned the moral façades which made most depraved Victorians outwardly respectable, ladies who chained themselves to railings, dropped bombs in letterboxes and blacked the eyes of policemen, all these owed some part of their inspiration to an evening when the Princess of Wales—the most admired lady in the land—entered the public dining room of a London hotel.

Chapter 24

MURDEROUS ATTACK

THE JUBILEE OF QUEEN VICTORIA had caught the imagination of Europe. When the time for her Diamond Jubilee approached, some of those who had been scornful before wanted to be partakers. Elderly Emperor Francis Josef of Austria-Hungary suggested he should lead the Sovereigns of Europe in array immediately behind the royal carriage. But the Queen wished for no Sovereign but herself at her Diamond Jubilee, even though the Treasury was willing to pay for their entertainment. They would be a great nuisance. She warned them all in good time so that the "Sovereigns" movement could be stopped before it grew too strong to oppose without offense.

Even so, the Emperor William thought he was exempt from this ruling. He cajoled his ill-used mother to write to her brother the Prince of Wales. Should Willy bring "Dona" (the Empress) and the elder children? Would he approach Mamma? That sent the Old Peacock to his mother in fearful agitation. The Boss of Cowes would come and boss the Jubilee! The Queen reassured him: she would have none of "them."

Ever since her widowhood Her Majesty had been seen in plain black, with perhaps a dash of white. It was darling Alix who persuaded her on the sixtieth anniversary of her accession to change that rule, and she who arranged with the dressmakers what that change should consist of. The Queen notes with delight in her journal that at the Palace dinner on the eve of the celebration "the whole front of my dress was embroidered in gold." On the great day the crowds saw her with panels of gray silk let into her black gown and "creamy white flowers" on her bonnet.

The Queen was very lame, and it was agreed that she must not get out of the carriage. It was suggested, therefore, that the statue of Queen Anne be removed at the foot of St. Paul's steps, that a ramp be run up into the Cathedral nave and the State carriage and six with postilions and attendants should drive up into the nave and come to a stop under the dome for the service. The project was abandoned when the Queen refused to remove Queen Anne. She is supposed to have said that if she deposed Queen Anne, then why should not somebody do away with a statue of *herself* one day?

The St. Paul's service took rather a second place in the celebrations: a brief affair with clergy, a great choir and military orchestra piled up on the steps, the carriage with the Queen broadside below and the mounted guests and officials in noble disarray ranged opposite.

Only two sat in the royal carriage, the Queen, with the Princess of Wales, gowned in lilac, facing her; and as they moved toward St. Paul's through the dense and frantic crowds the old lady with tears in her eyes kept muttering in shaking tones: "They are so kind. So kind!"

One of the first moving pictures to be exhibited depicts the Queen and her daughter-in-law sitting very still, face to face in the open carriage, while the surpliced choirs and the bandsmen rise up the Cathedral steps in a great bank behind them. The pair in the carriage hold their parasols over their heads and about them dance flickers and flashes as if the rain deluged down.

Queen Victoria was nearly eighty years old as she made her great circle through London with the horse, foot and guns of her Empire pouring before her, and people wept and fainted. Once the procession broke, the soldiers marched, the Queen stayed. The State carriage crossed London Bridge to the poor people on the Surrey side. Lord Howe, Gold Stick, hurtled over his charger's head, landing with a sickening clash of armor beside the State carriage.

Like a stone the old Life Guardsman lay across the road. The carriages stopped. The cheers died. Gold Stick staggered to his feet. The Princess of Wales standing up told him to get into one of the royal carriages. He glared at her: his tone, if not his words, was rude. He called for his horse. Amid cheers he climbed into the saddle, and the Queen for the moment was forgotten. The soiled veteran rode grimly onward behind the carriage, resolved to jog painfully after his Queen to the end.

But to Alix, the most interesting part of the Diamond Jubilee celebrations was a project of her own. She was noted for strange ideas. She was also noted for obstinacy. There were practical people, experienced organizers, who declared that if the Princess plunged into this one she was going to make a fool of herself and everybody connected with it. Her idea was to give the biggest banquet in the history of the world. She intended to be hostess to 400,000 guests; and those guests were to be the poor of London, or any hungry person, good, bad or downright criminal—no questions asked—who cared to present themselves. It was a brilliant idea; but hardly anybody wanted to subscribe their money to a fantastic scheme which would probably end in chaos.

A great friend saved her. Sir Thomas Lipton sent her two items in one envelope: a cheque for £25,000 and a satisfying menu with prices, which he could promise to provide at one time for 400,000 guests. He reckoned that to do the thing well she would require 700 tons of food—he was not yet sure how many gallons of beverages —and perhaps 10,000 waiters. That set the ball rolling. Subscriptions for the Princess's Monster Dinner arrived by every post. Almost every church hall and meeting hall in London was rented, the army of waiters began to be recruited, and Sir Thomas Lipton with the Princess sat at Marlborough House working out the details.

On the day after the Diamond Jubilee procession the great feast took place at the same hour all over London. Hungry people eat fast, and it was impossible for the hostess to attend these dinners taking place all over the capital. She concentrated on the three main centres: the People's Palace and the Central Halls in Holborn and Clerkenwell. Many of the diners were almost starving, but there could be no doubt that the appearance of the Princess of Wales among them, most elegantly gowned, was the highlight of those three feasts, and it probably gave courage to some tragically weary people who shrank from the future.

Looking at those soiled and tattered diners the heart of Alix filled with pity; for tomorrow some might be dining off the crusts from dustbins. Something could be done to stop that.

Again with the help of Sir Thomas Lipton she started the Alexandra Trust. From that time onward a person provided with one penny could buy a helping of hot food, and for two or three coppers could procure a large meal.

The official Jubilee festivities lasted a fortnight, and one of the best-remembered events in after years was the Palace Garden Party, where the old Queen and the Princess of Wales drove slowly round the gardens in a victoria among the crowded guests.

Viscount Esher has recorded one event in these celebrations which provided an unusual experience for the Princess of Wales. Joseph Chamberlain, her "Red" convert, was now Colonial Secretary, and on June 24 he gave an evening party at his house to the Colonial Premiers. He had asked far too many guests, or perhaps the un-invited were trying to look in at the house with lights blazing and doors open. When Esher arrived a scene of loud chaos raged in Piccadilly outside the house. The fiery Chamberlain had, perhaps, transmitted his indignation at the confusion to his staff. Great persons, including royalties of both sexes, were caught up in the street battle. "The footmen were the great offenders—ragging all the guests and using most filthy language—especially to respectable elderly ladies. The Princess of Wales drove up and had to drive away."

Esher also has an amusing sidelight on domestic life at Marlborough House at this period. On some Office of Works business he was sent for by the Prince of Wales to Marlborough House. After they had talked for half an hour in the royal study upstairs "two messages came from the Princess to say she was waiting, the second so peremptory that the Prince left hurriedly."

Jubilee time was not an unclouded period for Alix. Throughout the celebrations half her thoughts were on Greece. The Greeks had become troublesome again over Crete, and she feared her brother was by no means as blameless for the dangerous developments as she could have hoped. Perhaps his grown-up sons, inspired by Hellenic fire, had been egging on their father.

Greek troops were attacking the Turkish Cretan garrisons. The Greeks did not seem to care what the Powers had to say. It was with startled amazement that the Powers heard of the Greek answer to their threatened blockade of the Piraeus. With drums beating and martial songs, the Greek mainland army was surging into Turkish Macedonia. It was full-scale war in the Balkans, led by the brother of the Princess of Wales!

But the Greek army was not yet ready for so heroic an enterprise. Pursued by infuriated Turks, they were soon fleeing headlong in desperate plight toward Athens. Greece was prostrate at the mercy of an indignant Sultan. Nothing but the Powers could save her.

Emperor William refused to stir in aid of the Greeks. Even though his sister was married to the Greek Crown Prince, he said it was "more correct" to leave the Greeks to their conquerors. Since the Greeks were entirely to blame he was probably right; but his Aunt Alix never forgave him.

Whatever the Emperor might choose to do about his sister, it was perfectly clear what Bertie had got to try and do about his brother-in-law; everything, in fact, now depended on the Prince of Wales, and the pressure was high at Marlborough House.

Lord Salisbury, the Prime Minister, was somehow moved to firm and decisive action. He secured such favorable terms for the erring Greeks that they were actually allowed to put a Greek governor on Crete, but subject to nominal Turkish suzerainty! Marlborough House, and in this case Marlborough House was Britain, wanted the Greek governor to be one of King George's sons. Emperor William would not hear of that: it was the English family at work again, establishing new spheres of family influence. But he was beaten, for the rest of the Powers favored the selection of the Greek King's son, George.

This family worry carried Bertie and Alix into 1898. From the autumn of '97 to that of '98 was also a period of death. Late in October 1897, after an operation, Princess Mary, the Duchess of Teck, collapsed and died at White Lodge. There in the drawing room, where the carved oak coffin lay guarded day and night by ladies and servants of the household, Alix visited the body of the woman who had been so good to her since the days of her first arrival in a strange land. Unhampered by the official duties which were the lot of the Princess of Wales, Mary had literally given her whole life to the neglected poor.

In May 1898 Gladstone died at Hawarden. Their old friend was eighty-eight. Queen Victoria never displayed such lack of insight as she did in her attitude to Gladstone. A strange man with a host of unexpected interests, which some thought ill-tuned to his evangelistic urges, baffling, contradictory and dynamic on all subjects, he and his family had always been dear to Bertie and Alix, who, if they did not swear by the righteousness of all his works, believed in the great services he had given to the country for years.

The last paragraphs of the long letter which Mrs. Gladstone received after the funeral from the Princess of Wales reveal their depth of feeling for the Gladstones.

". . . We all individually grieve the loss of a great personal friend, from whom we have received innumerable kindnesses which we shall never forget. How my whole heart went out to you during last Saturday's terrible ordeal (the State funeral in Westminster Abbey), when I saw you kneeling by the side of the dear remains of him whom you loved best on earth, 'the People's William,' and your all.

". . . I was deeply touched by your kind lines when you thought there was a ray of hope left, and you may be sure our visit to you and your beloved husband only one little year ago, in your own beautiful home, Hawarden, will ever remain as one of our most precious and valued memories.

"With deepest sympathies with you and your children,

Yours very affectionately,

Alexandra."

Perhaps the Queen found it a new and last cause of complaint against Gladstone that he spoiled by his death her birthday celebrations. "I am sorry for Mrs. Gladstone," she said. "As for him, I never liked him and will say nothing about him."

The decision of the Prince of Wales to act as a pallbearer at the State funeral of the "G.O.M." (the Grand Old Man) roused the sharp indignation of his mother. It was unprecedented. Princes never did that—ridiculous and theatrical. There was apparently a move to get her to write an appreciation of her veteran servant for the newspapers, and Esher discloses that she absolutely refused to do this, saying that her private letter to Mrs. Gladstone was enough.

Then, as Michaelmas approached, Alix was called to Fredensborg. Her mother was dangerously ill. A telegram from Denmark came to the Queen from a daughter-in-law almost prostrate with grief. Queen Louise was dead.

When Alix later told the Queen that "no words could describe her sorrow," there was, perhaps, a note of reproach in her words; for her mother-in-law, though kindly to her at this time of affliction, had by no means made it easy or pleasant for her to take those annual trips to Denmark which had meant so much in her life.

It was in the early summer of 1899 that a telegram came to the Queen from Emperor William, who ever since his "Kruger Telegram" following the Jameson Raid in 1896 had been in ill odor, not only with the British nation but with his grandmother. The telegram announced William's regrets that he would be unable to join Her Majesty at Osborne that summer, because of an injury to Dona. It was surprising; he had not been invited.

Presently it became plain that William wanted an autumn invitation to Balmoral. He would like to bring the Empress. The German Ambassador somewhat delicately approached the Prince of Wales on the matter. The Emperor felt there had been misunderstandings. It was time to let Britain and Germany know that these were ended by a social visit.

This unquestionably would be a good thing, but personally it was disturbing to Uncle Bertie, who had just lost the Queen's Cup to the *Meteor II,* and who, of course, would have to be host. He went to the Queen and pressed the Emperor's suggestion. The Queen would not have William at Balmoral. On reflection she declared she would have him at Windsor in November. She supposed he would want some sport. Bertie could see to that: perhaps three days at Sandringham after Windsor. The invitation was accepted. William was coming with Dona, his two youngest sons, and a considerable suite, concerning whom he politely sent a list.

That was unfortunate, for this list nearly wrecked everything. Uncle Bertie discovered in the Imperial list an old enemy, Admiral von Senden, a stiff, supercilious Junker type, who till recently had been used by the Emperor to carry letters to the Queen. An unfortunate difference had arisen between the Prince of Wales and the admiral in the equerries' room at Marlborough House, and von Senden had given an insultingly colorful account of this to the Emperor. William was informed that the Prince could not accept von Senden. "I shall take whom I like, if I go!" came the sharp retort. Both men were furious; but so important was this good-will German visit considered to be that the Prince of Wales promised his friends he would give way—provided the German admiral apologized on arrival.

Meanwhile, on October 11, the Boer War broke out, and the German visit had to be shorn of all unnecessary ornament. Emperor William arrived with his family on November 19 for a five days' stay at Windsor. The Prince of Wales received his apology in writing from von Senden, and cordiality reigned in the Castle. Even the German Emperor's advice and sympathy for the British Army, which was doing very badly in South Africa and on the eve of Black Week, stirred no noticeable resentment.

Sandringham was keyed up for the Imperial three days. The last time William had been at Sandringham he had walked out of the house without an explanation, and the hostess went about her preparations with grim resignation.

But it was different this time. Even Aunt Alix was impressed and pleased, for William knew how to be attentive and charming. The Emperor, clad in a pale blue hunting suit with Tyrolean hat and black cock's feathers, and followed by four light blue Jägers with horns and loaded guns, performed some amazing one-handed shooting, seizing gun after gun and firing with startling speed, while his bag of pheasants earned the wonder of the shooting parties. Never did Emperor William part on such friendly terms with Uncle Bertie and Aunt Alix as at the end of this visit.

Even while the Emperor was at Sandringham the mind of Alix was largely taken up with her war schemes. Though her nephew's manner had improved, she resented the interruption to her activities. The most important of these was a hospital ship. It was entirely her idea. In the Crimea those invalids who did not expire in the horrors of Scutari were shipped home in the holds of hired cargo vessels. In the "small wars," homegoing troop ships had provided a miserable passage.

The hospital ship was to have every comfort, the latest medical facilities—even nurses. Sir Thomas Lipton, leading with his own liberal donation, soon got a fund going for her. Meanwhile she had to fight the same kind of battle with the War Office as Florence Nightingale had done in earlier days. Like Miss Nightingale, her obstinacy was equal to the task. Even Bertie seemed to think her idea rather luxurious, and somewhat grudgingly gave up an afternoon to visiting with her the hospital ship then fitting in London docks.

Some people aboard her hospital ship thought the Princess of Wales was very interfering: she seemed to imagine that she was captain, head surgeon, purser, foreman of fitters and matron rolled into one. In the end her ship was a very good one, except for the engines, which were beyond her. On one item she was beaten: they would not grant her ship a chaplain. She angrily accepted the assurance that captains read ships' prayers very well, content that she had won her major battle.

She was also concerned in a scheme for providing portable houses for the families of British dockers who had gone to unload store ships in South African ports. The cheapest huts, she was told, could be bought in Germany. "Nothing will induce me to get them from Germany!" was the determined reply.

Nurses were in short supply. She sent twelve of the best the London Hospital could provide as a start. These she paid out of her own fund, but demanded that they should wear the same uniform as the military nurses. Some jealous person at the front insinuated that her nurses were scarcely turning out as well as might have been hoped. Burning with indignation, she telegraphed to Lord Kitchener, demanding that "no stone should be unturned" to expose the truth. He replied that her nurses were excellent. He had tracked the libel to its source. The culprit had been asked for an explanation.

She did more than had ever been done before, except in a haphazard fashion, for the families of serving soldiers and for the war widows and orphans. But her chief achievement was in the nursing field.

There was a summer afternoon of 1901 in the gardens of Marlborough House—she was Queen then—when her biggest batch of nurses for the front grouped around her. An official offered to read for her "a fitting little speech" he had composed for the occasion. Nobody had ever expected the Princess of Wales to make speeches. She might perhaps on occasion say a word or two in that attractive foreign accent which she had never tried to smooth out. But this time she did intend to speak.

"Not a bit of it, my *speech,* I will speak it myself!" she announced in her clipped exclamatory manner.

It wandered somewhat from the point and a great deal from the text, but it stirred the nurses.

As Queen, she became President of the military Nursing Board. She was a virtual dictator, giving direct orders to government serv-ants on the staff; but nobody dared suggest that in this she was do-ing more than the King dared do. Her final achievement was the creation under the War Office of Queen Alexandra's Imperial Nursing Service, which has since so greatly distinguished itself in two world wars. For many years after its formation she was forceful and active in the interests and improvement of this corps, and she always talked of its members as "my nurses" till the day of her death.

In the year 1900, the last one of a sixty-three years' reign, Britain was without a friend in Europe. Everybody sided with the Boers. France thought she could never forgive Britain for the Fashoda in-sult. In France, where *"Vive les Boers!"* was shouted whenever an Englishman was recognized, both Queen Victoria and the Prince of Wales were so unrestrainedly insulted and caricatured by the Press that the Queen canceled her holiday in Italy because she would have to cross France, and the Prince did not visit his beloved Paris for the first time in eighteen years. He was President of the British section of the 1900 Paris International Exhibition, and had worked hard in the preliminary preparations. He now refused to attend the opening. In dismay members of the Government begged him to put a good face on things and go for the sake of policy. "If I did," said he, "the street crowds might insult the British uniform. That could mean War!" At this, Lord Salisbury agreed there was "no more to be said."

But Alix was interested, and she did visit the Exhibition with Charlotte Knollys. It was purely a holiday jaunt, and some people may have regarded their departure with anxiety. They stayed at the favorite Hotel Bristol, and no Parisian ever bothered them, though the presence of the Princess of Wales was no secret.

It had been earlier in the year, in April, that the event had at last happened which for one reason or another had been threatened for so many years.

Bertie and Alix had set out on a three weeks' visit to her father at Copenhagen. On the morning of April 4 they sat in their railway carriage in the Gare du Nord Station at Brussels. The whistle blew, doors slammed, and the train crawled slowly along the platform. Their carriage window was wide open.

Somebody leaped on the footboard. The scene outside was blotted out. The face of a youth, convulsed and wild-eyed, confronted them. The muzzle of a pistol quivered before them. Two crashes: they dazedly watched gray wisps of smoke curl from the barrel. The figure was torn backward from the window. Outside, fury and confusion raged on the platform. A hole in the upholstery between their heads showed where one bullet had lodged. The train jolted to a stop. Passengers, porters and police were beating and tearing at the assailant. The appearance of the Prince of Wales in their midst, ordering them to desist, probably saved the boy's life.

"It was fortunate that the miscreant was so bad a shot, as it seemed inconceivable he should have missed at two yards' range. . . . The Princess is none the worse, and bore everything with the greatest courage and fortitude," Bertie reported in a round of letters to his friends.

The miscreant was Sipido, a fifteen-year-old Belgian anarchist, the tool of older men who believed that by this deed they would profit the Boers in South Africa.

Sipido's bullet, taken from the upholstery, lies in an envelope in the Souvenir Room at Windsor Castle, and is labeled in King Edward VII's handwriting, "Sipido's bullet, Brussels, April 1900."

The Sipido attempt had a strange sequel. A Belgian jury acquitted Sipido's three accomplices, and the culprit because of his youth was ordered to be placed in a Home of Correction until he came of age. Sipido was then released for three days to prepare an appeal. He fled to France and vanished. It was King Leopold of Belgium himself who, turned detective, tracked the boy to Paris and in face of vehement denials assured the French police that the culprit was in the city. King Leopold proved to be right. Sipido was returned to the Home of Correction. But soon he was at liberty again. His letter of apology to King Edward was acknowledged but coldly received by the Foreign Office.

A person who seemed deeply upset by this affair and its shabby aftermath was Emperor William. Perhaps he imagined himself in the same circumstances. The morning after the attempt the Emperor arrived at the British Embassy in Berlin while the Ambassador was still in bed, to express his earnest condolences. When his uncle and aunt returned from Denmark, the Emperor, bringing the British Ambassador with him, boarded their train at Altona to congratulate them on their escape. Yet at this time "the friend of England" was moving toward a Franco-Russian alliance, the long-term motive of which seemed to be Britain's final destruction.

The last hour of the great reign was slowly drawing on. To none near the Queen did it approach unexpectedly.

At Osborne at 6:30 p.m. on January 22, 1901, Queen Victoria lay dead in the supporting arms of her grandson the German Emperor. Beside the bed knelt the new King, and all about stood the family. The Queen had rallied from time to time, and one by one she had recognized them as they called out their names. It was the new Queen who had wept most unrestrainedly.

The King must hurry off to London. It was Emperor William who, rejecting the undertaker's men, himself measured the Queen for her coffin; it was he who controlled everything in the house of death, who soothed the emotions of that tense evening; and it was he who joined the King on his return in the death chamber and with the Duke of Connaught gently lifted the little body of the dead Queen and laid it in the coffin. Strange, indeed, but it is the figure of Emperor William II, not King Edward, which dominates the public funeral of Queen Victoria; and it was the German Emperor, as much as the King, whom they cheered so loudly in London streets during the following days.

Part Six

EDWARDIANS

Chapter 25

AN OBSTINATE QUEEN

THE GOLDEN REIGN HAD BEGUN. It was the crystallization of the long Victorian age, which had almost but never quite found itself. Never were Britons so contentedly sure of themselves as in the first decade of the twentieth century, so amiably superior to a tinsel shabby world, never so comfortably immaculate. The brief Edwardian era stands alone in our history. Its glory derives much from the Sovereign couple who led the nation, and who by temperament were ideally tuned to the measure of the times.

After the State funeral the Sovereigns first showed themselves to the people on February 15, 1901, at the State Opening of Parliament.

It was two o'clock on a gloomy afternoon when King Edward VII appeared before the Throne. Suddenly the lights flashed up in the House of Lords, and there he stood holding the hand of Queen Alexandra. They had waited a long time. He was fifty-nine, she was fifty-six.

At sight of the Queen there was a gasp, a flutter in the air of the hall. The packed assembly saw a tall girlish figure with the crown gleaming above a black Mary Stuart coif and the deep black of her gown standing out from the brilliant State robe, a great rope of pearls falling to below her knees and the Koh-i-noor flashing in the golden light. Beside her the King, short and massive in scarlet tunic, offered a startling contrast. Esher noted that the Queen "was a little nervous," but her loveliness had "created a well-justified sensation."

But the Queen soon recovered herself. She appeared to forget that she was the constant target of all eyes. It was observed that she became almost undignified, and apparently unappreciative of the deep solemnity of the occasion, began to nod and smile to her friends, scanning every corner of the hall and evidently much amused by the "rugger scrum" at the Bar among the enchanted M.P.s who had flocked from the Lower House. People felt that there was a freshness in the air: that this first royal appearance inaugurated a new kind of royal regime, and they were right.

Two days before the State Opening, King Edward had convened an extraordinary Charter of the Garter, and by special statute he had made Queen Alexandra a Lady of the Garter. No woman had held this honor since the time of Henry VII. This the King had done because he was most anxious that the Queen should be seen wearing the Garter Ribbon at the Opening of Parliament. He was, as he told his friends, determined to show his appreciation of the way in which his wife had supported him during the long and perhaps tedious years as Princess of Wales. He meant to uphold her new dignity in every possible way; and, in the course of the new arrangements which were being worked out at this time, he received with great indignation a suggestion that when he was out of London the mounted Guard at Whitehall should be reduced. This detachment is symbolically the traveling escort of the Sovereign, and once actually was so in sterner days.

"Do you suggest that the Guard reduction at Whitehall takes place if the Queen still remains in London?" demanded the King.

The disturbed official mumbled, for he did mean just that.

"Certainly not!" snapped the King. "The Queen will always have the same traveling escort as myself."

He also directed that no kind of program of arrangements for the Queen must be made by an equerry without first consulting her, and any alteration that she wished must be attended to without further question.

The Princess of Wales had been thought of as easygoing during the last reign—at least, when she was not pursuing one of her pet ideas—but the unexpectedly outspoken resolve of the King to uphold his wife's Sovereign status was not at all ahead of her own views on this matter, as soon began to become apparent. She was going to establish for herself a peculiar kind of queenly omnipotence, which was, so to speak, the manifestation of Alix coming into her own at last.

Lord Esher, who was now coming much in contact with the new Sovereigns, told his son in a letter written shortly after the death of Queen Victoria that the Queen had objected to being called Queen Consort. She declared that "she meant to be Queen—although," he added, "she says rather pathetically she would prefer a peaceful and quiet station." Alexandra had also assured one of her close friends that now she was Queen she was going to do as she liked. With considerable exaggeration she declared that as Princess of Wales *she had always had to obey somebody,* but she *was not going to do so any more.*

Visitors to Windsor Castle, where the King and Queen were in residence, were impressed by the remarkable change in the atmosphere even within a fortnight of the death of Queen Victoria. In the royal apartments they suddenly realized that they were breathing fresh air and that previously they had gasped as they made their entrance. The gloom, the aroma of regal sanctity, was gone. The dead Queen's Indian servants were drooping about like "uneasy spirits," lost, unwanted, with nothing to do. Busy people pitied the plight of these faithful dusky servitors.

The Queen bustled about in her lively matter-of-fact way. The King sat with his friends in his own small set of rooms which he had used as Prince of Wales. Esher, who had known the last of the old days, thought that somehow the Throne was losing its dignity, and recorded his observation with nostalgic cheerfulness. It was all "too human."

Dinners at the Castle were shorn of all the old mysteries: the subdued lights, the holy hush, the sacred corridor where the old Queen had the shrinking diners brought forward to whisper one by one before the Chair. Now they all assembled in the Green Drawing Room, dined cheerfully in the White Room instead of in the dark oak room, and all went out arm-in-arm as they came in. The party remained in the Green Room. Sometimes the Queen played patience, or sometimes she played bridge with the King. At first she used to say that she could not play for money because her income had not yet been voted to her by Parliament and she could not tell whether or not they were going to be generous to her. Occasionally she risked penny points. But the real bridge began later when the ladies had retired.

Things gradually settled into a routine in which the Queen presided in the Green Room and the King soon carried off some chosen guests to the card table in the adjoining room. Every male guest summoned to the Castle knew he faced the possibility of having to sit up at the card table till at least one a.m. with the King. The new King may have been more good-natured in his tyranny than Henry VIII, but there was something about him which put people in mind of that monarch. Guests who had not been summoned to the King's table were at liberty to take their leave when the Queen retired to her apartments, and it was only the inexperienced who at this point approached the King's table to bid him good night. This was apparently not necessary, and old hands knew it was dangerous, unless you wished to risk the chance of being ordered to take a hand to replace someone who wanted to go home. As long as the Queen remained with her guests she was, says Esher, nearly always "full of rag and mischief."

The Secretary of the Office of Works soon discovered that he was destined for a busy time with the new King and Queen. They wanted to change everything at Windsor and Buckingham Palace. But they were by no means in agreement with the views of each other. During her last few years as Princess of Wales the Queen had grown very deaf, and this meant that conversations and arguments, bickerings and badinage were carried on in loud tones, which drew everybody's interest.

Two days after the Opening of Parliament, Lord Esher was called to Windsor to go over the State rooms and all the private rooms of the Castle with the King and Queen. Queen Alexandra declared that they ought to live in the State rooms. She could do a lot there with a little imagination.

"No," said the King loudly, "Mamma's old rooms are much the best for comfort when all the rubbish is turned out. I shall occupy my Father's rooms."

". . . Quite a smart difference of opinion," noted Esher in his journal that evening. A dutiful and more or less silent listener to this royal debate, which the King won, was the young Duchess of

Cornwall (the future Queen Mary), who accompanied them and whom Esher thought helpful with her quiet suggestions.

The Prince Consort's rooms, which the King intended to occupy, on that day presented exactly the same scene to the beholders as these had done on the day of the Consort's death, and his light top hat, gloves and cane still lay on the table in the anteroom. And, in the Queen's rooms, among the immense collection of rubbish, some of the first objects selected for destruction by her eldest son were several busts, statuettes and many photographs of Mr. John Brown. When the clearing-up began, King Edward is said to have triumphantly destroyed these with his own hands.

The bronze bust of Brown, which watched over his grave in Crathis Churchyard—the villagers whispered that in the twilight the eyes glared after passers-by, and they avoided the locality—was removed by royal command. One night while the family were in residence at Balmoral the big cairn of stones on the hillside, built by order of Queen Victoria, was seen to have vanished. Report soon spread that the heavy stones were scattered broadcast in all directions. The story was told that the King himself had gone out with a party by moonlight and had led them in the work of tearing down Brown's cairn. If any person about the Court was consulted about this, it was pointed out quite truly that the autumn gales were very severe that year.

Sir Lionel Cust, a very old friend and an art expert, was called in to reorganize and rehang the many magnificent pictures at Windsor and the Palace. He was awarded the title of Surveyor of the King's Pictures. Through casual rehangings the royal pictures had in the course of years fallen into laughable disarray: Landseer's stags, domestic scenes at Balmoral, worthless daubs of unknown German relations, and grand ducal family groups—a favorite kind of art with the old Queen—took pride of place or mingled with the most priceless Old Masters.

Shortly after Esher's visit to the Castle, Lionel Cust was going the rounds. He was not apparently escorting the Sovereigns on this occasion.

"As the King and Queen passed through the Castle," he recalls, "discussing plans . . . it was difficult to avoid being an eavesdropper owing to the Queen's unfortunate deafness and the King's rather penetrating voice.

"At one time, passing through the corridor, they passed by the marble effigy of a baby. Queen Alexandra asked who it was. The King replied: 'Don't you know?—if that child had lived you and I would not have been here.'"

The effigy dated from 1821, when Elizabeth, only daughter of William IV and Queen Adelaide, had died after a few months of life.

On March 5 a new royal command arrived for the Secretary of the Office of Works. Sir Francis Knollys required him to meet the King and Queen at the Prince Consort's entrance, Buckingham Palace, next day. He was to be "alone—please tell nobody." The assault on Buckingham Palace was to begin.

After that visit Esher wrote to his son that he was "tired to death." He was, in fact, contemplating giving up the Office of Works; but the King had cried out, "For God's sake, don't!" He promised to stay with them till after the Coronation.

The "fussing" over Buckingham Palace that day, with the two of them shouting at one another and not paying much attention, had been not unamusing. He was convinced that the Queen knew how to make the place really habitable. State rooms as well as living rooms had got to be completely overhauled. One of the first places they demanded should be done up at the public expense was the "Sepulchre"! This was the entrance hall below the Grand Staircase, walled in imitation marble, which damp and dirt had so blackened that the name given to it by the Sovereigns was very apt. Esher also learned on this occasion the interesting fact that Queen Alexandra had never in all the years entered her late mother-in-law's personal apartments in Buckingham Palace.

Three days later Esher was with the King at Hampton Court. He declared it was very beautiful. He would have to bring the Queen there. Shortly afterward it became known in the royal circle that the King and Queen were seriously considering transferring the Court for all time from the gloom of Windsor to the much happier environment of Hampton Court. This plan, however, presented certain obstacles, which could not be easily overcome.

Then Esher was back again at Buckingham Palace for a morning alone with the Queen. "She was in tearing spirits." She told him how she was going to arrange her personal treasures in all her apartments. She left, and in the afternoon King Edward arrived. Every room was visited again. Esher listened to the King's views, which in some respects were different. However, he felt sure that between them they would greatly improve the Palace.

Esher went to Marlborough House. The Queen wanted to see him. No "tearing spirits" this time: she was in "sore distress." She showed him all the treasures in her rooms. She did not know what she was going to do with all these "beautiful things." Suddenly she had realized that her Palace apartments would not hold half of them—unless, as she explained hopefully, she could be allowed more rooms than she was really entitled to use.

Meanwhile, the activity inside Buckingham Palace was great. They still lived at Marlborough House, but the King had his offices at the Palace. Between bouts of office work he might often be seen, cigar in mouth, sitting on a table or straddling a chair in rooms which suggested chaotic furniture warehouses. Decorators were at work and pictures were being hung up and pulled down. Nobody took any notice of him, and occasionally he shouted directions in high good humor, or arrived before some object and started to handle it himself. Sometimes the Queen came bustling in with Francis Knollys. She might not notice her husband among the men at work, and was evidently thoroughly absorbed and full of enjoyment.

One of the new enthusiasms of King Edward was for motor cars. He had bought several of these, but as yet he would not allow the Queen to have a car. There was a kind of chivalry in this, an anxiety for her safety, and perhaps also he felt that the sight of the Queen smothered in white road dust would be undignified; but his decision greatly annoyed Queen Alexandra, who saw many of her female friends traveling about in smart cars while she ambled after them in a carriage.

She managed, however, to acquire her delight in speed, for which she was noted, before she was mistress of her own car. When King Edward was away from Marlborough House she used to send out a lady in waiting to borrow a car from one of her friends. Members of the Court took a gloomy view of this habit, and wished the King would let her have her own car. Sooner or later, they prophesied, she would borrow "the wrong kind of chauffeur" and there would be a serious accident. It was, perhaps, this viewpoint which finally persuaded her husband to let her have a car for herself.

On the evening of August 5 news came that Empress Frederick had died that day at her Palace of Cronberg.

Eight days later King Edward and Queen Alexandra stood with Emperor William in the mausoleum of the Friedenskirche at Potsdam, where the body of poor Vicky was laid beside her husband. One of the brilliant women of her time, her lack of tact, perception and judgment had made her life a stormy and tragic one. Her eldest brother was deeply affected. He wrote to his friend Lady Londonderry, "She has now at last the rest and peace she wished," and doubtless he had in mind not only her physical agonies but the restless and unhappy years which had gone before.

This was the occasion of the first meeting of the King and the Emperor since the Queen's funeral. It was a restrained and amiable one, for William was inclined to accord a greater respect to Uncle Bertie in his new role. Perhaps he was moved to address himself to Uncle Bertie as a veteran Sovereign to a novice, but the only irritation he stirred came from quite a trivial cause. Seeking to show King Edward the greatest possible honor, the Emperor resorted to his favorite pastime, military display. When 15,000 troops, who had been lining the route to Potsdam, were suddenly summoned by the All Highest to march past King Edward at the Castle, he was secretly much annoyed, considering it to be a braggart gesture perfectly unnecessary and unsuitable to the sad occasion.

In the latter months of 1901 preparations for the Coronation, fixed for June 26, 1902, were in full swing. There having been no Coronation for sixty-four years, many problems offered themselves for settlement which have not arisen to trouble those concerned with subsequent Coronations. Historians and traditionalists had gone enthusiastically to work, and people listened attentively to their instructions. But one person at least heard them with some impatience. A number of experts, including fashionable dressmakers, had decided upon the right costume for the Queen at the Coronation. Traditional this may have been, but it was not attractive.

Queen Alexandra expressed her conclusions upon the matter to General Ellis, one of their oldest equerries, and then Comptroller to the Lord Chamberlain's Department.

"I know better than all the milliners and antiquaries," she announced in a brief note. "I shall wear exactly what I like, and so shall all my ladies. . . . *Basta!*"

Four of these ladies, who were to stand by her throne in the Abbey and "arrange" her crown, she was going to pick for herself. She was not interested in dusty claims or precedents, and was sorry to cause disappointment if somebody else had already selected them for her. She would have four Duchesses. The really important thing was that they should all be tall like herself. They must all be beautiful and they must all have a certain similarity of appearance. She was not going to have the effect spoiled by some lady who did not "match" the rest. The tenacity of the Queen on a number of points, not excluding the height of her footstool in the Abbey, was, indeed, one of the notable features of the 1902 Coronation. In view of this particularity of Queen Alexandra to have ladies who suited her to be in attendance by her Throne in the Abbey, instead of ladies who, whatever their looks, might have traditionally claimed to fulfill this office, it is of interest that the now elderly Augustus Hare, who was at the Coronation, refers in the last pages of his diary to the very bitter resentment aroused by the Queen's choice of four pretty Duchesses to bear her canopy, none of whom by right of precedence were entitled to perform such a duty.

As early as October 1901 rumors were rife not only in the provincial newspapers but among the leading London stores and tradesmen connected with the Court and society that the King was a very sick man and that the Coronation might be postponed or never take place. People about the Throne strenuously denied these stories, and strangely enough there is a good deal of evidence that these intimates believed that they were really speaking the truth. A growing irascibility in the Sovereign, a hastiness and impatience which sometimes discomfited them, they seem to have inclined to see as a sign that the monarchical office, after so many retarded years as Prince of Wales, had gone to King Edward's head. Royal servants, however, had probably formed a more accurate estimation of the truth.

Whatever people had chosen to think of King Edward while he

had been Prince of Wales, the tremendous reception which greeted his every appearance left no doubt of their gladness that he now ruled them. Perhaps they thought his robust geniality, his spaciousness, was more fitting in the kingly role. There has probably never been a more personally popular figure on the Throne than King "Teddy." The fact that he was resolved to spend as much or rather more time abroad than he had done as Prince of Wales—a quite unique procedure for a British monarch—and that he meant to rule without in the least abating any of his old amusements and activities, a traveling "country house" King, seemed to increase the love and admiration of everybody. He was colorful, and there had been a drab race of Sovereigns for nearly 250 years. And he could scarcely have had a more colorful Queen: her extraordinary appearance of youthful beauty was now becoming a national miracle. Perhaps she received even greater ovations than he did. She had said that she would have preferred a more "peaceful station." But she always encouraged the cheers. She loved them. Cheers and crowds made the King frown. He would look around for a way of escape. They upset him.

Lord Esher, among many others, confirms these opposite reactions to popular applause upon the King and Queen. He records a day in June 1902 before the Coronation when he escorted Queen Alexandra and Charlotte Knollys over the empty Abbey to see how things were being arranged. Nobody appeared to have seen them enter; but the word had gone forth. They came out, and there were all the Westminster boys in cricket flannels, all the clergy and domestics. A wild roar of cheering greeted them. It was the most sensational Abbey visit so far. "Such a row. The Queen was delighted. In that respect she is unlike the King, who dislikes a 'reception.'"

In 1902 a Coronation was such a novelty that it was natural that the nation should be intensely interested, and the added attraction that it was the first "Empire" Coronation made the event even more stirring; but it seems almost surprising that the middle-aged couple who were the central figures should have aroused such a flood of emotional excitement as was actually the case.

The first event of the glorious month was the Coronation Tattoo at Aldershot on June 14. The King, the Queen, Princess Victoria and the Prince of Wales (later George V) sat in the royal box, and there was frantic enthusiasm at the end when they were shown in a blaze of light. How could the spectators know that King Edward could scarcely keep his feet?

During the performance the King had been seized with violent pains. Nobody was aware of this but Queen Alexandra. But after the performance he appeared so ill that the family took turns at sitting up the night with him at Government House, Aldershot. He was better in the morning, but much exhausted, and rested that day at Government House. It was understood that the King had caught a "chill" from the rain and cold of the previous night. The family, however, were deeply anxious and puzzled. The Review of the Aldershot garrison was to take place on the following day. It was obvious the King could not undertake this: he appeared rather worse. On Monday morning, while the Queen with the Prince of Wales reviewed the line of 31,000 troops, King Edward was brought to Windsor in a traveling carriage with four horses. Queen Alexandra followed as soon as she could leave after the Review.

On Tuesday morning the King seemed to be recovered, and walked about his room. On Wednesday he lay in bed with a high temperature, but insisted on seeing important visitors, while his dog Jack lay on the bed and growled at everybody who kissed the royal hand.

Sir Francis Laking and Sir Frederick Treves, taking a serious view of the situation, were now talking of the need to postpone the Coronation till a later date. The King assured them he would sooner die in the Abbey than disappoint the people.

Councils were held and a final decision was come to that if there was no more than risk involved the King should go through with the ceremony; if real danger existed, in the doctors' opinion, the Coronation must be postponed. This presented the doctors with a difficult problem. The royal health fluctuated from day to day. They suspected the King suffered from an acute form of an inflammation now known as appendicitis. Only about two people in Britain had been operated upon for this complaint. They were aware that the King might die without an operation. They believed such an operation full of hazard. Meanwhile, King Edward, having very little idea what was the matter with him, was beset with anxiety that the public would hear of his illness. The only people who did get wind of it were the West End shop assistants.

Queen Alexandra attended Ascot. She was very calm and appeared in high spirits. It was said that Ascot was the one occasion upon which she could not supply the color which the presence of "Teddy" gave it. Coronation Ascot went flat, but still it was believed that the King suffered only from a chill.

Three days before the Coronation date, King Edward, according to arrangements, left his bed and with Queen Alexandra traveled by train to London, where they were to drive to the Palace in an open carriage with Escort. Laking had wanted the journey to be made quietly by road; but this would at once have caused comment, and King Edward was determined to keep his illness a secret.

This drive from Paddington to the Palace was the first occasion for thousands of Empire visitors and foreigners to see the King and Queen and vast excited crowds filled the streets. Among the spectators at Paddington was C. W. Stamper, who was shortly to be engaged as superintendent of the King's cars, and to become very intimate with the King and Queen.

At sight of the King, people were struck with horror and bewildered dismay, and so it was all along the route. Stamper describes his sensations:

"I stood among the crowd that cheered the King out of Paddington station. His eyes were closed, his head down, and his face grey and drawn. Her Majesty kept touching his arm to rouse him, and each time that she did so he lifted his chin a little, his hand struggled up to his head, and he raised his hat. He hardly opened his eyes at all. I was terribly shocked, and thought him as good as dead. . . . It is common knowledge that up to the last moment he withstood his physicians. . . . I have been told that he said to his doctors at Windsor: 'Afterwards you may cut me in two, but I cannot disappoint the people.'"

That afternoon, in the House of Lords, Lord Spencer asked Lord Salisbury for information about the King's health. A spectator records that "everybody took off his hat except dear old Lord Colville, aged 84, the Queen's Chamberlain, who sat on the 'sacks' looking a picture of sorrow." That evening the doctors came to the King. They told him bluntly he must submit to the operation and postponement of the Coronation or die.

It was noon on the 24th when suddenly, very fast, the grim news spread through the crowded streets, blazing and flapping with decorations. A kind of hush fell, broken only by the hammering of the workmen on the stands. That went on and on; and, indeed, the first thing the King did when he awoke after the operation was to complain about the hammering.

A Frenchman, staying at the Carlton, has left one of the best accounts of this occasion. His party had entered the gaily decorated restaurant, where laughter and loud conversation filled the room with an atmosphere of intense excitement.

"All at once there was an instantaneous and striking silence. We looked around with surprise, and, as the silence continued, we rose from our seats. Everybody was standing motionless, as if petrified. In the middle of the room Mr. Ritz, pale and dejected, was speaking in a voice muffled but clearly audible to all. He said, 'The Coronation will not take place. The King, after consultation with his physicians, is now undergoing an operation, dangerous, perhaps mortal, which has been deemed absolutely and immediately necessary.' "

The Carlton was to give a grand dinner and concert on Coronation Eve. By the King's wish all celebrations were to continue; but the expensive decorations seemed a heartbreaking mockery to the Frenchman.

"The concert," he says, "was a little shortened, and at one point a lady who sang was asked to give the National Anthem. The entire company rose and joined in it, but in some parts of the hall there were sobs. Whether foreigners or not, the women wept, and nearly all the men had tears coursing down their cheeks. The vocalist, affected by these tears and sobs, went into hysterics. The concert stopped, and the company, dejected and silent, left the hall. Nearly all went to their rooms."

The operation had been performed by Sir Frederick Treves, and as soon as it became obvious that the King would recover, Treves set to work to prevail upon everybody to persuade King Edward to be crowned during the first week in August, while he was still an invalid and the doctors had control over him. Otherwise he believed that the convivial temptations would be too great. *"Dinners,* Ma'am," he assured Queen Alexandra, "are far worse than a Coronation service!"

The July weather was brilliant, and the King was to convalesce for three weeks aboard the *Victoria and Albert* in the Solent. He was not as yet allowed to walk, and the prospect of being exposed to the compassionate gaze of his subjects in such a state much agitated him.

On July 14, the day before the royal departure for the Isle of Wight, sailors from the *Victoria and Albert* arrived at Buckingham Palace with a specially made carrying-chair. Their task was to carry the King from his bedroom to where a large closed omnibus would await him at the rear of the Palace. The sailors were brought up with the chair and were met by the Queen in the corridor outside the King's room. An equerry, at her command, seated himself in the chair and a rehearsal of the royal removal to the ground floor began, with Queen Alexandra anxiously supervising the party during the journey. Next day, in the morning, King Edward was safely carried down, shut into the omnibus with the Queen and passed out through Victoria Gate to Victoria Station without arousing the smallest interest.

One or two interesting glimpses have been recorded of life during the convalescence aboard the *Victoria and Albert,* where the King spent his days basking in the sun on a couch on deck, with the Queen frequently at his side. He always wanted someone to talk to, though it might be nobody more distinguished than a member of the crew passing on duty. Books were discarded one by one; he scribbled his illegible letters, which were broadcast across the counties of Britain and the face of Europe, and that was more amusing; but it was not long before by his command a stream of distinguished visitors began to present themselves at the gangway of the *Victoria and Albert.*

Kitchener was one of the first to arrive. "K."—the fabulous war-

rior, with those eyes of blue steel which made men shudder—
towered over the royal couch. He came straight from his South
African victories and the peace which he had achieved with the
Boers. "K." knelt and kissed the royal hand, and King Edward laid
the Order of Merit around his neck. Such was the harsh and ferocious reputation of Kitchener then that onlookers were touched at
sight of the giant kneeling with bowed head before his master.
Queen Alexandra burst into tears.

Lord Esher was summoned to the royal yacht. He always seemed
to find the Queen in "one of her ragging moods, too sweet for
words." Soveral was there, peering with sardonic good-humor
through his monocle, and always saying amusingly just enough,
never too much, to divert the King. Esher observed that the Queen
was greatly captivated by the Bishop of Winchester, as the old
Queen had been before her. The attraction seemed to be mutual,
and people watched with amusement as the solemn dignitary with
growing animation followed her about. She led him so far away
from the paths of virtue that he smoked his first cigarette with her.
Esher was at Osborne House when the Queen arrived with the
Bishop. She took him upstairs alone to the bedroom where Queen
Victoria had died. There, as she told everybody afterward, the two
of them held an impromptu service beside the empty bed. It was
"the mixture of ragging and real feeling" which Esher and others
found "so attractive about the Queen."

The return to London was made on August 6, to prepare for the
Coronation three days later. The Colonial troops and the foreign
guests had departed. People no longer looked for pageantry. Many
called the Coronation when it finally came "a family festival."

In the words of Queen Alexandra to the Archbishop of York:
". . . It was quite different from last time. Then people were thinking too much of the pageant, and not enough about the religious
part of the ceremony."

But if the tone of the Coronation was subdued, the Queen herself
caused a tremendous sensation, as she had done at the Opening of
Parliament in 1901. So inspired was one spectator, who watched her
in the Abbey, that he wrote, "It seemed as though there burst upon
the imagination for the first time the full sense of what a Corona-

tion means." Queen Alexandra was universally hailed as the most beautiful Queen who had ever entered Westminster Abbey.

Some public functions had inevitably to be undertaken by the King and Queen after the Coronation, and King Edward was advised to take a sea cruise, one of his favorite amusements, at the earliest opportunity.

Accordingly on August 22 they left Cowes for a cruise along the west coast of Scotland. When they visited the Isle of Man they were entertained by Sir Hall Caine, the famous Edwardian novelist. He has left a vivid impression of that occasion:

> "Just a gentleman in a lounge suit and two ladies wearing black sailor hats, driving in an ordinary hired landau, with a few friends and officials of the island in carriages and hackney cabs behind them, and three or four local journalists bicycling by their sides. . . .
>
> "I should have said that the King was a strong man that day. Looking at his sunburnt face, and listening to his full voice and hearty laughter (I told him some quaint Manx stories), I found it hard to realize that he had lately recovered from a serious illness. In conversation he rarely said more than a dozen words at a time, yet this conveyed no sense of reticence but rather of an unbroken flow of talk, consisting chiefly of questions. The Queen, on the other hand, talked continuously, hardly ever waiting for a reply, but this may have been partly due to her deafness, which, though not then extreme, must have made it difficult for her to hear what others about her were saying. She was all nerves and emotions, but it was clear that she was struggling to control both in order to spare or not displease the King. Our insular authorities, in the excess of their loyalty, had ordered that numerous guns should be fired during the luncheon hour from some unseen place under the Castle walls, and seeing how much the explosions were distracting her I suggested that I should ask the Governor to stop the firing, but she would not permit me to do so. 'No, no, please don't: the King would not like it,' she said.
>
> "It was the King with her first and last always."

Basically, Sir Hall Caine is doubtless right in envisaging Queen Alexandra as always concerned above all with pleasing her husband. Yet he contrives to suggest a subdued quality, a queenly submission, which another event of this same year scarcely corroborates. Sir Hall Caine would perhaps have been bewildered if he had heard of Lord Esher's story of the first Trooping of the Color Birthday Parade, which took place on October 27, 1902. Not many were aware of the truth at the time, and if it reached shocked newspaper editors they suppressed it.

King Edward had decided that his Birthday Parade was an occasion when the Queen ought not to appear. He told Queen Alexandra that she could watch the final march past the Palace from a window with the old Duke of Cambridge, whom she was to entertain. She received this announcement in ominous silence. But she seated herself beside the Duke at the window and watched King Edward depart in glory down the Mall.

Presently she declared, "I go!"—a celebrated exclamation of hers—and standing up, ordered a carriage to be brought round instantly.

In a few minutes the veteran Duke sat alone in stupefied incredulity with tears coursing down his cheeks, while below him the Queen's carriage seemed to race from the Palace gates to the Horse Guards.

The Queen arrived on the Parade almost unnoticed. Her carriage joined the tail of the King's procession, and with serene unconcern she followed in the wake along the line of troops. Esher does not disclose what happened when the King first became aware of the Queen. As a highly discreet courtier he was perhaps somewhat shaken himself, but he records the incident as "funny."

Nor was Queen Alexandra's action when Cecil Rhodes died in this year indicative of a respectful attitude toward the contemporary viewpoint of high authority.

Ever since the Jameson Raid and the disclosures and recrimination which followed, Cecil Rhodes had lived in retirement under a cloud. He had been put in official Coventry. When he died, one of the wreaths displayed at the funeral caused some raising of eyebrows among officialdom. The wreath was from Queen Alexandra: the only royalty bold enough to pay tribute to a disgraced man. Had anybody asked why she sent it, she would probably have answered, "Well, I liked Mr. Rhodes!"

The Coronation had given her an excuse for one of her original experiments in generosity, and she was anxious to make the most of the opportunity. One day in late spring she asked someone about her, "Who do you think are the unluckiest and most ill-used people in the country?"

After a moment's hesitation the answer came: "The maids of all work, Ma'am. They get a hard time!" This was offered half jokingly.

"Good," said the Queen. "I'll give them a tea party."

Having made a large subscription from her own purse, she soon found many eager to back her whim both with money and practical assistance. As a result, 10,000 maids of all work sat down to an elaborate tea in halls all over London. The Queen herself visited as many of her guests as possible, and beside each plate was a brooch mounted with a crown and the Royal Arms and "From the Queen" inscribed on the reverse side. Perhaps royal recognition did do something to better the unhappy lot of girls who were scornfully referred to as slaveys.

In November the Emperor William came to them for the Sandringham birthday party. It was considered a family attention which should be accorded him in Coronation year. He had, after all, been most anxious to come and "boss" the Coronation, believing that he had a claim to be invited even if other Sovereigns were not.

This was the last occasion upon which a meeting of perfect cordiality appeared to persist from beginning to end. Yet William had stirred Uncle Bertie to secret fury and tired out Aunt Alix. If King Edward could have read the Emperor's report to his Chancellor, "My reception here was hearty and affectionate as ever," a weary smile would have passed his lips. William, overflowing with All High geniality, was at his expansive worst. It was his pleasure to tell everybody how they ought to do everything. He assured Uncle Bertie that he was using the wrong motor fuel: hence the unsatisfactory results. He ought to use potato spirit. If the advice was heard with impatience, it was quickly forgotten.

But several days later a mysterious array of bottles and phials decorated the royal table. The ingredients of potato spirit had arrived from Berlin by Imperial command. The Emperor was the only person in the room who was totally unaware of the indignant explosion which the King suppressed by a supreme effort.

Sir Henry Irving, traveling day and night from Belfast, reached Sandringham to entertain the Imperial guest, returning the same night to his company in Ireland. It was his custom to accept no payment for such occasions. His reward was a generous outpouring of Hamlet-like advice accorded to him by the Emperor at supper.

When Emperor William departed, King Edward was heard to exclaim, "Thank God!" at Portsmouth; and Aunt Alix, resting at Sandringham, declared she was "perfectly exhausted."

Coronation year ended for Queen Alexandra with her Christmas Dinner in the Alexandra Trust building to 1,500 war widows and their families. This was to be a more intimate affair than the tea for 10,000, and she personally insisted upon supervising all the arrangements. The puddings were to be piped in by the Scots Guards, there were to be presents for all and a full program of famous variety artistes was prepared to enliven the proceedings. But when December 27, the great day, arrived, Queen Alexandra lay in bed in deep distress with a violent cold, and the much-looked-forward-to dinner had to take place without her.

Chapter 26

SOVEREIGNS IN A NEW PATTERN

THE YEAR 1903 was the year of the "Entente Cordiale." It was entirely the King's idea and it was his achievement. For years he had dreamed of a spiritual union between the British and the French, which in course of time must develop into something stronger and more binding than any signed treaty between statesmen. The time scarcely looked auspicious. Nobody else but "the Frenchman at heart" would have dared such a venture in the spring of 1903. He might bring frightful humiliation not only upon himself but upon his country. If he attempted this, he had got to succeed.

In the spring King Edward set off alone on a yacht cruise, which after a State visit to Portugal took him to Gibralter, to Malta and finally to Naples and a State visit to Italy.

The outward journey was done. All this had been very successful; but it was easy. Neither the Portuguese nor the Italians had sponsored the Boers as had the French, nor had they lost Fashoda. The royal suite could scarcely be blamed for dreading the State visit to Paris, which the King had pressed for so ardently from a surprised and somewhat reluctant French President.

It was May 1 when King Edward, pale and stern, stepped from the Bois de Boulogne station in Paris. *"Vive les Boers!" "Vive Fashoda!"* were the only cries to greet the British scarlet. There might well be a bullet before long.

"The French don't like us, Sir," murmured sardonically one of the resentful suite who trailed behind him.

"Why should they!" snapped the King.

They drove with the President through a chilling silence and an army of watchful bayonets. Catching the slightest sign of friendship in the crowds, King Edward bowed and smiled.

It is said that King Edward won the heart of Paris, and therefore the heart of France, on the following evening at the Théâtre Français. In the interval he strolled into the lobby smoking his cigar. Recognizing a Parisian actress who had visited London, he approached her and engaged her in loud and animated conversation.

Certain it is that three days later, when he left the Gare des Invalides, having come to the French with nothing to offer but his genial personality, he passed happily out of the station with the crowd roaring, *"Vive notre Roi!"*

The Entente proper was to follow later; but this in the eyes of history was the moment of miracle. It was the supreme achievement of his life, and nothing can have given him greater satisfaction.

After this their projected visit to Ireland in July must to him have seemed more hopeful. As for Queen Alexandra, she was full of memories of skulls and crossbones, and seemed to be looking forward to a new trial of strength. It might turn out a stormy passage. Irish M.P.s had actually risen in the House and cheered British defeats during the war.

The extraordinary success of the Irish visit took many by surprise. In Paris people had shouted, *"Vive notre Roi!"* In Ireland all over the place they howled: "Come back! Come back!" and simple people wept and sobbed in a kind of frenzy at their departure. The Dublin Corporation had refused them an Address of Welcome, but that did not stop the Dubliners giving them a colorful and thunderous welcome.

In one remote village where they stayed to inspect the carefully cleaned-out peasant cabins the ignorant and ragged inhabitants rushed about them screaming, "Hurrah for *Henry VII!*"

At Mallow station, where amid skull and crossbone emblems they had been all but torn from their train on their last Irish visit, they descended into a cheering throng. Mr. Hains, the father of Nurse Hains, who had nursed the King after his operation, was brought to the King and Queen. He was assured by the Queen that his daughter had probably saved the King's life, and that she seemed very successful in the post which the King had given her as Matron of the newly established Convalescent Home for officers at Osborne House.

These two outstanding events of 1903, the French and the Irish visits, were a great delight to a King and Queen at the outset of their reign, and an encouragement when they looked toward the future.

So delighted were they with the Irish visit that they decided to go again in the following year. Accordingly in April 1904 they were once more in Dublin. As on a previous occasion, the Dublin Corporation, faithful to tradition, refused them an Address of Welcome; but when they attended a gala performance at the theater the house rose at them at their entrance, and the gallery, alleged to be packed with the roughest elements in the capital, broke into "God Save the King" and carried it through to the end without a note of accompaniment from the band. The emotional Irish were amazed and stirred by the beauty and grace of the Queen, and this was a factor which undoubtedly played an important part in the first two Irish visits of the reign.

It was in July 1904 that Lady Walburga Paget, she who had done so much to bring Bertie and Alix together many years before, and had watched them with a friendly and discerning eye ever since, made a revealing entry in her diary:

"The King, as King," she wrote, "is much more useful than he was as Prince of Wales. He has a great deal of ability, but is always surrounded by a bevy of Jews and a ring of racing people. He has the same luxurious tastes as the Semites, the same love of pleasure and of comfort. Still, he is a *charmeur* and very able."

Augustus Hare, the diarist, noticing at the Coronation the gallery in the Abbey which was alloted to the King's friends, refers to the jealousy which their presence had naturally stirred in certain established circles and discloses that they were nicknamed "the Fallen Angels."

By 1904 the royal regime had got into its stride and the pattern was becoming clear. Buckingham Palace was scarcely as it is today, a royal dwelling-place for a part of the year: it was a royal stopping-place between country house visits. It was noticeable that the King and Queen were seen together a good deal more than they had been in their later years as Prince and Princess of Wales. As a rule, Queen Alexandra was a guest only at the greater country mansions such as Chatsworth or Blenheim. To the smaller houses King Edward usually went alone. But whether the house was big or small, the host had to submit to one rule when the King was coming. If the royal stay was to last over three days he must hand over a room to the local post-office authorities to be fitted up as a postal and telegraph office. During these country house visits King Edward did a great deal of work, as also when he was on the Continent, and he never departed to his pleasures till all was done. Statesmen were amazed at his grip on everything and his speed of execution. He was soon known to be an extremely jealous monarch, and to keep any detail from him courted a sharp explosion. His worldliness had imbued him with judgment of a very high order, and the influence of the country house ruler soon became immense. One rule which King Edward imposed on himself was that between country visits he always spent a few days at the Palace to straighten out any tangled ends.

New glory came upon Sandringham and Balmoral, which the local people hugely enjoyed. C. W. Stamper has given an interesting picture of Royal Sandringham when the upper and lower lakes were frozen over.

"Sometimes a hockey-match was arranged. Equerries, guests and servants of all grades were summoned to take part in it. The King would pick one side and the Prince of Wales another. His Majesty used to keep goal. It was only at these times that the servants were allowed to skate upon the upper lake, but the lower was always at their disposal. At that of the tenantry, too, and of everyone on the estate."

Queen Alexandra was "always first on the ice," the most skilled skater in a keen skating family.

At Christmas the suite and household gathered round the great tree in the ballroom, at the foot of which the King and Queen stood behind a kind of counter. Everybody held a numbered ticket corresponding to the presents on the tree. An equerry passed the presents down to the King: he called the number and handed out the presents; unless the number corresponded to his own present—a moment for applause. The Queen meanwhile flung bags of sweets and crackers in all directions. Sometimes she put distorting spectacles on her nose, which caused her to aim one way and throw another, a simple amusement which made her shriek with delight.

Guests at Sandringham in those days were the little flocks of birds which Queen Alexandra used to feed in winter. Among these many cock pheasants appeared, which she always addressed by name. If, as often happened, one of her pet pheasants was killed by the never-ending shooting parties, she became extremely annoyed with the King and the party in general.

Sir Felix Semon, the King's friend, tells of the Balmoral dinner-parties under the new Sovereigns, where "a deafening tribe of royal pipers in Highland garb, when the game was served, solemnly marched three times round the table and made a hellish noise with their bagpipes."

Once more Balmoral was dedicated to the noble stag, as in the days of the Prince Consort. But whereas a kind of earnest intensity had reigned there then, inspired by the princely Coburger, King Edward with a boyish gusto plunged his guests into the strenuous sport, and brimming with geniality and pride exhibited to them all the colorful ceremonial he could command. Stag shoots took place almost every day, and Queen Alexandra and often the Princess of Wales with her children drove to join the sometimes rather jaded sportsmen who came in from crag and forest for the picnic luncheon. And if the never-ending jokes and banter about "staggies," which indoors and out of doors poured from the stout and beaming royal host, seemed occasionally rather feeble to his guests, there was something wonderfully spacious and regal about it all which made a Balmoral visit a prized memory.

Only twice during the reign is Queen Alexandra known to have taken a hand in international politics—in the autumn of 1904 and the summer of 1905; and, as might be surmised, it was only her family connections which brought her to do so. For in the one case Russia and in the other case Denmark were dangerously involved.

On an October night in 1904 the Hull fishing fleet trawling off the Dogger Bank was suddenly illuminated in a blaze of searchlight beams. A minute later a storm of shells was exploding around them. The result was tragic, and no vessel appeared from the darkness to give them succor.

The Russian Imperial Fleet proceeding to the seat of war in Japanese waters had in a moment of extraordinary panic bombarded the Hull trawlers in belief that these were Japanese gunboats sent out to waylay them.

But the Russian admiral never even troubled to report his feat of arms on Dogger Bank, and only offered an explanation at all when violently pressed to do so.

No wonder King Edward, the British Press and the public cried out for the blood of the Russian admiral, demanded humiliating reparations and said many nasty things about Russia and her gallant fleet! Nobody hates apologizing more than a Russian, especially if he is in the wrong. Matters had soon been pushed to the brink of a war which nobody wanted.

"Nicky" himself was full of apologies to his English relations; and here was a key to the impasse, if anybody attempted to make use of it. For, though "Nicky" was rather weak and not so influential as the Czars before him, his mother Marie Fedorovna, the Dowager Empress, had a voice which was listened to in the most powerful Muscovite circles.

King Edward in his indignation pursued a recalcitrant attitude even toward "Nicky"; but Queen Alexandra meanwhile was doing all she could in her letters to her favorite sister to set the affair on a cool and even basis and to prevail on her to soothe rising tempers at St. Petersburg. She also probably played a part in causing King Edward to make a sudden *volte face*. For he suddenly seemed to recognize that the sharpness of his own attitude and the violence of the demands he was personally sponsoring must end in war. Quite unexpectedly the King wired the British Ambassador at St. Petersburg to modify Britain's demands. This moderate approach almost certainly kept Britain out of the Russo-Japanese War and gained her an ally which in the early days of the First World War proved to be of great value.

The German Emperor had been very much frightened at the

Dogger Bank incident. He had resolved that if a British fleet dared to storm the Baltic he would occupy Denmark and close the Kattegat.

This fear resulted nine months later in a clandestine arrangement made with cousin "Nicky" at Bjorko, that if at any time the British Fleet *did* attempt to enter the Baltic, Russia and Germany would jointly occupy Denmark, if possible peacefully.

To this end the German Emperor presented himself uninvited to the aged King Christian at Fredensborg. But before he departed for Denmark, warning of what was afoot had reached London through the Emperor's sister, who was married to the Crown Prince of Greece.

Here was a matter which Queen Alexandra could best handle: was she not her father's favorite and adored daughter? She rather feared that her father, who was eighty-six, might be a little feeble in face of the wheedling and blustering Emperor. But a strong letter from darling Alix would surely fortify him.

Her father had always been amiable and easygoing: it took a lot to stir him. Sitting at her desk she gave her emotions free play as she proclaimed her "horror at the bare thought of his *betraying* England." Such a thing, she declared, was beyond belief. Whatever old Christian might have done without his daughter's backing, he now assured her that he was in full agreement with her sentiments. The German Emperor retired crestfallen from Fredensborg.

A complicated and involved intrigue followed, during which the Emperor blamed not Aunt Alix but Uncle Bertie. "The arch mischief-maker of Europe is at work in London again!" he warned cousin "Nicky." And why had the Dowager Empress of Russia when visiting her father at Fredensborg summoned the Russian Ambassador to St. James's to cross the sea to meet her? He knew it was all aimed again at himself and wondered if "Nicky" realized what his mother was doing! As for "Nicky," having made a fool of himself at Bjorko, he was making excuses all round, sure only that he had had enough of cousin Willy.

By now relations between King Edward and Emperor William were obviously brittle and vicious. Uncle and nephew met abroad from time to time, and watching one another with beaming faces searched for twisted meanings in every word that was spoken. The bitter antagonism which had begun on the waters of the Solent had now spread to the high seas of the world. The naval armaments race was under way.

The fact is trivial but not unamusing that, in all their relations together, only once did Uncle Bertie admit the supremacy of nephew William. This concerned the German Emperor's hand "bugle-horn" or cornet with four keys, which cleared the way for the Imperial motor-car. A Jäger played this, sitting beside the chauffeur. King Edward could not resist the "bugle-horn." It was once the office of C. W. Stamper, superintendent of the royal cars, who sat in front whenever King Edward traveled, to play this fascinating instrument along the highways of England: a process which occasionally required prompting by a tap on the glass by the King.

Another international problem of 1905, rapidly developing into an energetic intrigue, inevitably involved King Edward and Queen Alexandra, although they would gladly have kept their names free of it. Maud, their lively youngest daughter, had married her cousin Prince Charles of Denmark. A marriage considered of no especial significance suddenly became an affair of European interest.

In the summer of 1905 Norway broke away from Sweden, amid scenes of considerable disturbance. Norway wanted a king for herself. Charles of Denmark appeared to be the most favored of several candidates. It was natural that the King and Queen should encourage the claims of their own son-in-law, especially as he was living in England with their daughter and was very intimate with the family. But unhappily, as the worst of several complications, the German Emperor, bursting with jealousy and viperous insinuations, was pushing a candidate of his own, chiefly, apparently, as a counter to the dynastic ambitions of Uncle Bertie and Aunt Alix! Nor was William inclined to suppress his unworthy suspicions, and whisperings about the "arch mischief-maker of Europe" being at work once again were heard in the Chancelleries of Europe.

All that the King and Queen had actually done was to declare their full approval of Charles's claim provided, and only provided, the momentarily highly indignant King of Sweden would agree to it. Privately they urged Prince Charles to betake himself abroad and press his own claims for all he was worth. This, after some reluctance, he was persuaded to do.

As a result, Charles and Maud were finally elected King and Queen of Norway in November 1905, and Emperor William secretly chalked up another black mark against his English relations.

When in the following spring news reached Charles (King Haakon VII) that the German Emperor was about to "steal a march on the English" by inviting himself and Queen Maud to pay their first State visit to Berlin, he immediately wrote to his father-in-law to declare that the first Norwegian visit "must be" on family grounds made to Windsor. Some statement of a sufficiently strong character to stave off the overtures of Berlin seems actually to have been put out, and the first Norwegian State visit—a somewhat unconventional affair consisting of a month at Windsor—took place in November 1906.

It was on January 29, 1906, that Queen Alexandra had been summoned to Denmark. King Christian, having reached his eighty-seventh year, had suddenly died of heart failure. Christian had indeed seen changes in the world since the days at Yellow Palace. King Edward was unable to accompany the Queen. Crown Prince Frederick succeeded his father; and so aged had their father been that it scarcely seemed to the children a time for deep or long mourning. It did not prevent Queen Alexandra going with King Edward to the revival of the Olympic Games in Athens three months later.

Before that, however, Dowager Empress Marie Fedorovna came from Russia to England for a private visit to her sister. Dagmar had not been in England for more than twenty-five years, and although the sisters had constantly corresponded they had seen comparatively little of one another. One afternoon she and the Queen had tea with their young cousin the Duke of Teck, who was commanding the King's Life Guard at Horseguards. It was said that Dagmar spent an hour gazing down enraptured and almost silent from the window upon the lively street scene of Whitehall. Royalties did not do that kind of thing in Russia.

On April 6, 1906, the royal yacht left Marseilles for Corfu with the King and Queen aboard, and from there proceeded to Phalerum. They were to be the guests of King George during the revival of the Olympic Games at Athens. The family meeting was, of course, delightful, but there was an inclination in the guests to anticipate the games as rather a bore—something likely to be tedious and amateurish. A huge new garish white stadium appeared too flamboyant for the nature of the expected display.

They were agreeably surprised by the unlooked-for efficiency of the Hellenes, and from being impressed began to take a lively interest, especially when the British fencing team led by Lord Desborough gained a resounding victory over the Germans, who had been expected to win. What followed filled the King and Queen with uneasy dismay. They had begun to feel uncomfortable when the spectators had laughed at the desperate but gallant antics of the fat German captain, who was severely whacked all over his body in saber play. The Germans had fought strenuously; they were simply a good team outmatched. With horror, therefore, the royal guests listened to the delirious roar of delight which went up from the Greeks at the German overthrow, and the more so because the Greeks were obviously trying to identify the British Sovereigns with this moment of celebration. The fact that the Germans were accepting their defeat like sportsmen added to their embarrassment.

King Edward and Queen Alexandra were observed to whisper urgently together. An equerry moved unobtrusively toward the British team leader. The moment the cheering died, Lord Desborough called to his team for three cheers for the German team, a courtesy clearly appreciated by the vanquished and not previously heard during the games.

On the last day of the games, Queen Alexandra was asked by her brother to present the prizes, and during this ceremony a little incident occurred which is a striking example of the freedom of speech that she allowed herself to adopt during the days of her queenhood. One almost wonders whether she was voicing her inner thoughts and uttered the words unconsciously, as is the way of some people in their later years.

Mr. A. Metaxas, the Greek Royal Court Architect, had won several of the shooting prizes. He approached, and Queen Alexandra shook his hand and gave him the winning smile which everybody expected of her. Then her expression assumed a rather more serious mien and she said something to him in English. Perhaps this surprised him, for he knew she could speak good Greek. Metaxas did not understand English, but he was delighted as it could only be a compliment: a compliment, moreover, which she had not awarded to previous prize-winners, upon whom she had merely smiled graciously.

The beaming Greek asked her nephew, Prince Nicholas, to translate the royal compliment. Nicholas, himself somewhat taken aback at his aunt's words to the royal architect, hesitated a moment.

"I'm afraid you will be rather surprised," explained Nicholas. "My aunt, you know, is rather an original lady. She said, 'I am very pleased to meet you—my brother's house is tumbling down!' "

The immediate cause of this severe pronouncement by the British Queen upon the Greek Royal Palace to the official responsible for its upkeep was because upon the previous afternoon some plaster had dropped from the ceiling and whitened her dress. Her accusation was not unjustified, however. Her brother's palace was indeed in need of attention, and it shortly afterward got it.

It was in 1906 that C. W. Stamper, who had not then been long in the royal service and was as yet not fully accustomed to royal vagaries, experienced an amusing instance of the imperious nature of Queen Alexandra. He was sitting in front of the Queen's car during a drive near Sandringham when the glass behind him was sharply tapped.

The Queen was gesticulating at him. Thinking something amiss, he followed his usual custom in such cases: he slipped out upon the running board of the moving car and came to the back window.

"Stamper," said the Queen, "I hear your brother is down here. Where is he staying?"

"At a hotel in Dersingham, Your Majesty."

"I hope he's comfortable. I have seen him acting in London. I should very much like to hear him sing."

"I know he would be proud to sing before Your Majesty at any time you please."

"Then ask him to come this afternoon!"

The afternoon concert duly took place before a household full of royalty in the Sandringham ballroom; but the breathless summons was a shock for the actor brother. Naturally it was a great honor, and Queen Alexandra was very sweet to him; but perhaps he never fully realized how glibly his brother had signed him on for this sudden nerve-shattering occasion.

The second week of February 1907 used to be long recalled by Queen Alexandra with an almost childish pleasure. King Edward took her to Paris for an incognito week of shopping and theater-going. Simple amusements of that kind were what she had longed for all her life and so rarely enjoyed. In all the years she had seldom been able to call her husband truly her own. But now they were just private people and the Parisians were happy to let them be. But if the French were delighted, as was obvious from their newspapers, the Germans saw things differently. One German journal announced that King Edward "wants to see for himself what is taking place in his branch establishment in Paris" (*Reichbote*), and the general tone was cynically offensive. *Reichbote's* remark amused King Edward, who made a point of meeting the German Ambassador. "Tell them," he said with faint scorn, "that the only reason I was in Paris was to please the Queen!"

With the death of old King Christian there was no longer any reason for the longed-for family reunions each year at Fredensborg. By the time 1907 came, Queen Alexandra and Marie Fedorovna realized fully what these had meant to them. A melancholy vacuum had come in their lives, and so it seemed it must be every year now. They yearned for Denmark as they had always done: yet what excuse had they still for often going there?

The two sisters in 1907 decided to buy a modest white villa called Hvidore looking out over the waters of the Baltic near beloved Bernstoff. Hvidore should be their annual meeting-place, and in Denmark Queen and Dowager Empress henceforth would be just private persons.

Here the two would meet every year until the Great War; and at Hvidore Empress Marie arrived as a fugitive with nothing but her jewels after the Russian Revolution.

July 1907 saw the last Irish visit of the reign. It was a bad year in Ireland: the year in which the Sinn Fein movement came into being, a year of cattle-driving and outrages. But the King and Queen, who confined their visit to the environs of Dublin, appeared to be greeted with almost universal enthusiasm in that part of the country.

This time they stayed aboard the *Victoria and Albert* in Kings-town harbor and made their visits from the ship. But this arrangement was not for the sake of safety, but because Lord Aberdeen, the Lord Lieutenant, an aristocrat whose domestic arrangements were reputed to be somewhat eccentric, had plainly showed an unwillingness to lodge royal guests at Viceregal Lodge: an attitude which King Edward curtly accepted with the comment: "All right. We shall stay on the yacht."

That, however, was only a minor cause of dissatisfaction. The King, unknown to the crowds who acclaimed him, was in the deepest ill-humor with everything Irish from the start. Just prior to his arrival, the Dublin Crown Jewels had mysteriously vanished from the safe in the Heralds' office at the Castle. Under the circumstances even the Heralds came under suspicion. The King, who did not think that sufficient concern was being shown by the authorities, nor zeal in pursuit of the thieves, who were rumored to be highly placed and possibly politically minded persons, was inclined to see the affair as a personal insult. Whether or not his attitude was justified, and he expressed himself with remarkable candor, nothing since has ever been heard of the Dublin Crown Jewels.

A peculiar transaction of the late summer and autumn of 1907, which came to concern intimately both the King and Queen, was that of the Cullinan Diamond. A matter which began innocently enough soon gave signs of developing into a political problem of some magnitude.

On August 19 Prime Minister Botha rose in the South African Parliament House and gave notice of a motion to authorize his government to buy and present to King Edward as a birthday gift the newly discovered Cullinan Diamond. The diamond had been brought up at the Premier Mine, Pretoria, and named Cullinan after the senior director. It was claimed to be the largest in the world.

This gesture of General Botha's was a mark of final reconciliation between the Dutch and the British. At first the British Government, and indeed King Edward, heard the news with enthusiasm. But presently it became known that although Botha's motion had been carried by 42 votes, there had been 19 Dutch members who had voted against the presentation. Those 19 dissentient votes must represent a considerable body of Boer opinion, and the King was quick to note this sinister fact and bring its import home to his ministers.

A gift of reconciliation in the purchase of which all Dutch tax-payers must participate, but which many seemingly regarded with distaste, might do more harm than good in South Africa. Then it became known that many Free State British had come to be against the presentation out of a kind of jealousy, because the Dutch were everywhere talking of the gift as "theirs."

In London there was much hesitation about accepting the gift even before the official offer had been received. Yet the affair had already gone so far that it would be very difficult to refuse the diamond. Indeed, nobody could suggest any diplomatic formula with which it could be refused. The King himself was deeply disturbed; he questioned whether it would be compatible with his constitutional sovereignty to accept a gift presented without unanimous agreement from the donors.

Lord Selborne, the High Commissioner in South Africa, was called upon for an opinion. He had no doubts: the Cullinan Diamond must be accepted by the King. His refusal would give mortal offense to the Boers. It would set the clock back. The man on the spot was so obviously appalled at the prospect of refusal that King Edward dispatched an official acceptance of the diamond.

It was the King's sixty-sixth birthday, and it was he himself, apparently quite unexpectedly, who solved the delicate problem of the Cullinan Diamond in the Drawing Room at Sandringham. When Sir Richard Solomons and Sir Francis Hopwood were brought in and placed in his hand the great cloudy uncut stone he turned at once to Queen Alexandra and gave it to her. He told them to tell the people of the Transvaal that it would be set in the Queen's Crown. Once again his marvelous flair for diplomacy had saved an awkward situation. Queen Alexandra, who had become personally known to most of the Boer leaders during their visits to London, was held in high esteem in South Africa. There the news of the King's action caused universal delight, and in Whitehall anxious ministers applauded it with equal fervor.

Stamper has recorded a picturesque motoring scene in the spring of 1908, in which the faithful Dighton Probyn figures in the service of his Beloved Lady. Probyn, now seventy-five, though with sixteen years of life ahead of him, looked his age. A venerable white beard replaced the groomed chin-tuft, and some found the giant patriarchal courtier a strange and amusing ornament to the train of the beautiful Queen.

Stamper himself was at Biarritz with King Edward at the time of the incident, but heard the story from a chauffeur involved.

Queen Alexandra had expressed a wish to break a train journey from London to Sandringham to visit the King's racehorse Perrier, the hope of that year's Derby. At Cambridge she alighted with Sir Dighton Probyn, where a car with two royal chauffeurs carried them to the stables. The chauffeurs were then ordered by Sir Dighton to take the Queen to Fordham Junction, where a special train would be ready to carry her to Wolferton.

Road maps were evidently a mystery to both chauffeurs, and the route to Fordham was unknown to them. The journey, though it should not have been long, was punctuated by jerky stops when the men searched desperately among the map squares. Nothing was said; but Sir Dighton as the truth dawned upon him grew very agitated. The road taken had brought them into open country, which he was sure was wrong.

A glance at his watch settled the matter.

"You must be miles out!" he cried. "We've been going half an hour already."

"The bearer of the map at once admitted that he did not know where he was, and Sir Dighton said they must ask the first person they met. So shattered, however, was his confidence in the chauffeur's power of direction and so great was his anxiety, that even when they had been set right by a passing wayfarer and were proceeding with all speed to the junction they sought, he himself interrogated with shouts every pedestrian they encountered. As they neared Fordham, these, I was told, became so frequent that the doubting equerry found it convenient to remain with his head out of the window, while to his repeated utterances of the word 'Fordham' he lent an inflection so pregnant that they elicited not only affirmative answers but many expressions of encouragement."

The Queen reached the Junction frowning with anger, not only because her special had waited three quarters of an hour and the line was dislocated, but because of their unnecessary dramatic entrance to the town.

June 1908 saw the *Victoria and Albert* with the King and Queen aboard lying off Reval in the Baltic. Two other royal yachts were there to meet them: the *Standart* with Czar Nicholas and the Czarina, and the *Polar Star* with Empress Marie Fedorovna and Queen Olga of Greece.

As the *Victoria and Albert* passed into the Baltic through the Kiel Canal, Emperor William had sent aboard his brother Henry and his wife to pay the Imperial respects. It quickly became evident, however, that the visitors had really come as spies. Assurances that the Reval meeting was merely a family affair were accepted with poorly disguised scepticism and further questions were asked.

Emperor William was convinced that "the family meeting" at Reval was to cement an arrangement for the encirclement of Germany, and he did not think fit to remain silent about his views. Rumors to this effect were soon rife all over Germany, and the name of Edward VII—the arch-conspirator—was spoken with bitterness and fear. When, shortly afterward, Count Metternich reported to Berlin that the British people and their King desired peace, the Emperor scribbled in the margin a comment which in view of what later happened is of curious interest: "Untrue. He (King Edward) aims at war. I am to begin it, so that he does not get the odium."

At Reval meanwhile the first dinner party aboard the *Victoria and Albert* had brought an embarrassing moment. By Russian Imperial etiquette the Dowager Empress took precedence over the Czar's wife. Normally Marie Fedorovna and her daughter-in-law met as seldom as possible. When they did, the Czarina was always looking for slights and inclined to defiant gestures. Just before dinner was announced the host and hostess perceived with dismay the signs of a storm brewing. It actually began to look as if the Czarina might refuse to dine if her mother-in-law went in before her.

King Edward was equal to the occasion. The instant dinner was announced he took an Empress on each arm, and, cheerfully bidding them keep step with him, he brought them to the dinner-table.

"Nicky" had arranged a surprise for Aunt Alix. That night in the moonlight a tug glided silently alongside the *Victoria and Albert*. Colored lights suddenly illuminated a gaily costumed party on the deck below: they were one of the most famous Russian choirs.

As the royal party leant on the rails listening to the beautiful voices on the still night air, the spell was somewhat broken for Queen Alexandra by the casual assurance of a Russian that "every single singer had been stripped to the skin at the quayside to see if they carried pistols or bombs!"

On June 11 they once more approached the Kiel Canal. This time Emperor William had a surprise for them. Whatever his personal feeling, he would observe the courtesies. He was, in fact, extremely proud of the stirring treat he had prepared for them. A regiment of dragoons, mounted, was drawn up at each side of the Canal entrance. As the yacht drew in, the cavalrymen wheeled and trotted at each side of the vessel as escort: an imposing spectacle, but not one which appealed to King Edward when on holiday. The scene was perhaps made the more interesting because the royal yacht was making the cleared passage at considerable speed. The cavalry trot broke into a canter, which was soon a disorderly chase: the officers purple with humiliation, the troopers blasphemously spurring their horses.

This Teutonic comedy might have amused Queen Alexandra. She did not see it. The sight of the flashing Imperial muster from her cabin window had stirred her hatred and scorn. She pulled down the blinds.

The first Olympic Games to be held in Britain took place at the White City in July 1908, and in the great arena before Queen Alexandra and 80,000 people of all nations occurred the dramatic closing scene of the greatest of all the marathon races of modern times. The name of Queen Alexandra will always be closely woven into the story of that epic day, for events caused her to make a rapid decision which few other royal personages, mindful of their traditional role of impartiality, would have ventured to take.

The arrival of the marathon runners was expected in the arena, and the crowd watched tensely the dark archway through which the winner would appear.

A figure lurched out into the sunlight—a tiny man in red running-shorts, bearing the Italian colors on his breast: Pietro Dorando! He staggered blindly as if the bellow of applause had struck him a blow. Dazedly, reeling, the little man started to trot round the arena.

The spectacle was stirring and agonizing. He swayed and tottered as he went. He gasped as if his heart might burst. He was like an unconscious man running. Even before the first collapse people knew they were watching a hero who had fought to the last ounce of his strength, and cheering madly they glanced anxiously from the sagging runner to the empty archway.

Italian friends, yelling with delight, weeping with ecstatic astonishment, were running beside him now. Suddenly all stopped aghast. An appalling silence fell in the arena. Dorando had fainted.

He stirred, scrambled to his feet. The man was scarcely more than crawling; it was horrible. But he had got to win now! Thousands of eyes returned questioningly to the archway.

He was gaining pace. He was almost running. He slipped forward on his face, and a shocked moan went up from the spectators. He rose again, shook himself, moved onward. Twenty yards ahead was the winning line. The stands shook with the applause and drumming of feet. His legs buckled under him like paper. He crashed to the ground like a stone. This time his friends caught him to save injury. Helplessly they stood about the limp body, staring round in terror at the archway. There was nothing to do but wait; it seemed the end for Dorando.

Through the archway came a big man running with ease, with the Stars and Stripes on his vest. His measured pace increased. He was closing on the body sprawled over the track. Dorando was on his feet. He was running, clutching and pushing at the air as he waded forward. The American had almost reached him. The crowd rose and strove with Dorando. They saw him plunge headlong over the winning line.

In the moment of hysteria and confusion the Italian flag raced up the mast. Then the flag slid down again. The Stars and Stripes fluttered in its place.

If the judges had lost their heads for an instant they had quickly regained them. They could in justice give no other decision than they had done. Dorando, hero as he was in the classic spirit of the first marathon runner, had plainly reached the winning post only with the help of his friends.

But people were in no mood for such rationalism. They had watched an epic. This was Dorando's marathon! A roar like the angry sea ran through the stands. Some were weeping at the tragedy. Some were ready to tear up the seats. Queen Alexandra was seen to be frowning and "to beat a tattoo on the floor of the stand unrestrainedly with her umbrella." A fashionable woman ran out as Dorando was being led away and, unclasping a valuable bracelet from her arm, fixed it upon his wrist. A workman shook his hand and left a shilling in it. And then, assailed by overwrought people on all sides, thumped on the back, caught by both hands with the tears trickling over his cheeks, the little Italian vanished from sight.

By that time Queen Alexandra had made her decision and declared what she intended to do. This was more than she could bear: she would give a cup to Dorando herself.

The news of this soon spread. Nobody was surprised in Britain: it was exactly what they might have expected of the Beloved Lady. Italy was delighted and honored, and in France *Le Matin* exclaimed that Queen Alexandra's Cup was "a more glorious reward than the first prize itself." Americans were not offended; they generously declared their gladness that Dorando would receive so honorable a recognition of his gallantry.

Dorando himself was evidently in agreement with the views expressed by *Le Matin*. On the day of awards he stood before the Queen. In her hands she held a cup inscribed with these words:

FOR PIETRO DORANDO

IN REMEMBRANCE OF THE MARATHON RACE

FROM WINDSOR TO THE STADIUM

FROM QUEEN ALEXANDRA

"When I was called to the Queen," said Dorando afterward, "I was trembling all over. I felt I should fall as I did on the day of the race. Then she spoke to me very kindly. 'Bravo' was all I could understand, but I knew what she meant by her smile. I tried to thank her in Italian, but I could not. I wept. This cup is balm to my soul. I shall treasure it to the end of my life."

Queen Alexandra was sixty-five in 1909: the youthfulness of her figure and her features still filled people with astonishment. Pierre Loti, the famous French writer, has left a remarkable description of her as he saw her at a ball at the French Embassy in that year, and his personal impression of her during a private interview at Buckingham Palace shortly afterward.

Writing of the Embassy ball, he says:

"I observed in one of the rooms a woman standing against the wall from whom the dancers appeared to keep at a respectful distance as they revolved past her—a slender, youthful woman with a smile on her face. She was dressed entirely in black of some diaphanous material with a sort of pale fire, like the flame of alcohol, round the bottom of the skirt.

"When someone said, 'It is the Queen,' deceived by her youthfulness, I should have doubted it. But I had caught a glimpse of her driving the previous day. . . .

"Later, when she left the hall, I observed her again. From under her cloak of grey fur peeped the dress of black gauze with its pale flames. Her head was uncovered, save for the scintillating *couronne fermee*. The cruel light fell full upon her. But she still looked young."

Loti was invited by the Queen to come to Buckingham Palace, for, having read all his books, she was anxious to meet the great Frenchman. One noon he arrived at the Palace. It had a deserted look. The King was abroad and the Queen was about to leave London. Blinds were drawn, and the Palace was, in fact, officially shut up. Loti was ushered into a waiting room, where

"a pleasant elderly lady-in-waiting entered and requested me to follow her, in French *sans accent*. She conducted me through dark, narrow corridors to a little lift with two seats which she worked herself. It stopped at the first story, and having passed through more dark corridors, we arrived at a room looking out upon trees.

" 'Remain here,' she said, 'and I will inform Her Majesty.'

"Left alone, I granted myself the privilege of glancing round this private apartment in the hope that it would reveal a little of the personality of the Sovereign. It contained no suggestion of splendour or luxury. It was a modest room with an air of neatness and simplicity, rather severe perhaps, but in perfect taste. It seemed as if it said that she who dwelt in it *submitted* to pomp and pageantry. On the walls, on the furniture, there were quantities of framed photographs, most of them in plain leather frames, but photographs of princesses and empresses autographed with grand names.

"Suddenly the Queen appeared—the Queen, as astonishingly young by day as by night, and clad so simply, had it not been for the supreme distinction of her person, nothing would have betrayed her rank. The pause before she spoke seemed to deepen the stillness of the empty Palace. . . . When the Queen spoke of my travels, my books, I experienced something like remorse as I thought of my attacks on England, and I entangled myself in embarrassed excuses.

"'Oh,' interrupted the Queen, with a trustfulness which touched me more than if she had reproached me, 'that belongs to the past, I am sure.'

"'Yes, madame,' I replied, 'that belongs to the past.'

"After a time which appeared to me very short but which was almost long for an audience, Her Majesty deigned to ask me if I would like to see the Palace. To see it in such company never should I have dared to hope! She rose, and I followed her for a never-to-be-forgotten promenade in the vast deserted pile. . . .

"The Queen, with her exquisite hand, unlocked and opened the heavy gilded doors as we passed through the deserted and silent rooms, in all of which, though about to be abandoned, there were clusters of blue hortensias, pink azaleas, orchids and lilies, arranged as if for a *fête!* . . ."

Pierre Loti found himself standing with Queen Alexandra before the portrait of the Duke of Clarence. She spoke with "an expression of wonderful tenderness" as she showed it to him. They passed on, and she led him to all the things which she thought would interest a Frenchman. Such was her "adorable simplicity" that Loti could scarcely persuade himself that this guide was the Queen, "who on great occasions entered these rooms in state, glittering with historic diamonds, and took her place on the throne which today was covered up like any ordinary chair."

At last they arrived "in a vestibule overlooking a monumental staircase. Her Majesty extended her hand. While I bowed over it she disappeared, and I found myself suddenly quite alone. . . ."

From the beginning of 1909 King Edward's health began to give anxiety to everybody who came in frequent contact with him. He was not himself aware that the little things which now always seemed to be irritating him, and his constant tiredness, were a symptom of failing stamina, and he sometimes looked childishly miserable when affairs did not work out for him in the delightful way he had planned. Even his cough, which he could not throw off and which occasionally without warning developed into spasms which seemed quite horrifying to other people, did not seem to concern him. He insisted on doing everything as usual. All his attendants were made to understand by the doctors that he must be most carefully guarded against bronchitis, as they believed that this malady might be very dangerous for him.

It was because of the King's health, rather than on account of her own strong distaste for the occasion, that Queen Alexandra was most reluctant to carry through the long-delayed State visit to Berlin, for which in tones of hurt complaint Emperor William had for so long been angling. King Edward was resolved to go, for he set great store by it as the only means left of improving steadily worsening Anglo-German relations; but it did not go unobserved by others that he regarded with dismay the onerous program which the German Emperor had prepared for him in Berlin, and which in the old days he would have anticipated with excited pleasure.

Berlin greeted them on February 8 with a military display of great magnificence. William was bursting with geniality: childishly flattered to receive a visit which should by right have come to him much sooner. The Berliners, flocking to see the arch-conspirator of Europe and his spouse, watched their passing coldly. The carriage procession was a disaster: gaps occurred, and the Emperor, continually glaring backward from his place in the first carriage with King Edward, appeared to be swearing out loud. Suddenly the horses in the carriage of the Empress and Queen Alexandra jibbed, reared and fell down, dragging the carriage across the road.

Queen Alexandra characteristically laughed, and the Emperor, beside himself with indignation at the clumsy mishap, took her levity as an insult. Members of the suite were turned out of the next carriage into the road and Empress and Queen mounted into it. The carriage still blocked the road. Not a Prussian guardsman dared to move. Spectators dragged the carriage from the roadway. At the first opportunity the Master of the Horse was publicly crushed by his infuriated Emperor. His subsequent introduction to the King and Queen was original. The Emperor gave no name. "Here," he snapped, "is the man who made such a fearful bungle with the horses!"

Even with the Berliners, King Edward was destined to be by no means unsuccessful. After a few days the British Sovereigns were almost popular. With Uncle Bertie William was doing well, but less so with his aunt. In public he was assiduous in addressing her as "dear Aunt" upon the slightest excuse. She retorted by calling him "dear Nephew." He was deeply annoyed. It was highly disrespectful.

Von Bülow, the Chancellor, who was the last remaining moderate, in the opinion of King Edward—he was shortly to resign in despair—has recorded that at the British Embassy luncheon Queen Alexandra, evidently primed by King Edward, earnestly expressed to him their hope that he would stay in control to aid in lightening the tension. It was at the end of this luncheon that suddenly King Edward collapsed in a terrible spasm of coughing. The guests watched helplessly. They were horror-stricken: Queen Alexandra ran to him and undid his collar. She begged everyone to leave the room and asked for a doctor.

Ten minutes later the guests were summoned back into the room. There sat King Edward in a rather crumpled collar, smoking a cigar. He called von Bülow to his side and began a political discussion. Presently the King referred to the State Ball, which he still meant to attend that night. Queen Alexandra declared that it was out of the question. She would go, but he would have to spend a quiet evening by himself and talk as little as possible; and for once the idea of a quiet evening did not seem entirely uncongenial to him.

On their last night they were to attend a State performance of *Sardanapalus* at the Opera House. The Emperor himself had been present at the rehearsals and made himself a great nuisance. Many of his grandiose ideas had had to be incorporated.

During the performance Queen Alexandra, who had been observing her husband, grew somewhat anxious. In intervals of listening to a long dissertation by the Emperor on *Sardanapalus* she succeeded in persuading King Edward to let her take his place in receiving the Ambassadors and Ministers during the interval. This was the kind of task she had always done her best to avoid all her life, and though perhaps her heart sank at the ominous symptom of the readiness with which King Edward abandoned his allotted task, she was now glad to undertake it, and was said to have carried it out with great charm and acumen.

The last act had scarcely begun when King Edward was seen to be asleep. Never before in his life had such a thing happened to this ardent theater and opera-goer. The Emperor, who might have taken umbrage, was deeply concerned: the truth was beginning to dawn on him. Perhaps deep down in his heart he felt some of that awed attachment for Uncle Bertie that he had felt for his mother Queen Victoria.

At the end of *Sardanapalus* the funeral pyre is lit and the stage appears to be bathed in the flickering light of flames. At this moment King Edward awakened. He thought the stage was burning. He was deeply agitated, and had to be calmed down amid a painful scene.

Next morning they departed, and although the Berliners acclaimed them much more vociferously than at their first appearance, the cheers were hollow. Three months later Anglo-German relations were said to be as bad as ever.

When on the return voyage Dover Castle came in sight the Queen happened to be on deck. Looking through a glass, she presently perceived with no little dismay that over the Castle flew the royal standard. To her it was a matter of not the smallest concern what flag the Governor chose to fly on his Castle, especially as the gesture was only meant to please them; but in view of the "dust-up" there had been on the outward journey, and with the King in his low state of health and so easily upset, it was most unfortunate. The royal standard had been flying above the Castle as they left the harbor, and King Edward had indignantly demanded to know what they meant by it: the royal standard must be flown only on a building where the Sovereigns were in residence. It showed gross ignorance in one of his high officials. He had wirelessed immediately to the War Office ordering that the matter should not occur again. And what was the result? There on their return was the royal standard!

Queen Alexandra hurried to the King's cabin and met the King about to come on deck, as was his custom as the yacht drew in to port. By some pretext she stopped him, brought him back into the cabin and kept him there till they were alongside. King Edward landed in blissful ignorance of this truly appalling offense.

In August, Cowes saw its royal Commodore for the last time. The Czar and Czarina arrived with their family in the *Standart*. "Nicky" was always good company, and as a nephew he was such a relief after William. Perhaps he especially appealed to King Edward and Queen Alexandra because in appearance he was so exactly like George, Prince of Wales. But the Czarina, who fell mainly to the lot of the Queen, was difficult. To begin with, she did not much like Aunt Alix, because she was the favorite sister of Marie Fedorovna. It was a time, moreover, when the Czarina was suffering acute nervous tension: for her little son, the Czarevitch, had been pronounced an incurable hemophiliac, liable to die at the slightest scratch, and in her desperation she had fallen under the sinister spell of the monk Rasputin, whose strange powers alone seemed capable of keeping the boy alive. Thus it was that the mystical ruffian who played such an extraordinary part in the downfall of Imperial Russia reached his high place.

At Cowes, Queen Alexandra persuaded the Czarina to bring the children shopping. Only with the greatest difficulty could the Czarina, set in the cautious ways of Russian royalty, be prevailed upon to venture herself and the family among the grim hazards of Cowes High Street. To the children, who had never before entered a shop in their lives, this was a never-to-be-forgotten occasion.

And so the dreary year 1909 dragged along. King Edward insisted upon doing all the usual things, and even went so far afield as Malta, but the cough was getting worse and more relentless in its attacks. Nevertheless, the King was never really ill, and people thought that if he could be made to take care of himself he might yet throw it off. But those very close to him were aware of a new symptom. Falling into fits of black depression, he would declare that it was time he handed over his office to his son George.

Even beloved Biarritz had seemed flat, and after the King had departed a shocked municipality read with consternation a communication from His Britannic Majesty that unless they completely overhauled the town drains he would not be visiting Biarritz again.

Chapter 27

HER LAST DEFIANCE

ON MAY 3, 1910, Queen Alexandra with Charlotte Knollys and a small staff arrived at Venice from Corfu for a week's stay. At Corfu she had been the guest of George and Olga of Greece.

That evening she sent for Charlotte Knollys. Miss Knollys saw that she looked extremely agitated.

"I'm worried about the King," she said. "I think he needs me. We'll leave for home tonight by the *Rapide*."

The Queen had spoken with such a strange tone that her resolve was not questioned. The dressers in speechless bewilderment were summoned to repack the trunks they had emptied that afternoon.

At Calais a telegram awaited Queen Alexandra. The King was in a serious condition. A heavy storm was in the Channel, but she crossed immediately. The Prince of Wales was standing on Victoria platform as her train drew in. Never before in her life when returning from a lone trip abroad had she looked from her train and not seen Bertie waving to her. She read the truth in George's face before he spoke.

She reached the Palace, and the King was sitting in his armchair with a cigar. He had been seeing visitors. And so he would sit dressed to perfection throughout the next day, the 6th, which was destined to be his last; but then the cigar would stay between his fingers, for he could not face it, and would own himself "miserably ill."

But that afternoon he smiled at her wanly.

"I'm feeling better and intend to fight this," he said. "I shall be about again in a day."

Then he told her that he had kept the royal box at Covent Garden. He thought she might like to see *Siegfried*.

"I have come back to be with you," was the quiet answer.

On that last morning King Edward again repeated, "I shall beat this," but his words seemed to trail away. He insisted against the doctors' orders on seeing his friend Sir Ernest Cassel. He never broke engagements.

In the late afternoon he woke from a doze in his chair. They told him his horse Witch of the Air had won at Kempton Park. It was a surprise, and he exclaimed, "I'm very glad," in something like his old firm tone.

He fainted twice soon after that, and he was too weak to resist any longer their putting him to bed.

One person outside the household saw King Edward in those last hours. It was a woman in society, and she came by permission of the Queen. This action of Queen Alexandra has always been quoted as being the most striking example of her selfless nature and great goodness of heart.

The Hon. Mrs. George Keppel was a woman whom society had observed to be a very frequent guest in those houses where King Edward visited, and to whom he paid notable attention. Throughout the golden reign Mrs. Keppel, whose tall and statuesque beauty was enhanced by a smile of celebrated enchantment and a nimble wit, had been a magnet in any room entered by the elderly King. A close sympathy and understanding appeared to exist between the two, concerning which the Queen was known to be aware and which it was believed she bitterly resented; for she saw in it a friendship for the King of a depth not enjoyed by herself in those later years.

The household were therefore astonished when Queen Alexandra in her grief ordered the woman whom she had long taken pains to avoid to be brought to the Palace. When Mrs. Keppel arrived, the Queen herself took her to the side of her dying husband, and there left her for a space. She then escorted her once more to the waiting car.

Almost the last words King Edward spoke before he slipped into the final coma were: "No, I shall not give in! I shall go on. I shall work to the end." He died as Big Ben boomed out the quarter to eleven.

Perhaps C. W. Stamper sums up the feelings of Queen Alexandra after forty-seven years of married life as well as any with one simple story.

In August 1910 he took a new car down to Sandringham for the Queen Mother.

> "While I was there she sent for me. It was the first time I had seen the Queen since His Majesty's death.
>
> " 'It's all terrible, Stamper,' she said. 'Even now I can hardly realize that he is gone.'
>
> "Then she spoke very kindly to me, and asked where I was to be found. . . . A day or two later she sent me a mourning pin in memory of the King—a pin of black enamel, with 'E VII' in white enamel, surrounded by little diamonds."

The rest is twilight lit by occasional gleams of Alexandrian flame. Sandringham remained the real home of Queen Alexandra, and King George V was content to occupy with his family the humbler quarters of York Cottage, once the "bachelor annex."

Even yet her beauty seemed astonishingly to remain; but the years were mounting upon her, and she was perhaps a little eccentric to the younger generation. A striking auburn wig, not always set straight, was somewhat startling at close approach. It was one of her little vanities, and yet she joked about her wig. "Is it straight, dear child?" she might exclaim gaily to people about her. Compared with herself, her staff appeared very aged indeed; and to the visitor they seemed to be muffled in antique garments. Her households, untidily flowing over with the sentimental rubbish of a life-time and many rare collectors' pieces, were bewildering. And the presiding figures, each reigning with the jealousy of age in their own departments, were Dighton Probyn and Charlotte Knollys: awesome and dismaying guardians to the new generations, but themselves helpless to control the cheerful whims of their mistress.

Queen Alexandra's godchild, Helen Hardinge, recalling youthful memories of her in those days, says:

"She would take you round the house, pressing gifts upon you. . . . She was an absolute target for robbers . . . and the people who lived in her household had the greatest difficulty in protecting her from every sort of imposition. No tramp would come to the door, no old woman, no gypsy and child, but if they were seen by the Queen they would get a present; she always felt that her staff were wrong to try and prevent her, so she just eluded them, and secretly sent out alms!

"She was extraordinarily unpunctual, and sometimes nobody got anything in the house, because the bells did not go for meals till the Queen was ready—and of course, at that moment nobody else was there."

She often dropped into the London Hospital after the old manner, making herself tea in the matron's room with Sir Dighton. She unobtrusively, but sometimes forcibly, followed many of her pet interests. In 1913 the famous Alexandra Rose Day was established, and from then oward annually on that day she would be seen driving through the streets with Princess Victoria in her open carriage to visit all the rose sellers.

When war came in 1914 and everybody blamed the German Emperor, she certainly was not surprised at what her nephew had done. "I always told you he was a bad man," she proclaimed to everybody. "Now, perhaps, you'll believe me!" But it was in character that after William's downfall she was never heard to speak hardly of him.

Then came December 1918, and Douglas Haig, on his first return after the Armistice, was to make a triumphal drive through London from Charing Cross. For the last time the Beloved Lady displayed herself in a flash of drama—the Alix of earlier days had come to life.

She had announced her intention of congratulating the victorious general in the street before Marlborough House. A polite letter from the Palace pointed out that the stoppage might seriously inconvenience the police and upset the smoothness of the procession; would she drop the idea?

No answer was received from Marlborough House: it was assumed that the matter was satisfactorily settled. It was thought that

Lady Haig and her two schoolgirl daughters, who had been invited to Marlborough House, were to watch the procession from the windows with the Queen Mother. The guests themselves were under that impression. Queen Alexandra with her three guests sat at the open window looking down on the Pall Mall crowds and each holding a cheap little Union Jack.

But when the procession seemed to be expected, Queen Alexandra suddenly stood up.

"I go!" said she firmly.

They meekly followed her, each of them still clutching a Union Jack. They emerged upon the pavement, and Queen Alexandra forcefully tapped her way through the gaping crowd. They stood with their flags in the open roadway of Pall Mall and a hush fell upon the people.

The first carriage with red-liveried royal servants and bearing Douglas Haig came in sight. They had no orders to stop. The Queen Mother moved out a little farther into the road. The carriage drew to a standstill. Douglas Haig stood up in the carriage. Queen Alexandra took his hand, and perhaps there were tears in his eyes as he bowed low before this unexpected welcome. What the Beloved Lady said to him was drowned in a roar of cheering.

After the First World War the members of the Greek royal family, so beloved by Queen Alexandra, were regarded with deep disfavor in Britain, because of the transactions of her nephew, the injudicious but much-misjudged King Constantine.

But the British royal family, led by Queen Alexandra, refused to recognize this undercurrent of hostility. They knew all the Greek family too well to believe a word of the cruel abuse which had been circulated against them. When the unfortunate Glucksburgs were cast into exile and scattered over the face of Europe, Queen Olga, the widow of King George, who had been assassinated in 1913 after the Balkan Wars, came to Sandringham to stay with the sister-in-law to whom she had so often been hostess at Athens and Tatoi in the old happy days.

They had not met since the death of King George, and the meeting of the two elderly women moved all who witnessed it. Both of them in their different ways looked back into a world which was dead.

Soon other members of the Greek royal family began to appear at Sandringham and went on to Windsor and Buckingham Palace. People seeing the Greeks received as dear relations in the royal homes began to wonder if all they had heard from Allied statesmen and Venizelist propagandists was true. The royal Greeks were soon welcome everywhere, and although some of them chose to live in Paris or Italy they began to look upon England as the nearest thing they knew to home.

Prince Nicholas, whose love for his Aunt Alix amounted almost to worship, joined her and his mother at Sandringham in the summer of 1923. He had not seen Aunt Alix since the war, and he recalled a trivial incident soon after his arrival which revealed to him that her memory, once so startlingly precise where people were concerned, was failing. His father King George had then been dead for ten years; but when he bent down to pick up Queen Alexandra's handkerchief, she broke into a peal of laughter and cried, "Why, Nicky, you are getting as bald as your father is!"

The favorite nephew could not fail to observe the pathetic oddness of the regime which had set in at Sandringham in those twilight days. Though Aunt Alix had always been a liberal giver, she had been jealous of her own souvenirs and possessions. They were part of herself. Now she had a mania for giving her valuables and her rubbish away. She chased everybody with them, and for exactly the same reason that she had once hoarded them: they were part of herself, and she desperately desired others to share in the happiness of them before it was too late. Nicholas was especially moved to watch his aunt at the end of a motor drive. It was the invariable custom. She was very lame now and she tottered on her stick. With a trembling hand she drew two packets of cigarettes from her bag. One she gave to the chauffeur and one to the footman. Nicholas' youngest daughter, Marina (now the Duchess of Kent), was then a beautiful girl in her teens. She was very like Queen Alexandra at the same age. Great-niece and great-aunt developed an extraordinary fascination for each other. Marina became the favorite great-niece, and the aged Queen could not take her eyes off her. In Marina she was seeing herself in the far-off days at Bernstoff, before the Prince of Wales had sought her out.

People observed with a shock of surprise that the two, so far apart in age, appeared constantly to be copying one another: they had exactly the same gestures, movements and mannerisms. Marina and her great-aunt would talk together for hours. Those who overheard them reported that although Queen Alexandra was sometimes perfectly coherent, quite suddenly she would be talking to Marina of people who had been dead more than fifty years as if the child knew them too. Marina, when this happened, never seemed in the least at a loss; it was almost as if she really had met them yesterday. When Marina departed, the very ancient souvenirs belonging to Alexandra's Danish days were the ones pressed upon her.

In the early 'twenties, of course, Marina had no reason to suppose she would ever be more closely related to the British royal family than she then was; but, in view of the fate in store for her, it is of interest that a remark made to her by her great-aunt in a moment of penetrating clarity has never been forgotten.

"The British are the most loyal friends in the world," Queen Alexandra assured her, "—if once you win their hearts. But there are no *half-measures* with them!"

Among the younger postwar people, mention of Queen Alexandra used to be made with bated breath: they whispered of a fabulous woman like Rider Haggard's *She*—incredibly old, with the beauty of a girl. She was neither the one nor possessed the other in those last days. But there was to the end the ghost of youth hovering somewhere behind her eyes, and the figure, though it tottered pathetically, was strangely girlish. She was in her eightieth year when on November 27, 1925, a gun carriage bore her on her last journey, while the snowflakes raced silently down and piled upon the drooping bearskins of the Guards.

INDEX

Abdul Aziz, Sultan of Turkey, 92-93, 105
Aberdeen, 68-70
Abergeldie, 80, 96, 115, 122, 188
Albani, Madame, 199-200
Albert, Prince Consort, 16-19, 22, 23, 25-27, 179-80
Albert Victor, Duke of Clarence, 76-77, 81, 106, 123, 154-56, 157, 171-72, 178, 190, 205, 219, 220, 221, 233
Alexander, Prince of Great Britain, 107
Alexander II, Tsar of Russia, 174-76
Alexander III, Tsar of Russia, 88, 174, 175, 185, 191, 203, 226-27, 230
Alexandra, 101-02
Alexandra, Egypt, 99, 105
Alexandra, Princess of Denmark (Queen Alexandra of Great Britain), accepts Cullinan Diamond, 282-83; activities, 121-26; activities during Boer War, 244-46; after King's death, 298-302; as Queen at Sandringham, 273-74; assassination attempt at Brussels, 247; Athens visited, 106, 150; at Portman Place, 209-10; at Reval, 285-86; at Rumpenheim, 126-29; Berlin State visit, 291-93; betrothal, 30-35; birth, 3; birth of George, 83; birth of Louise, 89; birth of Maud, 107; charities, 166-67; childhood, 4-5; conduct at seizure of Schleswig-Holstein, 78-80; confirmation, 14; continental tour, 96-98; coronation, 265-66; deafness, 254, 256; death, 302; death of Queen Victoria, 248; defies King at Birthday Parade, 267; defies the Queen, 67-75; during King's convalescence, 264-66; during Prince's illness, 130-136; education, 13-14; enthusiasm for changes in royal homes and royal habits, 254-58; first Denmark visit, 80-83; first London season, 62-66; first reception in England, 48-52; first royal appearance, 251-52; funeral of Alexander II, 174-76; funeral of Frederick IV, 201-03; girlhood, 13-15; gives world's biggest banquet, 239-40; grief at death of Clarence, 221-23; hospital activities, 163-66; hostess at Sandringham, 117-20; ideas on Queenhood, 252-53; in-

sists upon own ideas at Coronation, 259; international politics, 274-76; Irish visits, 94-95, 189-95, 271-72, 281-82; journey to England, 37, 45-48; Lambeth meetings, 181-82; lameness, 301; leader in new habits of society, 236; meeting with Prince of Wales, 24-25; Near East tour, 99-106; Olympic Games at Athens, 278-80; Olympic Games at London, 286-88; popularity as Queen, 260; postponement of Coronation, 263; premature birth of Clarence, 76-77; rheumatic illness, 89-92; Royal Closet, in, 37-38; Silver Wedding Day, 199-200; snubbed by the Queen, 197; sudden return to King from abroad, 296; suggested as bride for Prince of Wales, 20-24; supports Queen at Diamond Jubilee, 238-40; Tranby Croft case, 215-17; visits the Elephant Man, 165-66; wedding, 53-57; with Kaiser at Cowles, 210-15
Alexandra Rose Day, 299
Alexandra Trust, 240, 269
Alfred, Duke of Edinburgh, 174
Alice, Princess of Great Britain and Hesse-Darmstadt, 28, 29, 37, 38-39, 41, 93
Alix of Hesse, Princess, 225, 229, 230-31
Anitchkoff Palace, 175
Arabi Pasha, 178
Ariadne, H.M.S., 99, 105
Armstrong, Rev. B. J., 70-71, 119
Arthur, Duke of Connaught, 124, 179, 248
Asquith, Margot, 200-01
Assouan, 104
Athens, 106, 146, 150, 205, 278-80
Augusta, Grand Duchess of Mecklenburg-Strelitz, 23, 24

Bacchante, H.M.S., 154, 157, 171, 178
Baker, Colonel Valentine, 61, 145
Balmoral, 29, 30, 32, 68, 96, 122, 229, 274
Bancroft, Squire, 178
Battenburg, Lord Louis of, 92
Bayreuth Music Festival, 122
Beatrice, Princess of Great Britain, 54
Benson, E. F., 150, 180, 209-10

303

Benson, Edward White, Archbishop of Canterbury, 179-82, 217
Beresford, Lord Charles, 152-53
Berlin, 98, 182, 191, 228, 291-93
Bernstoff Castle, 12, 13
Biarritz, 121, 295
Birmingham, 138, 139-42
Bismarck, Herbert, 173, 188, 199, 202
Bismarck, Prince Otto von, 33, 34, 74, 78, 79, 94, 98, 173, 199, 228
Blackburn, Mrs. 107
Black Eagle, 37
Blumenthal, Field Marshall, 202
Boer Wars, 171-72, 244-46
Boganowitsh, 176
Botha, General, 282
Bouraki, General, 116
Britannia, 157, 212, 213, 214
Broglie, Duc de, 134
Brown, Dr., 76-77
Brown, John, 26, 27, 30, 31, 69, 83, 85-86, 93, 122, 126, 130, 145, 154-55, 156-57, 182-84, 255
Brown's Hotel, 113
Bruce, Colonel, 16-17, 60
Brussels, 32, 46-47, 247
Buckingham Palace, 10, 17, 87, 255, 256, 257, 264, 272-73, 289
Burke, Thomas, 59, 189

Caine, Sir Hall, 266-67
Cairo, 99
Cambridge, George, Duke of, 3, 13, 15, 61, 65, 86, 114, 145, 179, 267
Cambridge, Mary, Princess of (H. R. H. Duchess of Teck), 3, 4, 13, 15, 38-40, 54, 65, 107, 108, 118-19, 124, 125, 126-27, 219, 220, 221, 224, 225, 241
Cambridge University, 17
Cannes, 121
Caroline Amalie, Queen of Denmark, 2
Carrington, Lord, 92
Cassel, Sir Ernest, 234, 235
Cavendish, Lord Frederick, 189
Chamberlain, Joseph, 138, 139-42, 240
Chaplin, Harry, 92
Charles, Prince of Denmark (Haakon VII of Norway), 277-78
Charles XV, King of Sweden, 97
Charlotte, Landgravine of Hesse-Cassel, 2, 8-9, 12
Charlottenburg Palace, 202
Chislehurst, 115-16, 136-37, 158
Christian, Duke of Augustenburg, 8, 11
Christian VIII, King of Denmark, 2-9, 10
Christian IX, King of Denmark, 1-9, 11, 12, 13, 21, 30-32, 37, 39, 40, 49, 52,

71, 73, 89, 185, 187, 224, 226, 276, 278
Cole, Viscount, 111
Compiègne, 97
Constant, 66
Constantine, Prince of Greece, 106, 195, 205, 300
Constantinople, 105
Cook, Thomas, 102-03, 104
Copenhagen, 14, 21, 45, 97, 114, 186, 224
Corfu, 106
Cork, 194
Coronation of Edward VII, 265-66
Coronation Tattoo, 260-61
Cowes, 121, 125, 153, 205, 210-14, 294
Crimea, 105
Crimean War, 88, 91
Crystal Palace, 148
Cullinan Diamond, 282-83
Cust, Mrs. Lionel, 153, 154
Cust, Sir Lionel, 255

Dagmar, Princess of Denmark (Empress Marie Fedorovna of Russia), 3, 4, 5, 13, 14, 22, 45, 71, 82, 88, 174, 175, 185, 186, 191, 226-27, 230-31, 275, 278, 281, 285
Dalton, Reverend J. N., 157
Danner, Countess (Louise Rasmussen), 10
Dardanelles, 105
Darmstadt, 93
De Lessep, 96, 104
Derby, Lord, 86
Desborough, Lord, 279
Diamond Jubilee, 237-40
Dickens, Charles, 54-55
Disraeli, Benjamin (Lord Beaconsfield), 94, 112, 118, 134, 146, 147-48, 149-50, 157-58, 159, 168-69
Dolmabakshi Palace, 105
Dorando, Pietro, 287-88
Dublin, 94, 192-93, 271, 272, 281
Duff-Gordon, Lady, 104
Dunrobin Castle, 115

Edinburgh University, 17
Edward, Prince of Wales (King Edward VII) achieves the Entente Cordiale, 270-71; activities, 125-26; after death of Clarence, 223-24; assassination attempt at Brussels, 247; at Reval, 285-86; Berlin State visit, 291-93; betrothal, 30-35; Birmingham conquest, 139-42; Canadian tour, 19, 23; character, 58-66; confirmation of William Hohen-

Index

Index

305

Edward, Prince of Wales (*continued*)
zollern, 138-39; continental tour, 96-98; convalescence from operation, 264-65; coronation, 265-66; "country-house" King, 273; Cullinan Diamond dilemma, 282-83; death, 298; death of Queen Victoria, 248; defies Queen at death of Gladstone, 242; diplomatic skill and achievements, 168-69; education, 16-17, 19; enthusiasm for motor cars, 257-58; failing health, 291; first rumors of illness, 259; freemasonry, 97; funeral of Alexander II, 174-76; funeral of Frederick IV of Germany, 200, 201-03; funeral of Napoleon III, 136-37; host of Sultan, 92-93; host to Kaiser at Sandringham, 243-44; illness at Sandringham, 130-36; illness before Coronation, 261-63; India visited, 146-47; indiscretions, 112-13; international problems, 274-77; Ireland visited, 94-95, 189-95, 271-72, 281-82; Kaiser's Vienna insult, 203-04; last days, 296-97; leader in new habits of society, 236; meeting with Alexandra, 24-25; meets Mrs. Langtry, 143-44; Mordaunt Case, 111-12; Near East tours, 27, 28, 99-106; Olympic Games at Athens, 278-80; operation for appendicitis, 262-63; orders changes in royal homes, 254-57; photograph of Alexandra, 15; popularity as King, 259-60; postponement of Coronation, 263; problem of a bride for, 17-19; relations with Napoleon III, 91-92; temper, 169-70; Tranby Croft case, 215-17; wedding, 53-57; with Kaiser at Cowles, 210-15
Egypt, 99-105
Esbekiah Palace, 99-100
Esher, Reginald Viscount, 235, 240, 243, 251, 253, 254, 256, 257, 260, 265, 267
Eugénie, Empress of France, 97, 106, 115-16; 137, 153, 183
Eulenburg, 202

Fenians, 189, 190-95
Fisher, Herbert, 60, 120
Fitzroy, Lord Charles, 86
Francis Joseph, Emperor of Austria-Hungary, 98, 203, 237
Franco-Russian War, 114-15
Fredensborg Castle, 81, 97-98, 123, 185, 195, 243, 281
Frederick, Crown Prince of Denmark (King Frederick VII), 6-7, 8, 10-12, 14, 18, 45, 71

Frederick, Crown Prince of Denmark (King Frederick VIII), 3, 4, 14, 22, 45, 278
Frederick, Duke of Schleswig-Holstein, 2
Frederick, Landgrave of Hesse-Cassel, 3
Frederick of Augustenburg, 71, 74, 78
Frederick William, Crown Prince of Prussia (Emperor Frederick IV of Germany), 16, 69, 73, 74, 82, 98, 124, 182, 198-200, 201
Freemasonry, 97
Frith, 65-66
Frogmore, 76

George, Prince of Greece, 106, 186
George Frederick Ernest Albert (King George V), 83, 123, 154-56, 157, 171-72, 178, 214-15, 219, 220, 222, 224, 228, 261, 296, 298
Gibbs, 168
Gibson, 65-66
Gladstone, W. E., 73, 113, 114, 149, 168, 172, 177, 183, 184, 195, 242
God Protected, 101-02
Goodwood, 121
Gordon-Cumming, Sir William, 215-16
Granville, Lord, 77, 116, 123, 174
Greece, 72-73, 87, 106, 149-50, 240-41
Grey, Hon. Mrs., 99, 101, 108
Grey, Major Charles, 61
Guest, Montague, 92

Haig, Douglas, 299-300
Hains, Nurse, 271
Hamburg, 46
Hamilton, Ernest, 95-96
Hampton Court, 256
Hanover, 46
Hardinge, Helen, 127, 129, 298-99
Hare, Augustus, 124, 125, 259, 272
Hartington, Lord, 113, 177
Haymarket Theater, 177
Heidelberg, 25
Helena, Princess of Great Britain, 8, 37, 39
Hero, H.M.S., 22
Higgins, Colonel, 118
Hinzpeter, 139
Hohenlohe, Victor von, 17, 159, 220, 228
Hohenzollern, 210, 211, 212
Holzmann, M., 61, 108
Homburg, 203
Hopwood, Sir Francis, 283
Howe, Lord, 238-39
Hvidore, 281

Illustrated London News, 179

India, 147
Ireland, 92-95, 189-95, 271-72, 281-82
Irving, Sir Henry, 176, 178, 184-85, 205, 269
Ismail, Khedive of Egypt, 92, 99, 100, 101, 104

Jerichau, Madame, 77
Johnstone, Sir Frederick, 111
Jubilee Year, 197

Karnak, 103, 104
Keppel, Hon. Mrs. George, 297
Keppel, Lieutenant-Colonel, 61
Kiel, 8, 12, 46, 79
Kiel Canal, 285, 286
Killarney, 194
Kingstown, 94, 192
Kitchener, Lord, 113, 245, 264-65
Knollys, Charlotte, 120-21, 151, 164, 166, 171, 174, 176, 233, 246, 260, 296, 298
Knollys, Sir Francis, 120, 126, 137, 256, 257
Knollys, General Sir William, 36, 60, 120, 129

Labouchère, Mrs. Henry, 177
Laeken Palace, 30, 32
Laking, Sir Francis, 151, 261, 262
Lambeth Chapel, 181-82
Langtry, Lily, 113, 143-44, 151-53, 154, 176-78, 235
Lee, Sir Sidney, 112
Leicester, 179
Leopold I, King of Belgium, 18, 25, 27, 29, 30-32, 36, 41, 46-47, 84
Leopold II, King of Belgium, 177, 247-48
Life in the Highlands, 183
Lind, Jenny, 55
Lipton, Sir Thomas, 239, 240, 245
Livadia, 106
London Hospital, 163, 164, 299
Loti, Pierre, 289-91
Louis, Prince of Hesse-Darmstadt, 29, 38-39
Louise, Duchess of Fife, 37, 89, 91, 130, 205, 210
Louise, Princess of Hesse-Cassel (Queen Louise of Denmark), 1-9, 12, 21, 24, 28-29, 30-32, 37, 40, 49, 52, 89-90, 126, 129, 195, 224, 226, 243
Louis Napoleon, Prince Imperial of France, 115, 116, 136, 153, 154, 157-59
Ludwig, Emil, 202, 211
Lyceum Theater, 178, 185

Macclesfield, Lady, 62, 76, 130
Magee, Bishop of Peterborough, 117-18
Mallow, 193-94, 271
Marina, Duchess of Kent, 301-02
Marlborough House, 5, 41, 58, 60, 61, 62, 89, 96, 107-08, 111, 112, 117, 143, 150, 152, 187, 198-99, 216, 233-34, 240, 257
Mathilde, Princess of France, 97
Matin, Le, 288
Maud, Princess of Great Britain (Queen of Norway), 107, 277-78
May, Princess (Queen Mary), 219-20, 221, 224, 254-55
Meade, R. H., 61
Merrick, John, 164-66
Metaxes, A., 279-80
Meteor I, 212, 213
Meteor II, 214, 243
Metternich, Count, 285
Meyer, Joseph, 128-29
Michaelovitch, Grand Duke Alexander, 226
Millais, 177
Montagu, Oliver, 92
Mordaunt Case, 111-12
Morning Post, 102-03
Mountbatten, Lady Louis, 234
Mount Edgecomb, Earl of, 60-61
Moxon, Reverend Mr., 70
Muller, Max, 79

Napoleon III, Emperor, 91-92, 94, 97, 106, 114, 115, 136
Nassau, Adelaide, 107
New Palace, Potsdam, 20, 22, 24
Nicholas, Grand Duke of Russia, 82
Nicholas, Prince of Greece, 186, 195-96, 231-33, 280, 301
Nicholas II, Tsar of Russia, 225-26, 227, 228, 229-30, 275, 276, 285, 294
Nightingale, Florence, 163, 245
Nihilists, 175-76
Nursing service, 245-46

Oberammergau Passion Play, 126-29
Oldenburgs, 6, 7-8
Olga, Queen of Greece, 97, 104, 106, 146, 148, 150, 185, 198, 285, 296, 300
Olympic Games, at Athens, 278-80; at London, 286-88
Ornament of the Two Seas, 101
Orontes, H.M.S., 158
Osborne, 81, 83, 121, 153, 192, 211, 213

Osborne House, 16, 24, 29, 37, 56, 211, 213
Oxford University, 17, 67-68

Paget, Augustus, 20-21
Paget, Sir James, 89, 90
Paget, Lady Walburga, 20-24, 27, 30, 31, 272
Palmerston, Lord, 53, 79, 80
Paris, 106, 115, 121, 281
Paris International Exhibition, 246
Patti, 96
Penzance, Lord, 111
Phalerum, 106, 278
Philae, 103
Polar Star, 285
Potsdam, 20, 24, 201
Probyn, Colonel Dighton, 120, 121, 164, 174, 176, 283-84, 298, 299
Punch, 63, 77-78, 86, 141
Punchestown Races, 95

Rasmussen, Louise, 10
Rasputin, 231, 294
Resistance, H.M.S., 47
Reval, 285-86
Review of Reviews, 216
Rhodes, Cecil, 267-68
Ritz, Cesar, 236
Robinson, Peter, 103
Rothschild, Sir Anthony de, 118
Rudolph, Crown Prince of Austria, 177, 198-99, 203, 204, 205
Rumpenheim Palace, 3-4, 13, 14, 24, 38, 126-29
Russell, Sir William, 99, 101, 102, 103, 104, 105
Russia, 88, 175-76, 226-28, 275
Russian Revolution, 175, 281
Russo-Japanese War, 275

St. George's Chapel, 42, 53, 222
St. Helier, Lady, 63
St. James Palace, 62, 224-25
St. Paul's Chapel, 238
St. Petersburg, 175, 226-28
Salisbury, Lord, 241, 246, 262
Sandringham House, 41, 60, 70-71, 107, 117-20, 122, 166, 244, 273-74, 298
Sandwich, Lord, 118
Sanger's Circus, 190
Savoy Theater, 236
Schleswig, 46
Schleswig-Holstein, 7-8, 11, 26, 33, 34, 71-72, 73-74, 78, 87
Scotsman, The, 69
Selborne, Lord, 283

Semon, Sir Felix, 234, 274
Sinn Fein movement, 281
Sipido, 247
Solomons, Sir Richard, 283
Soveral Luis Marquis de, 187-88, 234-35, 265
Speier Castle, 24
Spencer, Lord, 82, 189-90, 193, 262
Spiritualism, 153-54
Stamper, C. W., 262, 273, 277, 280, 283-84, 298
Standart, 285, 294
Stanhope, Lord, 193
Stanley, Dean of Windsor, 184
Stanley, Lord, 87
Stanley, Mary, 54, 55, 57
Strauss, Johann, 236
Suez Canal, 96, 99, 104, 147, 178
Sutherland, Duke of, 59, 101

Tavistock, Lady, 180
Teesdale, Major Christopher, 61, 90
Terry, Ellen, 185, 205
Thackeray, 55
Thunderer, H.M.S., 153
Thyra, Princess of Denmark, 3, 22, 45, 55, 98, 126, 129, 186
Times, The, 18, 34, 79, 91, 99, 101, 102, 103, 105, 141, 216
Tomahawk, The, 86
Tranby Croft case, 215-17
Treves, Sir Frederick, 164-65, 261, 264
Trieste, 99
Turkey, 87, 105

Viceregal Lodge, 95, 189, 192, 282
Victor Count Gleichen, 33
Victoria, Princess of Great Britain, 222, 260-61, 299
Victoria, Princess Royal of Great Britain (Empress Frederick of Germany), 16-19, 20-24, 27, 28, 33, 54, 66, 69, 73, 74, 82, 98, 114-15, 124, 139, 173, 182, 192, 198-99, 201, 202, 204, 228, 237, 243, 258
Victoria, Queen, 18, 22, 26-29, 30-32, 33, 34, 36, 37, 41, 51-52, 53-54, 55-56, 64, 67, 69-70, 72, 74-75, 79, 83-84, 85-86, 87, 88, 89, 92, 93, 95, 96, 106, 114, 116, 120, 122, 126, 130-32, 134, 136, 147, 153, 155, 157, 173, 179, 181-82, 183-84, 189, 190, 193, 197-98, 203, 205, 211, 219, 223, 224-25, 237-39, 240, 242, 248
Victoria and Albert, 47, 48, 231, 264, 281, 285, 286

Vienna, 203-04
Von Bülow, Chancellor, 292
Von Doehme, 201-02
Von Eckhardstein, 212

Waldegrave, Lady, 125
Waldemar, Prince of Denmark, 3, 22
Walters, Catherine, 113
Warrior, H.M.S., 47
Wellington College, 157, 180
Whistler, James, 177
Wiesbaden, 93
Wilde, Oscar, 177, 235
William, Prince of Denmark (King George I of Greece), 3, 4, 22, 45, 48, 72-73, 87, 96, 97, 104, 106, 146, 148-50, 185, 198, 206, 278, 279, 296, 300
William I, King of Prussia, 93-94

William II, Emperor of Germany, 24, 55, 138-39, 172-73, 182, 188, 191-92, 199, 201-04, 205, 210-15, 228, 231, 237, 241, 243-44, 248, 258, 268-69, 275-77, 278, 285, 286, 291-92, 299
Williams, H. L., 145
Williams, General Owen, 215
Wilson, A., 215
Winchester, Bishop of, 265
Windsor Palace, 38, 255
Wood, Charles Lindley, 61
World War I, 299

Yellow Palace, Copenhagen, 1-5, 11, 12
Young, Sir Allen, 143

Zenia, Grand Duchess, 226
Zulu War, 157

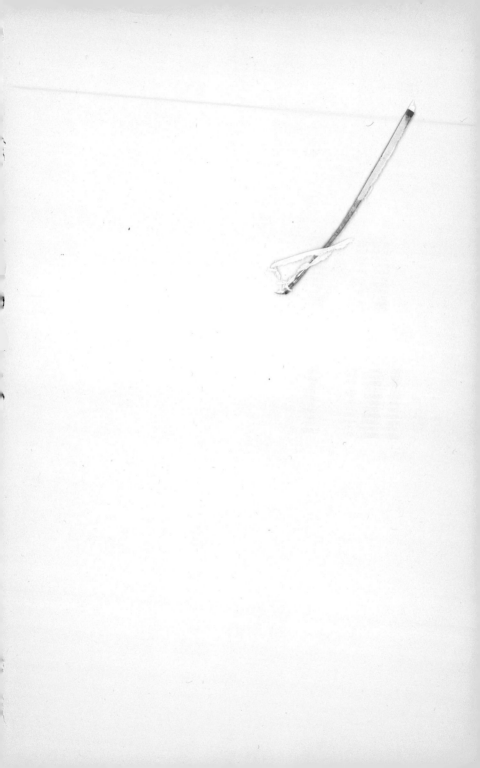